The Cross-Border Family Wealth Guide

The Cross-Border Family Wealth Guide

ADVICE ON TAXES, INVESTING, REAL ESTATE, AND RETIREMENT FOR GLOBAL FAMILIES IN THE U.S. AND ABROAD

Andrew Fisher

WILEY

Published by John Wiley & Sons, Inc., Hoboken, New Jersey.

Published simultaneously in Canada.

For general information on our other products and services or for technical support, please contact our Customer Care Department within the United States at (800) 762-2974, outside the United States at (317) 572-3993 or fax (317) 572-4002.

Wiley publishes in a variety of print and electronic formats and by print-on-demand. Some material included with standard print versions of this book may not be included in e-books or in print-on-demand. If this book refers to media such as a CD or DVD that is not included in the version you purchased, you may download this material at http://booksupport.wiley.com. For more information about Wiley products, visit www.wiley.com.

Library of Congress Cataloging-in-Publication Data:

Names: Fisher, Andrew, 1971– author.
Title: The cross-border family wealth guide : advice on taxes, investing, real estate, and
    retirement for global families in the U.S. and abroad / Andrew Fisher.
Description: Hoboken, New Jersey : John Wiley & Sons, Inc., [2017] | Includes index.
Identifiers: LCCN 2016039868 | ISBN 9781119234272 (hardcover) |
    ISBN 9781119234296 (ePDF) | ISBN 9781119234289 (epub)
Subjects: LCSH: Americans—Foreign countries—Finance, Personal. |
    Aliens—United States—Finance, Personal. | Families—Finance, Personal. |
    Estate planning. | Wealth—Management. | International finance.
Classification: LCC HG179 .F53378 2017 | DDC 332.0240089/13—dc23
LC record available at https://lccn.loc.gov/2016039868

Cover Design: Wiley
Cover Image: © Ian McKinnell/Getty Images, Inc.

Printed in the United States of America.

10 9 8 7 6 5 4 3 2 1

This book is dedicated to my three wonderful children—Ella, Mack, and Vivian. I love you guys like the whole world.

Contents

Part IV: *Real Estate*   *107*

Chapter 9   Real Estate Taxation and Other Considerations   125

Part V: *Cross-Border Taxation*   *143*

Foreword

Tim Kochis, JD, MBA, CFP®

For well over 40 years, I have had the great professional gratification of helping clients to optimize the achievement of their personal financial goals. The first third of that time was focused nearly entirely in the United States, and for clients with virtually no tax or investment or financial issues that extended beyond the U.S. border. Times, of course, have changed dramatically. Business, capital flows, and, importantly, human talent are increasingly globalized. Our clothes, our cars, our food, our neighbors, even our spouses and partners, often come from some other country; the same is true for residents of Italy, or Malaysia, or Chile. But, awareness of related financial issues and the optimization of financial consequences for those whose lives cross-national boundaries hasn't kept pace. In recent decades, I've been privileged to be a small part of a large effort to develop a global profession of personal financial planners, under the certification rubric of the CFP® mark. The number of these professionals and those on a pathway to this certification around the world now exceed well over 200,000. But this is a still tiny response to the immense global need—and, sadly, almost none of these have genuine competency to practice outside of their own country's laws and domestic financial structures. There remains a huge challenge and lots of room for further professional development ahead. Perhaps ironically, due to its size, prominence, and highly unusual and exceptionally complex tax laws, the biggest part of that challenge exists in, and because of, the United States.

So, here, finally, is a book that speaks to this most underserved set of personal financial planning issues! Andrew Fisher's *Cross-Border Family Wealth Guide* comes to the rescue of those many (perhaps 30 to 40 million people around the world, with 20 to 25 million of them in the United States) who may not even realize that they need to grapple with tax, financial, and investment requirements and opportunities that are extraordinarily complex and often surprising, where mistakes are usually costly, and for which there is, today, almost no competent, comprehensive assistance readily available. This guide sets out an easy-to-grasp understanding of how to recognize the unique problems faced by non-U.S. persons with any financial connection to the United States (residence, job, inheritance, property, etc.) *and* by U.S. citizens with any parallel connection (residence, job, inheritance, property, etc.) outside the United States. But more than just entering into this sometimes nightmarish terrain, *The Cross-Border Family Wealth Guide* reveals proven pathways out.

Fisher is quick to acknowledge that he doesn't have *all* the answers; but then, no *one* person does—and there are *very* few who are even somewhat conversant with some of them. That is one of the core problems this book attempts to solve. Fisher shares decades of experience of practical solutions to very common issues and some that are uniquely challenging. And, he points the reader in the direction of more in-depth assistance where more specialized resources are required. For the many individuals and their families in need of this guidance, none of their issues are "common." For each of them, the problem of navigating these challenges is direct, unique, and very often urgent. For many, this book will provide the complete answer; for others, it will permit a better-informed, more self-confident use of the additional advice that might be required.

The Cross-Border Family Wealth Guide makes an important contribution to the achievement of better financial outcomes for potentially very many people. The author's combination of talent and specialized experience is quite rare, but there is no attempt to self-promote or self-aggrandize here. Andrew Fisher's book reflects a genuine commitment to help.

Preface

The goal of this book is simple: to help cross-border professionals and globally mobile families to understand their personal long-term wealth management goals and align their assets and strategies to best achieve those goals, while minimizing taxes and other expenses, and reducing and controlling risk.

Whether you scan the table of contents, look for a specific issue in the index, or just read each chapter straight through, you will likely find information in *The Cross-Border Family Wealth Guide* that will shed light on critical financial questions and issues facing you and your internationally oriented family, including:

- Relocation, expat assignments, and immigration
- Banking, currencies, and cash management
- Real estate—both residences and for investment purposes
- Taxation in the United States and abroad
- Entrepreneurialism and business ownership
- Investments and asset allocation
- Retirement planning
- Estate planning

Every attempt has been made to make the information in this book as accurate, timely, and usable as possible. But since (a) every family's situation is unique, (b) financial rules, regulations, and treaties are constantly changing, and (c) international financial issues often involve great complexity, in almost every case it will make sense for you to seek out qualified, competent, and caring professional advisors to assist you. At least have someone look over your shoulder and check your assumptions; in most cases, it's worth spending the time and effort to find an individual or firm to work closely with. Please allow us to take this early opportunity to say a little about our firm and its founder.

Our Firm: Worldview Wealth Advisors

The members of our professional team here at Worldview have a passion for all things international, from travel and languages to culture and, of course, investing. That is, we were drawn to cross-border wealth management because we had a passion for international people, culture, and financial matters in the first place. We also enjoy learning and seeking answers to questions, which is a good thing, because wealth management laws and strategies for cross-border families are always changing and evolving. There is always something new to learn and apply.

Along with our international focus, our firm is dedicated to being a true holistic wealth advisor. We do not have commissioned salespeople who are always angling to make the next sale or otherwise generate a commission. Instead, we specialize in advising clients through a personalized financial planning process, for which we charge a fixed one-time fee. For clients who want our ongoing help with managing their investments, we work on a fee-based model—charging a small percentage of the total amount of financial assets that we oversee—which allows us to better sit on the same side of the table as our clients.

We abide by a fiduciary standard; we do what is right for our clients and put their best interest first. Because we employ a professional advisory approach rather than the more traditional sales-focused approach of most financial advisors and stockbrokers, we are able to focus our time on first understanding our clients challenges, and then finding solutions and answers for them. Furthermore, our professionals have the highest level of credentials in our industry, including CPA (certified public accountant), CFA (chartered financial analyst), and CFP (certified financial planner).

For over a decade now, we have operated in this advisory manner and professionally dedicated ourselves to learning about all of the issues and questions facing cross-border families. Over time, we have worked hard to consolidate much of what we have learned into the volume you are now holding. What you find in *The Cross-Border Family Wealth Guide*, then, is the result of our research and experience in working with hundreds of families with cross-border issues, as well as what we have learned from interviews held with dozens of cross-border experts working in this area.

Worldview's Founder, Andrew Fisher: A Personal Pledge

As a CFA (chartered financial analyst) and a CPA (certified public accountant), there are many directions I could have taken my career. I chose to focus on advising cross-border families not only because I enjoy the intellectual challenge and constant learning that is required, but also because I love meeting and getting to know the many exceptional people who come my way.

Our firm's clients tend to be extremely interesting, globally oriented, multicultural, highly intelligent, and well-educated people. They are generally very appreciative not only of the quality of the investment, tax, wealth management, and long-term planning advice that we provide, but of our inherent appreciation for who they are and what they have accomplished.

For all these reasons, I have personally dedicated myself to doing whatever it takes to make sure that we give our clients the best possible advice. For example, we consciously cultivate and rely on a large network of trusted professional partners and colleagues in many different fields, an absolutely necessity given that no single professional or firm can keep track of it all.

In just the same way that I have dedicated myself to helping my clients, I have also pledged myself to putting together the best possible, most understandable, and most useful book that I could. If you are reading this, I want you to know that I am committed to your long-term financial future and to helping you and your family not just survive, but thrive, wherever you are in the world.

Andrew Fisher

Acknowledgments

I want to first thank my dear friend and long-time business partner, David Colvin, who is with CLVN Tax and Financial Advisors in Amsterdam, The Netherlands. His friendship and our intellectual banter have been a constant part of my life since we met at university in 1989, and it was with his encouragement that I began to specialize in cross-border wealth management so many years ago. He taught me the basics of cross-border taxation, and our wealth management brainstorming sessions have been the single most important contributor to my growth over the years into an expert in this field. Thanks DC!

I would like to express my gratitude to Tim Kochis, who in addition to writing a terrific forward for this book, has been a wonderful supporter and mentor to me since we met in San Francisco. He is a big picture thinker and a true visionary for our industry. I really appreciate him taking an interest in me and in my vision for Worldview.

I have been fortunate to have gotten to know many respected professionals working in various fields of cross-border advice, including business and estate planning attorneys, tax advisors and accountants, bankers, HR professionals, immigration attorneys, association leaders, insurance brokers, and relocation providers. I'm glad to have been welcomed into the world of cross-border advice by these professionals, and many of them were very generous with their time by allowing me to interview them for this book. During these interviews I was able to learn about the most common questions and challenges they see among their clients, which helped me to expand the advice within this book greatly.

I want to make a special mention of the contributions of Russell Mansky, who is with Spott, Lucy & Wall CPAs in San Francisco. He has a vast and technical knowledge in the area of cross-border taxation, which he so generously put to use in his review of certain chapters of this book. Other professionals who generously contributed their knowledge to this effort include: Jordi Argente, Shaun Dublin, Ming Fang, Stephen Foster, Jacob Glickman, Michael Gottschalk, Jason Graham, Scott Jones, Gary Kaplan, Eng Khoo, Vince Lau, Gopal Shah, Carol-Ann Simon, Carole Jodi Trent, Mark Walters, Mark Weaver, and Ajay Whitmore.

I'm lucky to have found a small but passionate group of employees and colleagues who've shared in my journey of building World-view into the leading wealth management firm serving cross-border families. I want to acknowledge my current and former team members for their significant contributions to this effort, and for their genuine and unfailing concern for serving our clients and their best interests.

The cross-border area of wealth management is highly complex and is always changing. As such, to be successful one must be energized by the need to constantly research and learn new things. I've been fortunate to have a wonderful community of wealth management peers to rely upon throughout my journey. I'd like to especially thank all of my friends at the CFA Society of Portland, and in particular the people with whom I served on the Board of Directors for so many years. Also, I very much appreciate the FPA and financial planning community around San Francisco for welcoming me and for inspiring me to continue to make financial planning a larger element of my firm's core value proposition.

I want to recognize the significant contributions of my writing partner, Jordan Gruber, to this project. His professional skill and passion for doing good work, combined with the personal interest he took in my project, without question made this a far better final product. Throughout the two years it took to finalize my manuscript, Jordan never waivered in his commitment or his optimistic outlook for what this book would become. We did it!

Thank you to my parents for inspiring me to seek out new challenges and international experiences, and for instilling me the confidence that with hard work I can accomplish anything I put my mind to. And finally, I'd like to thank my family for their wonderful support throughout this project. My wife and three wonderful children have always been there for me, and their love and support make me tremendously happy.

About the Author

Andrew Fisher is widely regarded as a leading wealth advisor to cross-border families. He frequently writes and speaks to the unique financial planning and investment complexities faced by international families, particularly when an individual is a tax resident of the United States.

With a broad base of experience in international investing, taxation, and wealth planning, Andrew enjoys helping clients find creative solutions to complex financial problems. More than having all the answers, he prides himself on being able to identify the most critical financial questions clients face and then build a team of experts to find solutions.

Andrew is the president and founder of Worldview Wealth Advisors, an independent wealth management firm advising globally oriented families—both Americans living abroad and foreign citizens living in the U.S. In addition to leading the investment team, Andrew serves as senior client advisor. In this role, he assists families with their complex, multinational affairs, seeking to optimize wealth, which is often located in multiple countries.

Prior to founding Worldview, Andrew was an international stock research analyst for Montgomery Asset Management in San Francisco. Previously, he worked in international research at Donaldson, Lufkin & Jenrette (now Credit Suisse) and HSBC Securities, both in New York City. He began his career with PriceWaterhouseCoopers in Los Angeles.

Andrew graduated cum laude from Cal Poly University, San Luis Obispo, with a degree in finance and a minor in Spanish. He also completed a year of study at the University of Madrid in Spain. He holds CFA and CPA credentials, and is actively involved with FPA and STEP organizations.

When out of the office, Andrew can be found enjoying the San Francisco Bay Area with his wife and three children.

PART

I

Financial Challenges
of a Cross-Border Life

CHAPTER 1

Who Are These Cross-Border Families?

There remains little doubt that in the twenty-first century, capital—the factors of production and the resources that make it possible to grow wealth—has become fully globally mobile. Like water seeking its own level, capital invariably flows to where it will be most valued and provides the greatest returns. We tend to think of capital first and foremost as financial capital, but financial capital is *not* the only kind of capital. In fact, globally mobile financial capital is almost always supported by something else: *globally mobile human capital*, that is, cross-border professionals and their families—people with the skills, talents, and drive to succeed and rise to the top, and who are willing to go wherever in the world they find the most opportunity.

Put differently, the large, powerful international companies and interests who deploy their financial capital where it is most advantageous also know that the best and most effective professionals, managers, and other high-level employees for any given situation usually do not come from only one country, including the country the company is headquartered in. These companies regularly recruit, hire, and redeploy professionals to assist, enhance, and even anchor their efforts in different countries depending on the company's overall strategic and tactical needs and the situation at hand.

As a result it is increasingly common to find top-notch individuals who start with a company in one country (usually where they are born), then move to work in another country (often but not always with the same company), and then go on to yet another country or perhaps back to their country of origin. Over time (and sometimes very quickly) these individuals invariably accumulate assets of various types in more than one country; and, over a decades-long career arc, things can—and usually do—become very complicated.

International professionals have families, parents, children, and other relatives. They have dreams, goals, desires, and long-term plans. And like everyone else, they have personal responsibility for making many significant decisions regarding the long-term management of the wealth they accumulate.

But these individuals must also face *a bit of a quandary*. On the one hand, the spirit that led them to excel and become desirable professionals, thought leaders, and managers of all types is the very same spirit that makes them want to achieve the very best for themselves and their families in the financial long run. On the other hand, the desire to intelligently grow and manage personal wealth can be frustrated or outright quashed by insufficient information, overwhelming details, and a dramatic shortage of places to turn for help.

The purpose of this book, then, is to assist cross-border professionals and their families, and in particular those with a financial connection to the United States, to make better, smarter, and more optimal personal financial and wealth management decisions, both in the short term and long term. Managing wealth efficiently and effectively is never easy and always takes careful thinking and planning, but cross-border professionals and their families—even the best and brightest of a class of individuals who are by definition at the top of the international class—find themselves in a particularly tricky and potentially problematic situation.

The Growing Need for a Definitive Guide

In 10 or 20 years, perhaps, we will look back and wonder with amazement how it was that as late as 2014, when initial drafting on this book began, there was no comprehensive guide to help cross-border families with personal financial decisions and the long-term effective management of their wealth. That is, as made clear throughout this chapter, cross-border professionals and other globally mobile families wishing to align their financial assets and strategies with their long-term goals and life planning objectives currently face a distinctly uphill battle.

Not only do they face three unique challenges—lack of uniformity, complexity, and scarcity of helpful resources—but also, they find themselves smack dab in the middle of the rapidly changing legal, financial, and regulatory landscape described in the last section. And then, on top of all that, while the community of cross-border professionals and globally mobile families is growing dramatically, the number of firms and individual advisors qualified to help them is simply not keeping up.

More and more, talented professionals from all around the globe are found working—all around the globe. If nothing else, the increasing economic expansion of emerging nations in Latin America, Eastern Europe, and emerging Asia, as well as the continued long-term expansion of China and India, is only going to create more opportunities for education, advancement, and cross-border work scenarios for exceptional and successful individuals living in all those places.

At the heart of this trend, of course, we come back to where this chapter started: to the global mobility of capital, including the human capital that goes along with it. This growing global mobility of capital, then, is coupled with the fact that outstanding individuals of all types, whether they are from a small village in India with only dirt roads or from a privileged background in London, are being sought out by companies and organizations and asked to relocate—often to the United States, which is still the world's strongest economic engine. So then, just as there has never been more global mobility of capital, there has also never been more global mobility of talented individuals of all kinds, from programmers and coders to security experts to managers and marketers to entrepreneurs and those who support them.

At my firm, Worldview Wealth Advisors, we have long recognized the lack of good information, advice, and places to turn to related to wealth management for cross-border families. Given the growing need, we simply felt that now was the time to pull together what we've learned about all of these issues and put it in a place where successful cross-border people from around the globe can access it and benefit from it.

Put differently, the need for a definitive guide at this point in time simply felt obvious to us. This volume is our response to that need by attempting to pull information together and provide usable, practical answers for those who are not in a position to afford to bring together their own high-level advisory team of financial advisors, attorneys, and tax professionals. And even for those folks who can afford to pull together their own professional team, we believe this book will provide a tremendous head start, because it looks at issues comprehensively and systematically. That is, when an expert is consulted with deep knowledge of a single cross-border relevant area like tax, real estate, investing, or immigration, he or she may not have a sufficiently robust understanding of the big picture to be able to offer advice that is digestible, relevant, optimal, and usable. With *The Cross-Border Family Wealth Guide* at your side, you'll be better informed, better able to work with the professionals you consult, and more able to achieve your goals in the long run.

Who's Who: Who This Book Is Meant to Serve

This book is intended to serve globally mobile families who have a financial connection to the United States, either by being a citizen or resident of the United States or by simply having assets located here. There is a relatively large community of people throughout the world who have financial affairs in both the United States and at least one other country. International or cross-border knowledge workers and other middle- and senior-management professionals, usually working for large corporations, constitute the majority of this community, but of course there are retirees, students, and children as well.

Some of these individuals are originally from the United States, and their knowledge and skills have brought them overseas. More often, people born outside the United States with substantial knowledge and skills are brought here and then stay for a while, and some stay permanently.

Often, top-notch individuals (and their families) move from one country to another, and then to still another, so that before coming to the United States they may have previously lived and worked in one or more other countries. Along the way, these cross-border professionals may accumulate personal relationships as well as financial accounts, real property, and other assets. And then, one day, these individuals may end up inheriting property or money from their parents—or their parents' parents—money and property that is located in a country other than the United States.

Examples of Who Might Benefit from This Book

For example, suppose a brilliant young Swiss marketing executive works for a major company in Switzerland. She is then brought over to the Hong Kong office before being further promoted and transferred to U.S. headquarters. Along the way, she leaves certain bank accounts, retirement funds, and other assets in both Switzerland and Hong Kong. Before coming to the United States, though, she falls in love with and marries a Chinese man, with whom she has two children. The whole family then moves to the United States, and while the children will obviously be of Swiss-Chinese descent, they will grow up in the United States.

Education is often a strong priority for international professionals, given their exposure to language, cultures, history, and travel. It's not surprising that by the time they are done moving through the U.S. school systems, their children will talk like, think like, and act like Americans. But at the same time, these children will also have their national history and background, and in some cases, their citizenry, in more than one country. Whether or not the children grow up in the United States, it is very common for cross-border professionals to want their children to get their college education at U.S. institutions, which are very well-regarded internationally.

Let's consider another example: a high-level programmer from India who works for a while in London, and then gets transferred to Chicago, New York City, or the Silicon Valley. Regardless of whether he ever moves back to India, he will likely accumulate assets of various types along the way. Bank accounts, retirement accounts, brokerage accounts, real property, and business interests might be part of the equation, not to mention such things as precious metals, collectibles (paintings, antiques, jewelry), and other items of value.

Something else he is likely to gain along the way is a family—a wife and children. Successful young people with busy lives often do not spend a great deal of time focusing on their assets and planning for the future, but with family and increasing maturity generally comes a heightened sense of awareness and responsibility. As the need to intelligently plan for the short, medium, and long-term economic future becomes clearer, our Indian programmer may find the following:

- He faces unique financial challenges of which he wasn't previously aware.
- He is immersed in, and must necessarily deal with, a complex and changing legal, financial, and regulatory landscape.
- Very few authoritative, reliable, and comprehensive sources of information are available to help guide him.

Diagramming a Cross-Border Person: Residency and U.S. Income Tax Status

In some cases, the cross-border professionals (along with their families) who come to the United States will get a Green Card, and will then decide to stay here permanently and become dual citizens. In other cases, they will return to their country of origin or to some other third country. Similarly, many U.S. citizens will decide to stay abroad permanently—in some rare cases even renouncing their U.S. citizenship—while others choose to come back to the United States. What's common to all of these scenarios, however, is that there will be assets—financial accounts, real property, and other tangible assets—in more than one country, and thereby subjected to the tax laws and other rules and regulations of more than one tax authority.

Traditionally, many individuals would hold onto their Green Cards for many years after they had more-or-less permanently exited the United States, since the ability to return to the country at some point is highly valued. Recently, however, the rules and regulations that make it possible to hold onto a Green Card—for example, how regularly the individual must spend time in the United States—have tightened. Additionally, there is greater awareness today about the need to continue to file tax returns in the United States as long as a Green Card is held; previously, this requirement was often not as well known or followed.

To help clarify things, please consider Figure 1.1, which illustrates a kind of "Who's Who" for purposes of this book—that is, it shows the six main categories that people fall into, based on whether they reside in the United States or abroad, and their U.S. tax status (either tax resident or non-resident).

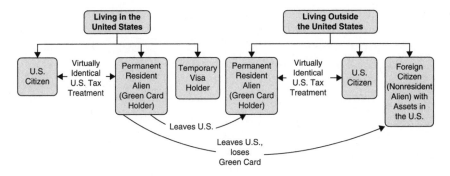

Figure 1.1 Who's who for the purposes of this book

Moving left to right, the Who's Who chart begins by dividing individuals into those living in the United States and those living *outside* the United States. Individuals living in the United States are U.S. citizens, permanent resident aliens (with Green Card), or temporary visa holders (either tax residents or nonresidents). We will return to this in detail, but note that a U.S. citizen and a permanent resident alien generally receive identical tax treatment by the IRS, although permanent resident aliens are more likely to have foreign income or assets that are also subject to foreign tax liabilities (like a rental property). Temporary visa holders may or may not be U.S. tax residents, based on whether they have a substantial presence in the United States. Also, temporary visa holders who must pay taxes in the United States may or may not owe taxes on their foreign income, depending on their specific situation. (They may only by subject to U.S. tax on their U.S.-sourced income.)

For those living outside the United States, there are three main categories. The first is the permanent resident alien, generally someone who lived in the United States but no longer does, and still has permanent residency in the United States (possesses a Green Card). Next is the U.S. citizen living abroad, someone who receives virtually identical tax treatment as the permanent resident alien living abroad. Finally, we have someone who is not living in the United States, and who is not a tax resident of the United States, but who has assets in the United States. The U.S. tax code considers such a foreign citizen to be a nonresident alien (NRA), or more simply a nonresident with assets in the United States.

Note that while the six main categories of individuals are based on *tax* status, the book ultimately goes far beyond taxation issues. Still, taxes are inevitable, and in many ways they form a core background against which each and every one of us has to be aware of and navigate. So while taxes aren't the only issue, and shouldn't necessarily be allowed to be the financial tail that wags the wealth management dog, they also are a vital part of the analysis and recommendations throughout the book and therefore provide the best possible starting point for describing "Who's Who." Moreover, while tax considerations are found throughout the book, all of Part V is devoted to taxes and will review, synthesize, and clarify points about taxes made elsewhere.

Having looked at Figure 1.1, you should be able to fairly easily identify which category you fall into, although your category can change over time if you change your physical residence (moving into or out of the United States), or if you change your work status and therefore tax status in relationship to the United States (Green Card or not, work visa or not, etc.). If you are married, it might be the case that you fall into one category and your spouse or children fall into another, a possibility we'll stay attuned to throughout the book.

How Many Cross-Border Professionals and Families Are There?

How many individuals and families fall into the different categories? Although there are no definitive numbers, a variety of estimates have been made. To begin with, there are estimated to be over 40 million foreign-born immigrants currently living in the United States, whether permanent resident aliens or temporary resident aliens, based on U.S. Census Bureau data. We further estimate that roughly 10 million to 15 million of these people could be considered cross-border *professionals* living in the United States (with higher education and income levels).

In addition, the State Department estimates that there are nearly 8 million nonmilitary Americans living abroad.[1] Although not all of

---

[1]The Association of Americans Resident Overseas (AARO). "8M Americans Abroad," AARO.org. Available at: https://aaro.org/who-we-are/8m-americans -abroad.

these people can be labeled cross-border professionals, we estimate that roughly three million of them are either working professionals or retirees (again, with higher education and income levels).

It is impossible to know the exact number of foreign-born individuals who once lived in the United States and now live somewhere else—whether permanent resident aliens or nonresident aliens—but the number might easily be between 10 million and 20 million people. Although there are once again no definitive statistics here, we can assume that the number of cross-border individuals who may benefit from this book is very large (perhaps as many as 30 million or 40 million people).

Unique Challenges Faced by Cross-Border Families Connected to the United States

There are three main unique challenges faced by cross-border professionals with assets in the United States:

1. *Lack of uniformity:* The asymmetric nature of tax regimes and reach—that is, U.S. federal and state tax law reaches much farther than the tax laws of almost any other country.
2. *Complexity:* The complexity of U.S. and foreign laws and regulations.
3. *Scarcity of resources:* Lack of sufficient help and information, especially for those who are not ultra-affluent.

These challenges are further outlined in Chapter 2.

2

Unique Challenges and the Regulatory Landscape

The Unequal Nature of Tax Regimes and Reach

To begin to understand how different the United States is when compared to other tax regimes, let's take a step back and consider things from the perspective of cross-border families from the past. Traditionally, it has been fairly common for certain types of professionals, especially those in Europe, to have a fairly high degree of mobility and find themselves living and working in multiple countries over time. A Frenchman might work in London for a while, or a Spaniard might find himself in Zurich for a few years before returning to Spain or going elsewhere.[1] Generally speaking, these individuals did not need a great deal of tax planning or other guidance with respect to how living in multiple countries might affect their personal financial and long-term wealth planning decisions, because much of their tax responsibilities to the former nation would end upon their move to a new location.

For example, suppose two Spanish brothers move to Germany to start a business building fine guitars. Upon leaving Spain, they were no longer required to report to the Spanish government on their financial affairs, nor were they required to pay any taxes to the

---

[1]Highly valued and talented individuals also often find themselves spending some time in former colonies of the European countries that they are from, assuming those countries still have significant economic relationships with their former colonies. Thus a British professional might find himself in India for a while, and a French woman might find herself in any one of numerous African countries that France still has substantial ties to.

Spanish government unless they left some kind of income-producing asset there, like a business or a rental property. Likewise, when they moved to Germany, they did not report to Germany on assets that they held outside of Germany—that is, those back in Spain (or held in offshore accounts). This may or may not have been technically correct under German tax law, but this has been common practice for decades, if not centuries.

Put another way, most countries *tax on residency*: If you are living and working in Germany, then you will be taxed by Germany. But if you are German and you are not living there—let's say you are living in New York City—then even though you are a German citizen, Germany claims no right to tax you on what you are doing in the United States.

The Unique Worldwide Reach of the U.S. Tax System

On the other hand, once an internationally mobile individual touches the United States in his or her working life—whether that is made possible by a short-term work visa or a permanent assignment with a Green Card—then that person generally becomes a U.S. tax resident, and things become both different and more complex. The United States is the only major nation to tax all citizens and residents on their worldwide income, regardless of whether they currently reside in the United States. So, once an individual becomes a U.S. tax resident, the person is mandatorily subject to the worldwide nature of the U.S. income tax, and *the IRS will seek to tax him or her on worldwide income and assets, no matter what country that income occurs in or where those assets are found in.* This is even the case if you were to sell highly appreciated property, where the appreciation occurred before you even moved to the United States (like a rental property in London that you purchased 20 years before moving to the United States).

Fortunately, a fairly complex system of foreign tax credits ensures that there is little or no double taxation—if you are working in the United States on a visa or Green Card, income from a business in a foreign country will often be taxed there first, and you will be given credit for the amount paid there when the amount of tax you owe in the United States is determined. However, there are many tricks and traps that the unwary can fall into, and a little bit of information and planning with regard to minimizing tax can go a long way and make a big difference. Similarly, with regard to assets such as bank accounts, brokerage accounts, retirement accounts, and real property, there are a wide variety of long-term planning possibilities and ways of leveraging and managing one's wealth for the long-term that are made more complex by U.S. tax law and regulations.

Complexity in Taxation and Other Regulations

Most cross-border professionals are quite surprised when they learn about the many financial requirements that go hand-in-hand with residing in the United States. Becoming a U.S. tax resident brings with it a great deal of potential complexity, both with regard to U.S. tax laws as well as other allied rules and regulations affecting things like moving funds from one country to another, opening accounts in more than one country, investing, business ownership requirements, and retirement planning. The U.S. system, then, is generally more complex both with regard to its tax code (many European countries have flat taxes or tax codes that are much simpler than the U.S. code) and the many other rules, regulations, and requirements that the United States imposes. For those cross-border professionals and globally mobile families with the most interest in wealth planning—which involves not only taxation and tax minimization strategies, but also questions of investment structure, asset allocation, savings and retirement plans, currencies, and so on—it can be a truly daunting task.

Why is the U.S. tax code—which takes over 70,000 pages to explain—so much more complex than that of many other countries, with many more deductions, rules, alternative rules, and so on? It's partly because the U.S. tax code, unlike those in other countries, makes more of an attempt to achieve certain social goals by encouraging and discouraging certain types of behaviors. However, the effectiveness of the U.S. tax code in achieving these goals is not always clear.

Likewise, for U.S. citizens living abroad, the long reach of the U.S. tax system complicates things—as you will remember from the discussion of Figure 1.1 earlier, a U.S. citizen living abroad is treated for tax purposes nearly identically with a permanent resident alien living abroad—but for a number of reasons, this has not troubled too many people or been seen as much of an issue. Why not? Well, first, many U.S. citizens abroad haven't been aware of their requirement to file. Upon becoming aware of the requirements, such individuals generally must seek professional tax assistance and come to an arrangement with the U.S. Internal Revenue Service (IRS) for missed taxes. Second, many U.S. citizens living abroad are doing so because they are working in Western Europe, and most countries there have substantially higher tax rates than the United States has, which means that by the time a tax credit offset is given (along with the Foreign Earned Income Exclusion which will be discussed later in Part V), they likely do not owe any U.S. taxes.

Consider, for example, a software coder from California who has moved to Germany indefinitely and is aware of his need to file with the IRS (since he is still a U.S. citizen). To begin with, in most cases he won't have to file a California state tax return. This is because, like most states, California bases its taxation on a person's intent and residency, and allows you to break residency should you move to another U.S. state or internationally. Now, without California tax in the picture, this software coder might be subject to a top U.S. tax rate of 28 percent (after applying the foreign income exclusion), but he will *first* be paying approximately 45 percent in tax and various withholdings on his earnings in Germany (since he physically resides there, Germany gets to go first). With the tax credit he gets for what he paid in Germany, he is likely to end up owing no additional U.S. taxes.

Scarcity of Professional Help and Information

In addition to the lack of uniformity and the significant complexity, there is a third unique challenge: *the lack of—the scarcity of—readily available help and easily accessible information.* While those who are ultra-affluent can afford to put together a specialized team consisting of accountants, attorneys, and other professionals, most successful educated families find themselves facing a lack of good information and guidance. With so many unknowns and so many unclear (and shifting!) rules and regulations, it can be difficult for such families to gain a clear sense of their financial situation, to clarify their goals for the future, and to make sure that what they're currently doing is aligned with and optimized for achieving those long-term goals.

Unfortunately, not only are there very few resources like the book you are now holding, but there are also very few places that a cross-border professional can turn to for help with even relatively simple problems. Not only do well-known financial and brokerage firms fail to make comprehensive service offerings available for cross-border families, in most cases they actively prohibit their advisors from giving cross-border tax, financial, and retirement planning advice.

There are, simply, very few if any good sources of information available. If you are British and walk into a U.S. brokerage firm and explain that you have been with Intel for 15 years and now are retiring back to the United Kingdom and that you merely need someone to help you make sense of it all, especially what to do with your 401(k) that is worth a few hundred thousand dollars—you will in all likelihood be told that you can't be helped. This is mainly because the complexity of what is involved is beyond the ordinary capabilities of the financial advisors involved, and the companies they work for do not want to risk giving bad advice and being liable for that advice.

Similarly, for the most part, foreign investment firms and banks will not give advice to, assist, or otherwise get involved with a U.S. citizen living abroad who has questions or problems. The world may be becoming increasingly mobile, but knowledge about what to do with cross-border financial planning has not yet become so. There's simply too much red tape, too much complexity, and too much potential liability, not to mention the additional potential difficulties that can arise from language, translation, and assorted cultural issues.

Interestingly, even those global financial institutions that have divisions in other countries are loath to advise cross-border professionals. For example, a large European bank will typically not work with a European citizen residing in the United States, even if that person is from that bank's country of origin. Similarly, many U.S. brokerage firms have a substantial international presence for offering financial planning and investment advice; but if you are a U.S. citizen and walk into one of their branches, they will likely not work with you. Why not? Well, in most cases this foreign operation will be staffed by citizens of the foreign country, and their focus will be on serving people from that country; working with Americans is not their mission, and once again, would involve too much red tape, complexity, and potential liability. (This is the same situation with the branches of large international banks in the United States.)

A Changing Legal, Financial, and Regulatory Landscape

Today, not only is capital more globally mobile than ever before, but we live during a time when technology and the Internet allow for the rapid dissemination of news and ideas in a way that vastly eclipses what had previously been possible. One byproduct of this informational bonanza has been more awareness and focus by national governments everywhere on those who attempt to evade taxes or otherwise keep the extent of their wealth at least somewhat hidden or secret. Similar attention has been turned towards unsavory, illegal, and outright criminal individuals and organizations, such as arms dealers, counterfeiters, and terrorists.

A Prediction

Going forward, it is unlikely that any new CEO of a Fortune 500 company will not have had overseas experience. Many of them, in fact, are likely to originally hail from a country other than the United States.

There is, of course, nothing new about individuals and organizations going to great lengths to keep their affairs and the extent of their wealth private. The evolving interplay between those who claim they are owed taxes—rulers and governments of every type—and those individuals or families who are wealthy enough to resist paying what they feel is more than their fair share of such taxes, goes back many centuries, perhaps even to the beginning of civilization. What *is* new is the combination of relentless needs for more government revenue combined with a greater technological ability to track wealth. As a result, governments everywhere—as well as the large financial institutions compelled to adhere to the standards of these governments—are taking a more aggressive and proactive stance on uncovering assets that they claim they have the power to tax.

Even before the advent of the Internet, national governments have done their best to track wealth and assets for many decades.

For example, a great deal of effort has gone into tracking the wealth—as well as tangible assets such as valuable paintings—that was illegally confiscated during World War II. More recently, in 2008 news came out about the biggest investigation ever initiated for tax evasion in Germany. The German intelligence service had purchased a stolen list of accounts and account holders at LGT Bank in Liechtenstein from a disgruntled former LGT employee. They were eager to learn the identities of their citizens who were potentially hiding assets and evading taxes.

This German effort spurred a series of tax investigations in numerous countries whose governments suspected that some of their citizens also may have evaded tax obligations by using banks and trusts in Liechtenstein and Switzerland, and it set off a firestorm of debate as to how aggressive governments should be with regard to pursuing illegal tax evaders. A similar controversy followed involving the Swiss bank UBS, whose management had allegedly directed its Swiss wealth advisors to actively solicit U.S. taxpayer clients by offering them access to offshore financial vehicles to hide their assets and avoid taxes.[2]

Most recently, on April 3, 2016, the first news stories were published concerning what would become known as the "Panama Papers," perhaps the largest ever leak of confidential attorney-client information related to the use of offshore corporations and tax evasion on behalf of wealthy—and often well-known—families around the world. Approximately one year before the story broke, an anonymous source leaked some 11.5 million documents from Panamanian law firm Mossack Fonseca, a leading player in incorporating and operating shell companies in friendly jurisdictions around the world, on behalf of large financial institutions and their wealthy clients.

Mossack Fonseca's specialty is creating "complex shell company structures" that, while legal, also allow the firm's clients "to operate behind an often impenetrable wall of secrecy." More leaked documents are expected to be released in the future, and investigations into the leaked information are being initiated in nearly every major

---

[2]Lynnley Browning. "Wealthy Americans Under Scrutiny in UBS Case," *New York Times,* June 6, 2008. Available at: http://www.nytimes.com/2008/06/06/business/worldbusiness/06tax.html?_r=1.

country throughout the world. Fallout from the "Panama Papers" will be far reaching and should unfold over many years.[3]

The Far Reach of the Foreign Account Tax Compliance Act (FATCA)

These controversies, along with other similar events and a general climate of more assertive policies, led the United States Congress to pass the Foreign Account Tax Compliance Act, or FATCA, a federal law designed to enforce the requirement for all U.S. citizens and tax residents to file annual reports on their non-U.S. financial accounts. FATCA, the first phase of which became effective in March of 2010, requires all non-U.S. financial institutions that wish to do business in the United States to put in place a process that probes their clients to see if they are U.S. citizens or tax residents (Green Card holders), and if so, to report their holdings to the U.S. Department of the Treasury. FATCA was, understandably, not well received by international financial institutions for two reasons.

First, the global economy was still working its way out of the 2007–2009 global economic downturn (the Great Recession[4]). Second, it forced international financial institutions to make extremely costly technology investments to comply with the act. Those international financial institutions that do not comply with FATCA risk being barred from doing business in the United States and having their U.S. accounts—including potentially their clients' accounts—confiscated. Noncompliance with FATCA, in a nutshell, could easily put such financial institutions out of business if they have any meaningful affairs and business relationships in the United States, which is the case for most major financial institutions.

Importantly, even though financial institutions around the world are dismayed by FATCA, foreign governments have cooperated with it because of their general interest in increased information sharing on financial accounts. While FATCA is a phased act and there

---

[3]Lisa Main and Elise Worthington. "Panama Papers and Mossack Fonseca Explained," ABC News Australia, April 4, 2016. Available at: http://www.abc.net .au/news/2016-04-04/explained-what-are-the-leaked-mossack-fonseca-panama -papers/7270690.

[4]With four consecutive quarters of negative GDP growth in the United States, it may be that an "ordinary depression," not a "Great Recession," is what actually occurred.

is still much to be put in place globally to comply with it, it is rapidly heading us all toward a new world order of increased informational sharing relating to financial affairs and transactions wherever they occur on the planet.

Recommending Against Secretive Offshore Wealth Strategies

Although a large variety of complex offshore wealth strategies exist,[5] this book is not the place to turn if you are interested in making use of them. First, for those following U.S. tax laws—which we assume holds for most readers of this book—few of these options are viable or without risk. Second, FATCA and the general environment of increased regulatory scrutiny make it increasingly more difficult for people to make use of these jurisdictions. (Corporations, of course, have additional options, from holding international profits offshore to avoid U.S. taxation to moving their headquarters to different countries with more favorable tax laws.)

Cross-border professionals and globally mobile families, then, must be aware that we have already entered and are going even deeper into a world of financial transparency and full reporting. It is becoming increasingly difficult to conceal taxable assets or even absentmindedly forget about them. In such an increasingly transparent world, above-board compliance with every country's laws is called for, and increased planning that optimizes one's long-term wealth vis-à-vis tax requirements, money movement, asset allocation, retirement planning, and so on, becomes more important than ever.

---

[5]These strategies emanate both from the larger and more well-known jurisdictions like Switzerland, Liechtenstein, and Singapore, to smaller offshore locales such as Isle of Man, Guernsey, Cypress, the Cayman Islands, the Bahamas, or Bermuda, to name a few.

PART II

Saving and Investing: Building Your Personal Net Worth

3

Building a Strong Foundation

The larger goal of this chapter—and in some ways, this entire book—is to help cross-border professionals and globally mobile famlies protect, maintain, and grow their wealth and achieve their long-term financial goals. For most people, these goals will include creating and accumulating sufficient wealth over the span of their working lives so that at some point—ideally before retirement age—they will achieve true financial independence.[1]

As for investing itself, then, the ultimate goal must also be to protect, maintain, and grow your wealth—and the very best way to do that is to *diversify* or spread out your wealth and investments, as we'll turn to later in this chapter. This includes growing your wealth so that it maintains purchasing power—the ability to actually purchase the things you need and want in the face of inflation. This means your wealth must grow over time at a rate that is at least equal to the inflation rate. Ideally, however, your wealth should grow at a rate that is *above* the inflation-adjusted level. When that happens, your existing wealth can contribute to the creation and accumulation of still more wealth on your behalf, which is referred to as "real" inflation-adjusted investment growth.

Retirement Destination Unknown: Invest Globally

Many globally mobile families understand that their wealth should be diversified across a variety of countries, regions, and currencies.

---

[1] *Financial independence* can be defined as having sufficient net worth (including existing assets and income sources) to provide for your complete financial needs for the rest of your lifetime.

In fact, in today's world most all investors have an increasing sense that economies all across the world are deeply intertwined and heavily dependent on each other; and, therefore, having global diversification, at least in terms of investments, makes a great deal of sense.

This intuitive sense is—or should be—bolstered by the reality that many cross-border families simply do not know exactly where they will retire to. They may remain in the United States (or remain abroad in the case of an American expatriate), they may return to their home country, or they may perhaps move on to some third destination that promises a pleasant climate or favorable tax laws. Many of our clients are uncertain where they will eventually retire, although some kind of split retirement between the United States and some other country is often—at least hypothetically—pretty appealing.

Spreading It Around

Given the likelihood of having some ongoing physical presence somewhere other than the United States after (and often before) retirement, we believe that it's very important for cross-border families to take an explicitly global approach to investing. This means that the investments they make in stocks and bonds (as well as in real estate) should be distributed across the regions or countries of the world where they are likely to physically be during retirement. The more global a family becomes, the more they need true global diversification and worldwide currency exposure through their investments. Regular U.S. investors typically have at most only 10 to 20 percent of their investments in countries outside the United States, and we believe this is far too little for international families contemplating retirement.

Put differently, for those who are considering splitting their time between two or more countries upon retirement, investing one's assets in a sensibly diversified way becomes even more desirable (and somewhat more complicated). To fail to do this is to risk losing substantial purchasing power in any of the regions or countries where you might plan to retire.

As a quick example, suppose you own residences in both the United States and Australia, and your stocks and bonds are primarily invested in U.S. companies even though you plan on retiring to Australia. So, you retire and move to Australia, and then in the first five years of your retirement, the dollar loses 25 percent of its value against the Australian dollar. If you had kept most of your investments in U.S. assets, you would have literally lost 25 percent of your purchasing power in the country that you knew, all along, you would be retiring to (Australia in this case).

Wealth Creation and Accumulation

Let's consider how financially successful families create wealth over time. Generally speaking, there are six primary ways of creating and accumulating wealth:

1. Saving from earnings
2. Real estate ownership
3. Stock-based compensation
4. Entrepreneurship and businesses ownership
5. Investment gains and reinvestment
6. Inheritance

Wise Words

"A penny saved is a penny earned."
— Benjamin Franklin, United States Founding Father and Inventor

---

Saving from Earnings

The first way to create wealth is *saving from earnings*. This is the most basic and fundamental means of accumulating wealth, and is also by far the easiest method. You need to save some of what you earn on a regular basis, or put differently, you must spend less than you bring in. International families—especially compared to typical American families—are generally very good savers. By living under their means, they are often able to save a significant percentage of their take-home pay on a regular basis.

One important method of saving from earnings is to *take full advantage of any tax-advantaged retirement savings programs available to you*. That is, you should make full use of opportunities to save money before paying taxes on it. So, be sure to participate in your employer's 401(k) retirement plan (especially those that include a matching amount from your employer), as well as any other similar plans (such as a 403(b), 457(b), IRA, SEP IRA, etc.). Roth 401(k)s and Roth IRAs can be quite valuable because they are one of the few structures that allow you to grow wealth tax-free; however, they may not be a good choice if you plan to retire abroad (see more in Chapter 7).

Another way you can create wealth through savings is to *make investments of your after-tax savings*—with funds you've already paid taxes on—in such things as stocks, bonds, real estate, and other possibilities that will be covered later in this chapter. This is by far the most common and most important means of building wealth, and the approach has been understood since the beginning of the concept of money. You are nearly gauranteed financial success if you can "live under your means" by saving a percentage of your after-tax earnings and investing those funds sensibly over time. This is the makings of the "millionaire next door," the seemingly poor neighbor with a low-paying job who chooses to live frugally yet dies a rich man.

Importantly, before you begin to save aggressively, it is *absolutely critical to pay down high-interest personal debt and build an emergency cash reserve of between 6 and 12 months living expenses.*

Real Estate Ownership

A second way of creating wealth is through *the ownership of real estate over time.* This can be through owning a personal residence or rental home, but can also include owning commercial properties like multifamily apartments, office buildings, and retail and industrial buildings, as well as more speculative land ownership (either for future development or for it's valuable mineral, timber, or other rights).

For most people, we commonly see wealth created through the ownership of primary and vacation residences, as well as a small number of single family rental properties—which are often former residences that were converted to rental properties. From the early 1990s until now—notwithstanding the housing crisis and accompanying Great Recession (officially, December 2007 to June 2009)—many people have experienced significant gains in the value of the residential properties that they own. However, it is unlikely that these unusually large price increases will continue in the future, particularly once interest rates begin their inevitable march higher (from today's levels, which are among the lowest in history).

Stock-Based Compensation

The third means of creating wealth is through *stock-based compensation*, that is, through gains on employer-based stock that is given to an employee either through stock options, share grants, or stock purchase programs.

Stock options offer an employee the right to buy shares of stock at a fixed price over a long period of time (often as much as 10 years, provided that you remain an active company employee). This can be a particulary powerful means of generating wealth, especially if the share price of the stock rises considerably higher than the *strike price* of the options (the price at which you can buy the shares).

Many employers grant shares of stock or RSUs (restricted stock units, which are a kind of phantom stock), which vest over several years of employement with the company. Stock purchase programs allow for employees to buy shares at a discounted price through the company's regular monthly payroll mechanism, usually up to maximum dollar amount per year. All of these methods, used consistently over a long period of stock price appreciation, can lead to significant gains and the creation of substantial wealth.

Entrepreneurs and Businesses Ownership

The fourth means of creating wealth is through *entrepeneurship and the direct ownership of individual businesses.* This can mean anything from a small business that provides you with extra income, to a going concern (such as a law firm or other professional practice) that serves as your primary source of generating income. This also includes being one of the founders (or other early shareholders) of a start-up business that is eventually sold or merged with a larger business, or taken public in an IPO (initial public offering).

Ultimately, it is the ownership of business assets that is generally considered the most powerful way to grow significant wealth. Being a direct and active owner, however, will almost always come with both higher risk and more stress than simply being a minority shareholder in a large company. Starting an entrepreneurial endeavor—having all the weight of success or failure rest on your shoulders—can be very stressful and inherently carries with it a much higher degree of risk than does being an employee of, or investor in, a larger organization.

Investment Gains and Reinvestment

Fifth, many individuals are able to create real wealth through investing. This investment success can come in many forms:

- Those who save well and start to invest early in their lives, generating solid investment returns that compound over time (e.g., someone who invests in a sensible portfolio over a long period and thus reaps the rewards of doing so);
- Those who possess extraordinary investment skill and are able to generate wealth through their own research and trading (this is difficult to do, and usually such investors will have some form of special access or knowledge about their unique area of investment);
- Someone who gets lucky, such as those who invested early in Apple, Google, or Amazon;
- Someone who buys a work of art or other collectible that rises hugely in value; or
- Someone who is very lucky who "invests" in a lottery ticket and wins.

Inheritance

The sixth primary method of accumulating wealth—which is a bit different in that it is nearly completely passive—is through *inheritance.* Many globally mobile individuals anticipate inheritances from their parents, their grandparents, or another member of their family, and some of these inheritances will be from family members outside of the United States. We will talk more about the implications and ramifications of cross-border inheritances later in this book.

Diversification: Protecting and Growing Wealth

If you want to one day achieve financial independence, your first priority is to create wealth through the most potent means you can, as described in the last section. Once you have accumulated some wealth, *your most important goal becomes the diversification of that wealth.* The goal of this is to first protect and maintain the wealth, and then to correctly situate it so that it can grow at a reasonable rate without exposing it to unnecessary risk. In this section, we will explore in greater detail the concept of diversification.

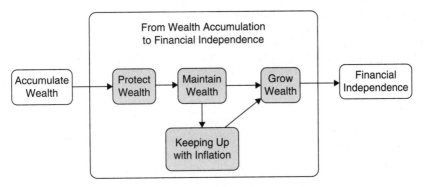

Figure 3.1   A balance-sheet approach to diversification and asset allocation

Considering Your Entire Balance Sheet

Whether your wealth is created through a specific event—like a company going public—or whether it is simply accumulated over time through savings, once you have accumulated that wealth, it's important to always be thinking about diversifying it—or spreading it out. As shown in Figure 3.1, after you have accumulated wealth, we recommend that you apply a *balance sheet approach* to diversification and the allocation of assets in your investment portfolio. By doing so, you both remove the risk of overconcentration and put yourself in a better long-term position for protecting, maintaining, and growing your wealth.

As an example, one way to protect your wealth through diversification would be to move from a concentrated stock position—all or a significant percentage of your stock investments in one company—to one that is more spread out. If, for example, you are working for a public company that has given you stock options now worth $1,000,000,[2] you should probably exercise a substantial percentage of those options and sell the stock to lower the risk that there will suddenly be a significant drop in the stock's price. Even if you really believe in the company, and feel that the stock will certainly go up in the long run, you still don't want to have an overconcentration of your personal wealth devoted to it.

---

[2]Suppose, for example, that you have options for 10,000 shares with a strike price of $10 per share, and the stock has risen to $110 per share. Once you execute the options and sell them, you will have $1,000,000, before the impact of transactions costs and withheld taxes.

The same thing holds if you purchased a piece of real property that has greatly appreciated. Suppose you purchased some property in San Francisco (or London, Berlin, or Mumbai) a few decades ago, and now it is worth 5 to 10 times its original purchase price. If that property represents a majority of your net worth, it would be wise for you to find a way to diversify that investment, even if that means selling some or all of the property.

Put differently, *it's just not prudent to put too many of your eggs in the same basket for too long.* While most people intuitively understand this concept—which is at the heart of the general notion of diversification—they often have a hard time knowing when to take action. Some people, unfortunately, simply end up taking too long, much to the detriment of their long-term financial health.

The Meaning of "Diversification" Versus "Asset Allocation"

The terms *diversification* and *asset allocation* are used differently by different books and writers on investing and personal finance, so it's not surprising that a bit of confusion sometimes results. To limit such confusion here, let's review these terms.

Spreading Thing Around

Diversification, the broader term, derives from the activity of diversifying or spreading out your wealth and assets, as well as any risks or hazards you face. The idea of "not having all your eggs in one basket" perfectly captures this: If you have an asset basket with *all* your eggs in it and you drop it, things will obviously be much worse for you than if only *some* of your eggs were in that asset basket.

The principle of diversifying one's wealth has long been recognized. For example, the Talmud, a text of Rabbinic Judaism thousands of years old, says, "Let every man divide his money into three parts, and invest a third in land, a third in business, and a third let him keep in reserve." Similarly, in 1738 the mathematician Daniel Bernoulli wrote, " ... it is advisable to divide goods which are exposed to some small danger into several portions rather than to risk them all together."

Asset Allocation in Investment Portfolios

Asset allocation is a newer term often associated with the Nobel-prize winning economist Harry Markowitz who, starting in the 1950s as an economics graduate student, came up with many of the basics of what is now called modern portfolio theory. He studied how entire blended portfolios—not just individual stocks or bonds—work together, and showed how to maximize return while limiting risk. (More specifically, he showed how it is possible—at least theoretically and retrospectively—to minimize risk for any given level of return, or to maximize return for any given level of risk, by using a mathematical construct known as the *efficient frontier.*)[3]

The most typical usage of asset allocation, then, refers to how an investment portfolio is allocated between the major asset classes, which are usually broadly defined as including: (1) cash and cash equivalents, (2) equities (e.g., stocks), (3) fixed-income investments (e.g., bonds), and (4) alternative assets such as commodities, real estate, and precious metals.

Later, in a famous study published in 1991, Gary Brinson and his co-authors were able to show that on average 91 percent of the total variation of actual returns among different pension funds was directly attributable to the weightings of the various asset classes, not to the choice of the specific stocks, bonds, or funds held nor to any market timing (Figure 3.2).[4] Note, too, that when an individual or family diversifies its wealth, it is in effect putting its assets into one of

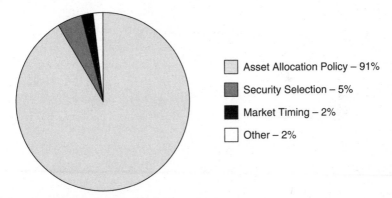

Figure 3.2   Determinants of Portfolio Performance

---

[3]The efficient frontier is the set of optimal portfolios that offers the highest expected return for a defined level of risk. http://www.investopedia.com/terms/e/efficientfrontier.asp

[4]G. P. Brinson, L. R. Hood, and G. L. Beebower, "Determinants of Portfolio Performance II: An Update," Financial Analysts Journal (May/June 1991); and Kleinwort Benson, 2011.

these same four categories as well. The implication here is that the growth of any family's long-term net worth will be mostly dependent on just how well its assets are allocated to begin with.

A Well-Allocated Portfolio Can Still Lack Diversification

However, even if a family's portfolio of assets is well allocated, it still may not be sufficiently diversified or spread out between different types of sectors, industries, and companies of different sizes within the major asset classes. We are, then, always interested in making sure that your wealth—whether taken in the largest sense, or just in regard to your investment portfolio—is not just sensibly asset-allocated, but also sufficiently diversified.

In sum, diversification is the general principle of spreading out one's wealth. This general principle has been specifically applied by economists to come up with the idea of portfolio asset allocation, which usually refers to spreading out investments in a portfolio between major asset classes. But even when this is accomplished, more diversification *within* those classes of securities may be desirable, such as diversification across geographic regions, sectors of the economy, industries, and specific companies within specific industries. By purchasing a pooled investment fund (like a mutual fund or ETF), it becomes possible to instantly diversify the amount invested across thousands of companies or other investments.

For more information on asset allocation generally, see *The Intelligent Asset Allocator—How to Build Your Portfolio to Maximize Returns and Minimize Risk* by William Bernstein (McGraw Hill, 2001), and *The Winner's Circle: Asset Allocation Strategies From America's Best Financial Advisors* by R. J. Shook (Horizon Publishers Group, 2007). Bernstein's book in particular provides an excellent tutorial at the layperson's level for understanding the efficient frontier and some of the theory and mathematics that eventually resulted in Markowitz winning the Nobel Prize for economics.

Allocating Your Net Worth: A Balance Sheet Approach

We recommend that all investors follow a balance sheet approach when considering the overall distribution of their assets (their net worth). This means you should be quite deliberate about the process of diversifying the entirety of your wealth, including the thorough and intelligent allocation of your portfolio investments.

We recommend that successful families carefully consider the distribution of their net worth (total assets minus liabilities), to ensure that they are reasonably well diversified. As you become more organized (perhaps with all of your information summarized in a spreadsheet), a sensible and suitable plan attuned to your personal long-term needs and desires can be developed and eventually executed.

Six Primary Asset Categories

There are six primary asset categories that likely represent the majority of a typical family's net worth. From roughly the lowest to highest risk, these include:

- Cash and cash equivalents
- Personal residences
- Income property
- Publicly traded securities—bonds and bond funds (fixed income)
- Publicly traded securities—stocks and stock funds (equities)
- Concentrated ownership of businesses

Three Additional Items of Importance

In addition, we will also briefly discuss three other related items of importance:

- Personal debt
- Collectibles and other hard assets
- Other private investment vehicles

We'll now look at each of these in turn.

Cash and Cash Equivalents

First, it is very important to always maintain a healthy reserve of cash or cash equivalents, which are highly safe and short-term investments such as money market funds or certificates of deposit (CDs). Cash and cash equivalents are liquid—they are immediately available to you if you have a need to buy something or want to invest in something else (like a great opportunity)—and they generally do not change in value (except as a result of exchange rate fluctuations).

The downside of cash and its equivalents is that this asset class is very low yielding (you will derive little interest income from it), and any income that is generated will generally be fully taxable (unless your cash is held in a tax-deferred account like a 401(k) or IRA). Overall, the after-tax return from cash and cash equivalents is generally always below the rate of inflation. While the real return (the inflation-adjusted return) on this asset class is therefore negative, it still has an important holding in everyone's balance sheet. In fact, as stated elsewhere, *you should strive to always maintain a cash reserve for emergencies equal to between 6 and 12 months of your living expenses.*

Personal Residences

Next, we generally recommend that you own your personal residence whenever possible and practical. For younger families, saving to purchase a residence is often a smart goal early on—provided that you are reasonably stable in your living situation and don't plan to move for at least five to seven years. There's been a good deal of writing and research about the wisdom of owning your own residence, and we strongly support this notion. Among cross-border families, the ethic of owning real estate is very popular, especially among those with Asian and European roots. They generally believe that property ownership is a fundamental element of being a financially successful person.

As for whether owning one or more residences is a smart investment, the general thought is that by owning your own home you are essentially paying yourself rent; and, as you pay down your mortgage, you are accumulating more and more equity in a property that will probably also go up in value. Furthermore, mortgage interest is a tax-deductible expense (in the United States, but not always in other countries), making the cost of mortgage financing especially attractive to higher income professionals. Historically, residential homes have tended to rise in value at around the rate of inflation, which, by any measure, is not that substantial. In the last 25 years or so, however, we've seen a much higher rate of appreciation among residential property in most large urban areas around the world, even after factoring in the effects of the Great Recession of 2007–2009 and the associated housing crisis. Because of this, one may expect the future returns on real estate to be somewhat lower in the next several decades, perhaps even below the rate of inflation (or even negative).

Income Property

A category related to personal residences is income property. In our experience working with many cross-border families who are originally from outside the United States, most still own at least one property abroad, usually in the country they were born in or in another city where they once worked. In addition to generating rental income, these single-family residences have very often appreciated significantly over time and are an important element of these family's overall net worth. However, there can often be a significant amount of time required to manage a rental property, which is not for everyone.

Another class of income property is known as commercial real estate. This generally includes larger and more business-focused properties, which can either be completely owned or partially owned with other investors, and which often employ professional property managers. Commercial real estate can include multifamily apartments, office buildings, and retail and industrial buildings, as well as raw and undeveloped land. In many cases, these investments require larger amounts of capital and more specialized industry knowledge; however, they can prove to be an important and valuable asset in the long run.

Real Estate: How Much Is Too Much?

Compared to typical Americans, international families generally hold a much higher percentage of their wealth in real estate. Real estate—including residences, rental properties, commercial holdings, and raw land—tends to be a very highly regarded asset that international people accumulate as they grow their net worth.

Overall, property investments can prove an excellent way to diversify your personal net worth. However, regardless of the extent of your real estate holdings, you will probably also want to invest in stocks and bonds to lower your overall risk and to increase the likelihood that your wealth will grow.

Publicly Traded Securities: Stocks and Bonds

As wealth is created, and then in turn diversified, the next two elements—which are liquid public securities that can easily be diversified—will likely become a larger part of most people's investment holdings.

Bonds and Bond Funds (Fixed Income)

Bonds are obligations generally issued by large corporations or governments (whether at the local, state, regional, or national level) that are meant to raise money for the issuer. They typically pay an annual interest rate and then, at some point in the future, they mature and pay back the bondholder the initial amount of money that was borrowed. The benefit of such fixed income investments is that while they are not entirely risk-free—a corporation, municipality, or even a sovereign nation could go bankrupt or otherwise default on its debts—they tend to be highly safe and stable and often pay a much better yield than cash or cash equivalents (such as those from a bank account or timed deposit).

Furthermore, bonds are public securities that are traded on an exchange. They can be purchased either individually or through a fund structure that owns many different bonds (e.g., a mutual fund or an ETF)—which offers the benefit of diversification. That is, by purchasing a variety of bonds or a bond fund, you have in effect placed your money with many different borrowers, whether governments or corporations. This dramatically lowers your risk and the long-term damage that you will incur if one or more of your bond issuers defaults on its obligations.

The three primary benefits of owning bonds are (1) capital preservation, (2) income, and (3) price movement that is generally inversely correlated to the stock market.

Finally, by owning bonds within a diversified portfolio that also includes stocks, you can significantly improve a portfolio's overall stability and its ability to protect and preserve capital. Why? Well, stocks and bonds are generally inversely correlated to each other, which lowers overall risk. This is because when the stock market falls, interests rates will usually come down, which is usually very good for those who own bonds. Conversely, when the economy is going very well, interest rates will often rise, which is bad for bonds and marginally lowers their value. But of course, during these good times the overall returns on a portfolio will typically benefit from rising stock prices.

Today's Unusually Low Interest Environment

As this book is being written in 2016, interest rates are still at or near all-time lows. Interest rates in the United States have been kept super-low by the Federal Reserve since the 2007–2009 Great Recession in order to stimulate economic growth and bolster asset prices. (In December 2015, rates were raised for the first time in nearly a decade.) This extremely low-interest-rate environment has reduced the value of having bonds in a portfolio in two ways.

First, a big part of the benefit of having a portfolio that include bonds as well as equities is that these two types of assets are inversely correlated—one tends to rise as the other falls, and vice versa—thereby providing a decrease in overall risk by owning both. Now, when interest rates go down bond prices rise, but since interest rates really can't go much lower, this dynamic has reached a kind of upper limit. Put differently, bonds aren't likely to go up much more in value should we encounter a difficult economic period … because interest rates really can't fall much further.

Second, bonds are not providing much immediate return on investment, again because interest rates are so low to begin with. So, if the benefits of bonds are (1) capital preservation, (2) a reasonable income stream, and (3) price movement, which is inversely correlated to stock markets, right now they are mostly only providing the capital preservation.

Stocks and Stock Funds (Equities)

Stocks are minority shares that represent fractional ownership of large public corporations. They are attractive in part because ownership of a business—even a very, very small piece of a business—is among the best ways to grow wealth, as discussed earlier in this chapter.

Basically, then, the public stock markets are an opportunity for investors—as minority shareholders—to own very small slivers of public companies. These minority shareholders are then benefited—even if only to a small degree—by the company's ongoing profits, both in terms of dividends and the increasing value of the overall enterprise (which in theory will be reflected in the price of its stock). Since you can buy shares of companies in such very small slivers, it affords the opportunity to build a much more diversified portfolio of minority ownership in a variety of companies across a variety of industries and regions around the world than would otherwise easily be possible. A well-allocated portfolio, then, will give you a stable and diversified exposure not just to a single concentrated position in one company, but in up to thousands of very small positions in a wide range of companies.

Whether you invest in shares of individual companies or through a fund structure—like a mutual fund or an ETF that itself owns a large pool of investments—diversified stock investments represent a very important element of your overall asset allocation. Why? Well, among your various assets that are passive and do not require an active management role (like running a business), stocks are *the asset class that has the highest likelihood to grow at a rate in excess of inflation over time.* That is, diversified equities can create real, after inflation, wealth over the long term; yet because of the benefits of diversification, they also provide a good measure of wealth protection and risk control, at least when compared to owning a single or small group of individual stocks. At the same time, because they are a *passive* investment, you can rely on the professional managers of the companies you are invested in, as opposed to being intimately involved with running the businesses you're investing in.

Downsides of Owning Stocks

There are also some downsides associated with being a minority shareholder of a company. Although you can in theory attend the annual shareholders' meeting, for the most part you won't have any say in business operations. And in some situations, minority shareholders can be disadvantaged relative to management. Moreover, it's quite typical for companies to make less than the maximum dividend payouts that they could in theory make to shareholders. Instead, they'll often retain a significant percentage of their profits and only payout a small percentage in dividends, justified by the need to reinvest and redeploy those profits so that the business can become more successful and produce a greater long-term return. A company like Apple, for example, despite huge earnings, pays out only a small amount in dividends because it feels it can effectively redeploy and leverage those retained earnings to produce greater long-term value for everyone involved. In many cases, this is correct.

Successful companies likely can better deploy capital by reinvesting it to earn a higher return than you could achieve by reinvesting the after-tax proceeds of those dividends.

The other major downside of owning public equities is that stock prices can be very volatile from year to year: In any given year, a stock or stock portfolio can suffer a dramatic loss in value. Stock market investing, then, should always be viewed with a long-term perspective—often a good 7 to 10 years or more—that endures at least the ups and downs of one entire business cycle. So while it is very likely that in any 7- to 10-year cycle there will be years when your stock market investments lose value, it's also true that there has hardly been a 10-year period (at least in the United States) when the overall stock market did not earn a positive return.[5] In short, the downside of stock market investing is volatility, in that the markets can fall precipitously in any given year; but over a full economic cycle, diversified stock market investing has proven to be a smart move.

Concentrated Business Ownership

The last element of a typical family's overall wealth mix is concentrated ownership of an operating business, either solely or with partners. In our experience, the most typical path to significant wealth creation for families is through the meaningful ownership of a company that grows substantially larger, more successful, and more profitable over time. Eventually, earnings are accumulated and some of that ownership can also be sold, and the resulting wealth can be diversified into the other categories of wealth described in this section. In any case, we recommend to clients approaching retirement age that they do not hold more than 10 to 20 percent of their net worth in the stock of any single company—even a company they started or helped grow—because of the risks inherent in being overconcentrated and insufficiently diversified. This rule can be difficult to follow in practice; a family can own a business that accounts for a huge majority of their net worth. Note that this rule becomes less important once a family has become substantially wealthy, and has accumulated enough other assets to completely provide for its long-term financial security.

---

[5]According to Morningstar, since 1926 the historical 10-year average of the U.S. stock market (S&P 500) was slightly negative only four times, in the 10-year periods ending in 1938, 1939, 2008, and 2009.

Before leaving this section, in addition to the six primary asset categories already discussed, there are three more items that should be mentioned.

Personal Debt

The first of these is personal debt.[6] The vast majority of cross-border families that we meet with and advise have little or no debt, other than mortgages on one or more residences or other real estate holdings. Families with international backgrounds will often work hard to pay down their mortgage debt as soon as they can, and generally do not find it wise to take on additional debt even if they have access to it. In other words, most foreign-born individuals place a high value on being debt-free or on having as little debt as possible.

Overall, we feel that the desire to have as little debt as possible, and the practice of paying it off as soon as is feasible, makes sense. However, debt—especially advantageous mortgage debt that provides a tax deduction—can provide substantial leverage in one's personal balance sheet that can enable further diversification in other ways. So, for example, suppose a family buys a million-dollar home, which they can either pay for outright or finance with a low-interest $600,000 mortgage. If they take on the mortgage, they in effect have an extra $600,000 readily available to them for investment, which they can use to further diversify their wealth. In the end, you should always be cautious about leveraging your assets with debt; it might be a smart move, but it can also increase risk to the degree where it can be catastrophic if not managed properly.

Finally, there is also the possibility of borrowing against one's investments (a margin loan) in order to make other investments. This is generally done to magnify the return on investments, because an investor can use leverage to purchase investments in excess of his or her total actual investment capital. We generally discourage people from using borrowed money as an investment strategy because of

---

[6]Business debt necessitates an entirely different conversation, with well-known methods available for evaluating whether it makes sense to borrow in order to build or expand a business.

the increased risk—after all, in the same way that gains are magnified due to leverage, so too are losses. It is also possible to utilize margin loans to further diversify a concentrated portfolio. In those situations, it can actually add value by lowering overall portfolio risk.

Collectibles and Other Hard Assets

Collectibles and other hard assets include precious metals (especially gold), gems, art, and other rare collectible items. Generally speaking, if you are not intimately aware of a particular market, you should probably not direct a substantial portion of your wealth in this direction. Investments in these areas can be highly subjective and volatile, and in many cases those who are not insiders to a market can be taken advantage of. Of course, many people purchase collectibles out of a passion for the objects (such as classic cars), and in those situations the actual investment returns are generally secondary.

Other Private Investment Vehicles

The final item to be considered is other private investment vehicles (also known as *alternative investments*). These are often private funds that invest in any number of strategies, and the most common include hedge funds, commodities pools, private equity and venture capital, pooled real estate funds, options, and quantitative trading, among others. In many cases, the fees charged by these funds can be high, and transparency and liquidity can be low. Furthermore, many of these funds are structured as investment partnerships with K1 partner distributions, making your financial affairs somewhat more complicated. Lastly, many of these strategies involve more frequent trading and therefore tend to be tax inefficient.

Investing in private investment vehicles can often carry significantly higher risk than other more traditional investments, but they also hold an appeal in that some will generate tremendous returns. Generally speaking, these strategies are generally best left to more sophisticated investors who have a particular knowledge set or special access into that specific investment strategy. If you aren't already involved with these sorts of things, you should probably not invest a substantial portion of your net worth in private investment vehicles.

Conclusion

Why is it important that you invest in such a way that your wealth maintains its purchasing power? As we discussed in Part I, in today's world things are changing more rapidly than ever before. In particular, consider the defined benefit pension system, which was once, for many decades, the predominant retirement vehicle for many people throughout the world.

The bottom line is that in today's world, people have to take on much more of the responsibility—and the risk—for making smart, approriate decisions with regard to their wealth throughout their lives. That includes the main subject of this chapter, which is to show how they should diversify the wealth that they accumulate along the way and intelligently invest and allocate assets for the long run.

4

Investing in the Markets: Stocks and Bonds

In Chapter 3 we looked at how following a thorough and deliberate approach to the allocation of your assets ensures good diversification and risk control. That process begins with putting together an accurate, detailed account of your actual net worth, including both all of your assets and all of your liabilities. In this section, we will take a more detailed look at the proper role of diversified investing in stocks and bonds within an overall wealth plan.

Three Important Attributes

Investing a good portion of your net worth—both through after-tax accounts as well as through 401(k)s or other tax-deferred retirement accounts—in stocks and bonds serves three very important purposes. These include the ease of diversification, the minimal need for your direct involvement, and the growth of wealth with reduced risk.

Easy Diversification

First, both stocks and bonds provide you with a simple way to diversify your investments, in a way that is both easy to implement and monitor. Utilizing pooled investment vehicles (like ETFs and mutual funds) allows you to achieve an even broader degree of diversification at little to no cost.

No Active Involvement

Second, because they are passive investments, you don't have to get involved in day-to-day management. (Think of the effort involved in owning stocks and bonds compared to owning an apartment building or operating a business.) For the most part, the management of your investments—especially if you are working with a qualified financial advisor—will require only a very minimal investment of ongoing time, freeing you to focus elsewhere (whether that focus is on other ways of accumulating more wealth, or is just on enjoying your life).

Source of Growth and Risk Control

Third, from a long-term strategic perspective, the primary purpose of these investments—especially stocks—is to grow your wealth in real terms (meaning after inflation). While the United States has been in a low-inflation period for quite some time, it is likely that at some point this will change and inflation will heat up. The goal, then, is to at least maintain your purchasing power by keeping up with inflation. Better still is to grow your portfolio and net worth so that they produce a net return—after all fees and expenses—that is above the long-term inflation rate. Whether you call it "real return" or "real growth" or just "increasing your purchasing power over time," this is a fundamental goal of diversified investing and is primarily accomplished through long-term exposure to stocks.

Bonds play an important but different role. Their purpose is to generate stable income through an interest rate that is better than what you can get at a bank or in timed deposits (like CDs). Bonds also provide an important element of stability and capital preservation to your overall investment portfolio.

Stocks and Bonds Work Better Together

Combining stocks and bonds together to build a portfolio generally produces lower overall risk. Why? Because stock and bond prices are generally inversely correlated to one another. This means that when the economy does poorly, and stock prices fall, interest rates generally come down to stimulate the economy, which makes bond prices rise. Conversely, when the economy is soaring, profits will be rising and most often stocks do very well. With such economic growth comes inflation and rising interest rates, which typically creates a more difficult period for bonds (whose value will tend to fall as rates rise). However, over a full market cycle (typically five to seven years), it has been proven that combining stocks and bonds lowers overall risk and produces better long-term returns.

Setting a Risk Objective

An important decision for investors is the percentage of their total investment portfolio that should be in stocks versus the percentage that should be in bonds. For larger institutional investors such as pension plans, foundations, and endowments, the most common allocation is a 60 percent/40 percent stock-to-bond mix. This division is thought to provide the optimal ongoing trade-off between long-term growth (from stocks) and capital preservation and income (from bonds). Although these large institutions—such as pension funds—are generally investing with a very long-term (often indefinite) time horizon in mind, they are also usually already paying out a significant amount every year in ongoing distributions.

For individual investors, however, the younger an investor is, the more risk they are generally able to take on because of the longer investment time frame they have available to them, and so a higher percentage in stocks versus bonds is usually recommended. Thus, younger investors are often advised to hold a portfolio of stocks and bonds with more than 60 percent in stock, and the remainder in bonds. As retirement approaches, the investor may decrease risk to a level approaching 50 percent stock (thought to be a moderate risk approach), or even to a level more conservative than this. There is some debate about how much risk a retired person should take with their investments, in part because this is highly dependent on their other sources of retirement income. Some retired investors will continue to invest in a moderate risk way, while others will choose to be much more conservative (and others still will be more aggressive).

In the next section, we will go into more detail as to the relationship between your investment priorities and objectives, and how to allocate your portfolio investments between stocks and bonds.

Managing Emotions While Focusing on the Long Term

Successful investing in stocks and bonds requires that you learn to understand and manage your emotions, particularly around your feelings of fear and greed. All too many people try to time the markets, that is, try to determine when they are about to go up or go down. But overall, this has proven remarkably difficult to do. The randomness of the markets has been well studied and written about, and we believe that markets are efficient and therefore an individual investor should not waste valuable time trying to outsmart the markets.

In fact, market timing has proven extremely harmful to many people. For example, a terrible mistake made by many investors during the aftermath of the 2007–2009 financial crisis and Great Recession was to sell their equities *after* they had already declined precipitously and lost tremendous value—effectively locking in their losses. Had they not reacted with fear, but rather stayed invested or even added more stocks to their portfolio when stock prices were low, they would have been far better off for it. This phenomenon is not new; in fact human beings have forever battled their instinctive reaction to follow the crowd when investing, much to their financial detriment.

Keep in mind that by investing in the stock market, you are essentially investing in the economy as a whole. And, naturally, economies tend to have business cycles (often lasting five to seven years or more) in which there will be periods of tremendous growth, periods of relative stability, and periods of substantial economic decline. You should, then, expect to see the stock portion of your portfolio deliver returns over time that are lumpy, nonlinear, and jump about quite a bit. That's just the way the whole system works. You will be best served to decide on a risk objective in the beginning that you can commit to maintaining, even if the market should fall significantly.

Stock Picking—Maybe Not

Greed also arises with regard to *stock picking*, which is related to but somewhat different from market timing. With stock picking, an individual or financial professional decides that based on different modes of analysis, or on access to information not yet generally known, or based on a gut feeling, that the next big winner or winners can be determined ahead of time. Economic science has proven over and over that all or nearly all known information about any given publicly traded investment is already embodied in its price (the *efficient market hypothesis*), and that stock picking very rarely works; and if it does work, almost no one can do it for the long run.

Warren Buffett seems to be an exception, but his model involves concentrated investing in a small group of companies that he personally investigates with a keen eye as to how they do business—an investing model that is quite difficult to properly execute. Moreover, if you take a close look at the lists of best-performing fund managers that come out regularly in financial magazines, you'll see that the best managers tend to only stay on top for a year or two; and very often by the time the next year has come around, those who were at the top have fallen squarely into the ranks of the middle or even bottom performers. For most people, then, our recommendation is to avoid trying to pick the next hot stock, sector, or fund manager. Instead, focus your serious investment capital on broadly diversified passive investment funds.

Investment Advice to Live By

If it is greed than leads people to the mistakes of market timing and stock picking, it is fear that makes people take precipitous action, ignore or fail to seek out competent advice, disrupt their long-term plans, sell the wrong things at the wrong times, and lose all momentum and direction. One way beyond fear and the whole fear/greed dynamic is to follow Warren Buffett's famous dictum regarding the timing of investments: "Be fearful when others are greedy, and greedy when others are fearful."

What this means is simple. On the one hand, if it looks like things are climbing to the sky and that, for example, you'd be a complete fool not to invest everything you have in something because everybody seems to be doing it and making tons of money—well, that's *just* when you want to pull back. Similarly, if it is 2006 or 2007 and everyone seems to be investing in real estate and making out big time, that's a good time to not let greed lead you into making a bad mistake. On the other hand, when everything looks terrible and it feels like there is no hope—when people start to say that "everything is different this time"—it will inevitably turn out that everything isn't really different, and pretty soon the economy and the markets will be humming along again.

The Value of a Financial Advisor

After starting my career as a PricewaterhouseCoopers accountant, I quickly moved to Wall Street to perform stock research to find winners and losers—undervalued and overvalued securities—in the international markets. After doing this for several years, I became somewhat disillusioned about Wall Street and the business of active stock picking. Why? Well, because I did not feel that my work was adding significant value to the portfolios we were managing.

I eventually founded Worldview Wealth Advisors in order to provide specialized wealth advice to families with cross-border lives. What I've learned through my journey is that what makes the greatest impact on client's investment results is developing a personal relationship with a financial advisor who considers their situation and goals, and helps them develop a long-term investment plan.

This kind of holistic financial planning—whether focused on budgeting and saving, investment management, tax strategies, or big-picture decisions about diversification and asset allocation—is by far the most valuable part of the investment advisory relationship. This is not something that can be delivered by a robot or a mathematical algorithm, and the specific investment strategy used is likewise less important.

Avoiding the Herd Mentality

As a good rule of thumb, then, if you see a lot of greed around you, that's a good time to be fearful, and if you see a lot of fear around you, that's an excellent time to look for opportunities and keep moving forward with your long-term plans. Unfortunately, most studies show that for the average person, investing in this manner is difficult because it's against human nature to not follow the herd.[1] Given our flight-or-fight programming, we are naturally predisposed to follow the herd in both good times and bad times. And even if you know that you should resist following the herd, it's very hard to do unless you have an unbending focus on the long run.

What you should aim to embrace, then, is the idea of long-term thinking. Whether the general atmosphere is one of market stress or one of market euphoria, you are always better off acting in a measured and controlled way, as opposed to in an emotional and reactive way. You certainly want to have feelings about your investments—they represent the security for you and your family's future—but you simply must control your emotions. It's been proven, both in academic studies[2] and through life experience, that decisions made during times of high stress rarely turn out to be wise ones—think of all the

---

[1]Studies consistently show that the average self-directed investor underperforms the overall stock market by between 3 percent and 4 percent a year. Individual investors fail to capture the same returns as market averages both because of greed (chasing returns) and fear (panicking in times of stress and selling).

[2]Daniel Kahneman, *Thinking, Fast and Slow* (Farrar, Straus and Giroux, reprint 2013), is a bestselling volume on behavioral economics—the science of how and why people make decisions relating to money and finance—that showcases the work that won Kahneman a Nobel Prize in economics.

people who sold their stocks at the depths of the recent 2007–2009 Great Recession only to watch the markets (but not their portfolios) quickly recover.

Staying Calm in Times of Change

As this book is being written in 2016, we find ourselves in a fairly peculiar time in the investment markets. We are (presumably) at or near the end of a 35-year cycle that has seen interest rates fall lower than they have ever been before in modern America (and around the world). This presents a particular challenge for those looking to maximize income from their investments. Why? Well, there really isn't a lot of opportunity to earn a reliable income from a portfolio without either lowering the quality of the bonds owned (increasing yield, but also risk), or moving a greater percentage of one's portfolio into stocks.

This dynamic is particularly challenging in the light of dramatically increasing life expectancies, which of course puts even more of a priority on the growth of one's investments (to preserve and grow one's purchasing power through retirement). Plus, as mentioned earlier, all of this is happening against the backdrop of a rapid decline in pensions and other defined benefit programs found both in America and abroad. The end result is that there is more pressure on everyone to work longer, to save more for their own individual retirement needs, and then invest wisely while avoiding the temptation to make "thinking fast" emotional decisions with their investments during times of market stress or euphoria. It is, therefore, more important than ever to stay calm and maintain focus on the long term.

Determining Investment Goals and Objectives

With regard to the structure of your investment portfolio, it is very important to have the right balance between stocks and bonds. The mix between these two asset classes is a highly personal decision, and depends in part on factors such as long-term goals, special needs, and your own personal risk tolerance.

Overall, though, most experts recommend that you progressively transition from more risky assets to more stable assets as you approach retirement, given that the time horizon for when you'll need to use the assets gets shorter. On the other hand, given that people are living longer and longer, you will likely need your portfolio to continue to grow throughout your retirement years, so it is important to strike a sensible balance between growth (from stocks) and income and stability (from bonds).

Ultimately, then, in order to make sure that you maximize your chances of financial success, you need to understand your investment priorities and objectives, and make sure that these are in alignment with your *risk tolerance*—that is, your psychological/emotional reactions to potential portfolio losses. Put differently, risk tolerance refers to how much loss you and your family can tolerate; for some people, even a little bit of portfolio loss is psychologically difficult, while others are able to ride the up-and-down waves of the markets with more equanimity.

Each investor must decide on his or her own risk tolerance level.[3] There are many ways to approach the question of risk tolerance, but ultimately it comes down to balancing the need for portfolio growth (which brings with it volatility) with the need for reliable income and safety. A big part of this consideration is time horizon—how soon investors will need to draw on their portfolio to fund their living expenses in retirement. Another factor is net worth, as those who begin with a far greater net worth are less likely to require significant portfolio growth to maintain their lifestyle. A third major factor here is the desired standard of living that is being reached for, since more expensive lifestyles require more income, and the requirements for more income requires greater asset growth and thus more risk, which brings us right back to questions of risk tolerance and psychological comfort levels.

Four Common Investor Objectives Defined

Generally speaking, when building a portfolio of stocks and bonds, there are four common categories of investor objectives (and resulting stock/bond mixes):

1. Conservative—income-oriented
2. Balanced—growth- and income-oriented

---

[3]Note that a wide variety of risk tolerance questionnaires and calculators are available online by doing a simple Internet search. While we don't endorse any particular risk tolerance calculator, spending some time with two or three of them will give you a pretty good idea of your risk tolerance.

3. Growth-oriented
4. Aggressive growth-oriented

A conservator investor is one whose primary motivation is to preserve capital and maximize income, with the potential of some limited portfolio growth. Generally, these investors have a time horizon of five years or under—that is, within five years they'll be looking to begin drawing off of their portfolio (if they are not already doing so). A typical conservative investor might hold 30 percent or less of his or her investment portfolio in stocks, with the rest in bonds or other fixed income vehicles.

Going up one notch in riskiness—for people able to handle more volatility—a balanced growth and income investor is looking for both capital preservation and current income, along with modest growth and appreciation at the expense of some additional portfolio risk. These investors often have time horizons of between 5 and 15 years, and will hold between 30 percent and 60 percent of their portfolio in stocks, with the rest in bonds.

A growth-oriented investor is someone primarily seeking asset growth but with somewhat lower volatility than displayed in the overall market. Their average time horizon is in the 10- to 25-year range, and their exposure to stocks would generally range from 60 to 80 percent of their entire investment portfolio.

Finally, there are those investors looking for aggressive growth in the value of their portfolio assets. These investors typically have a time horizon of greater than 25 years, and are willing to accept a great deal of volatility—lots of ups and downs—in exchange for the promise of higher long-term growth. Aggressive investors typically have 80 percent or more (up to 100 percent) of their investment portfolio allocated to stocks.

For a comparison of how asset allocations often change with investor age, see Figure 4.1.

Fundamental Investment Guidelines

Given everything already discussed in Part II, what is the best approach to take in investing your portfolio? Overall, as a quick summary, the best thing you can do is to take a deliberate and steady approach in order to gain exposure to the worldwide economic landscape, with an appropriate allocation between stocks and bonds.

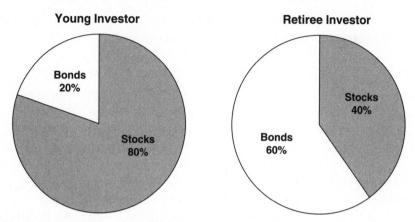

Figure 4.1 The chart on the left shows an example of stock allocation for a younger, growth-oriented investor. The chart on the right shows an example of stock allocation for a retiree who is more conservative.

In this section, we will now turn from the big picture to more of the nitty-gritty details of investing by reviewing a set of investment fundamentals based on our beliefs and experience. Each of these fundamentals will be considered in turn.

Low-Cost Passive Investing

We believe strongly in low-cost investing, which often means making passive investments through mutual funds or ETFs to gain exposure to a broad section of the investment markets. There has long been a spirited debate about whether it is possible for a professional investor, working with all publicly available information, to actively trade in and out of various securities and to sustainably beat the overall market, after subtracting the costs of management fees, transaction costs, and taxes. While it might be true that some few professional investors possess the skill to actively trade and beat the overall market over short periods of time, it is highly unlikely that any actively managed fund you could invest in would be able to beat the market over the long term.

Therefore, most individual investors are far better off sticking with lower-cost passive investment funds (as opposed to using actively managed funds). That is, lowering costs through passive index-based investments is likely to deliver greater returns than active management will over the long term, once all of the various transactions costs and taxes are taken into account.

Tax Efficiency Is Huge

Tax efficient—tax aware—investing is extremely important. This seems especially true for today's world, which is likely to see lower returns on stocks and bonds, as well as higher taxes around the world.

For example, you should absolutely take maximum advantage of any tax-advantaged savings vehicles at your disposal, such as 401(k)s (especially when there is a matching contribution from your employer). With these kind of pretax vehicles, your investments can grow in a tax-deferred way for many, many years before you actually end up making use of them. The benefit of tax-deferred compounding of returns is really very powerful.

Tax-free bonds, when available and appropriate, are also worth considering. State and federal tax-free municipal bonds are generally best for those investors already in very high tax brackets. Finally, tax-efficient investing embraces tax optimization strategies like tax loss harvesting and other strategies that are designed to minimize taxes on an ongoing basis, although most investors will need help from an accountant or financial advisor to best make use of these strategies. The bottom line here is that you, or someone you're working with, should always have one eye on minimizing taxes, an ongoing imperative that never goes away and that can make a big difference in the long run.

Global Diversification for All

The need to be globally diversified—to have portfolio exposure to different regions and currencies around the world—is of critical importance, which is why it pops up so often throughout this book. Ultimately, we all find ourselves in an increasingly global economy, so we all need to have exposure to that economy through globally diversified investments, or we may find ourselves—in a truly global sense—both left behind and left out of participating in worldwide economic growth. Many cross-border families have more global lifestyles, and may even be planning to retire in a foreign country, making the need for global diversification of their investments even more important.

Risk Control Through Asset Allocation

We believe that every investor's investment objectives must be synchronized with their ability and willingness to take on risk, as determined by their net worth, their age and time horizon, and their income, along with their overall attitudes toward investing and volatility.

With this in mind, your portfolio risk can be controlled both through your portfolio allocation between stocks and bonds (the greater the percentage of stocks, the riskier your portfolio will be), as well as the distribution of your overall net worth and assets (the allocation of your total assets between your investment portfolio and other assets like cash and real estate). The most important thing with regard to your asset allocation is to be in a position where you can and will stay fully invested through good times and bad—it's the sudden leaps into and out of the market that really hurt people—even if that means you need to have a relatively more conservative portfolio asset allocation to begin with.

Regular Rebalancing Adds Value: Don't Invest and Forget

It's very important to periodically rebalance your portfolio between risky assets like stocks and more stable investments like bonds. Ultimately, this amounts to a simple (but somewhat counterintuitive) process of selling winners and reinvesting the proceeds in losers. For example, if you have a traditional 60 percent stock and 40 percent bond investment portfolio, and the markets are currently favoring equities, then the percentage of your portfolio invested in equities will start rising (to a level above 60 percent of your total portfolio).

Every six months, every year, or every few years, then, you'll want to sell enough equities to return your allocation back to 60 percent–40 percent. The reverse is also true, and if your equities have been falling but your bonds have been doing well, you should periodically sell some bonds and reinvest the proceeds back into stocks to return the portfolio to its target allocation. Think of this rebalancing as a way to force you to act in a contrarian manner compared to the overall market, so that you end up being a buyer when others are selling, and vice versa.

Strategic Versus Tactical Asset Allocation

As previously discussed, the specific allocation of the assets in your investment portfolio is of critical importance. As a number of academic studies have shown, the vast majority of your portfolio's return will be dictated by the asset mix (the allocation amongst various asset classes) in your portfolio, and not by the underlying securities found in those various asset classes. But then, many investors are confused about how to best build and monitor an investment portfolio. For this reason, we thought it would be important to briefly address the ongoing debate between proponents of strategic asset allocation (SAA) and tactical asset allocation (TAA). Below we will define each of these portfolio management techniques.

Strategic Asset Allocation (SAA)

This approach calls for the establishment of a long-term target allocation among major assets classes such as stocks, bonds, and cash, based on an investor's unique portfolio objectives, risk tolerance, and time horizon. Furthermore, a particular allocation should be established within each of these core asset classes; for example, within stocks you may choose to invest in large and small U.S. stocks, as well as international and emerging market stocks. Over time, this target portfolio mix is periodically rebalanced when various asset classes have veered too far from their target portfolio allocation or weighting. No attempt is made to predict which asset class is likely to outperform the others; rather, relative winners in the portfolio will naturally be sold down and reinvested in relative losers as a simple result of the ongoing process of periodically rebalancing the portfolio.

Tactical Asset Allocation (TAA)

Here, the investor attempts to add value to a portfolio's return by selectively overweighting those asset classes that are expected to outperform on a relative basis in the short-term, and underweighting those expected to perform poorly. This approach is considered to be more active in terms of the investment management time and effort that is required (even though the investor may make use of passively managed investment products to achieve the desired investment exposure). Importantly, TAA fundamentally relies on the premise that an investor possesses the ability to determine which asset classes are likely to do better than others in the near term—something that is quite difficult to consistently accomplish.

Take It Slow

Our general advice is that for most people, following a good strategic asset allocation is the wisest move. Investment markets are very efficient over the long run, and maintaining broad portfolio diversification across the major asset classes best ensures investment success. The concept of "reversion to the mean" points to the fact that most asset prices tend to move back towards their mean or average value over the long run. Thus, the strategy of making periodic and incremental portfolio shifts (buys and sells) to get back to your target allocations (when the assets being sold have risen to an overweighted position relative to the positions that are being added to) works in a way like an autopilot. It guides you to taking profits on positions that have appreciated, and to adding to positions that are currently relatively out of favor.

This is not to say that it is impossible to outperform by making tactical asset allocation (TAA) decisions. In fact, we do believe it is possible to assess various asset classes with regard to their current valuations and recent performance history, and to make adjustments so that those assets that are historically overvalued (expensive) are held at a smaller weighting, and those that are historically undervalued (inexpensive) are weighted higher. However, this type of active investment management is very difficult to do well over a long period of time, and the process of consistently researching and monitoring the portfolio is beyond the capacity (skillwise and timewise) of most individual investors. For most people, a well-considered strategic asset allocation (SAA) approach to portfolio management is likely to deliver the best long-term investment result.

Our Approach: A Global Growth Portfolio

At Worldview Wealth Advisors, we have developed our own approach to investing over our many years in the business. Over time, we've modified our investment approach as a result of our increasing specialization in serving internationally oriented clients, ultimately realizing that there was a strong need among cross-border families for a customized solution for their U.S.-based portfolio assets.

Our investment solution was designed to be a low-cost, globally oriented portfolio held inside of a U.S. brokerage account in the name of an individual investor, whether or not he or she lives in the United States. The investments within the portfolio are ETFs (exchange traded funds), which in turn hold hundreds of underlying stock and bond positions. These underlying investments are located both in the United States and abroad, and are held in a variety of currencies and regions around the world. The weightings of the various investments are proactively adjusted—using a combination of both strategic and tactical asset allocation approaches—across asset classes, sectors, and currencies, based on our view of the economic landscape, in an effort to both improve returns and manage risk.

This investment solution comes in a variety of different configurations suitable to different risk objectives, ranging anywhere from aggressive to conservative. For the large community of internationally oriented people who have (a) worldwide retirement issues, (b) a very busy schedule, and (c) not a lot of options to choose from, this can be an effective, low-cost, broadly diversified, and globally aware solution.

A Jurisdictional Review: Where to Hold Investments?

Where do—and where should—cross-border families maintain their investment accounts? Until now, we have mainly focused on the *why* and the *what*: why investing is important generally, and what things should look like as you diversify your wealth through the investment process. In this section, we will review the *where* and the *who*—that is, the different geographic, national, and jurisdictional options for *where* investment accounts should be located and maintained along with the closely allied question of *who* cross-border professionals and their families are working with—or should be working with. In terms of opening, maintaining, and overseeing their accounts, then, our experience shows that cross-border families tend to hold their portfolio investments in one of four primary locations:

1. *Large foreign banks:* Typically foreign onshore retail banks located in the major countries in Europe or Asia;
2. *Large offshore private banks:* Often larger banks located in major offshore tax havens like Switzerland, Lichtenstein, Hong Kong, and Singapore;
3. *Smaller offshore banks and insurance companies:* Offering private banking services and various private pension schemes from both the larger tax haven countries and often from smaller

tax havens like the Channel Islands (Jersey and Guernsey), the Caribbean, Panama, Cyprus, and others; and

4. *U.S. brokerage accounts:* Either at one of the large national financial institutions, or at an independent investment brokerage.

Large Foreign Banks in Europe or Asia

The first approach we see is the use of large onshore banks both in Europe and Asia (these are onshore in the sense that they are not located in an offshore tax haven), the kind of big banks that have many branch locations throughout one or more countries, such as Deutsche Bank in Germany, Lloyds Bank in England, BNP Paribas in France, ABN Amro in Holland, HSBC in Hong Kong, Commonwealth Bank in Australia, and so on. (These banks are the equivalent of a Wells Fargo, Chase, or Bank of America in the United States.)

When international people become young adults and start to need banking services, they generally will open a bank account wherever they live. Eventually, when they start working and their savings build up, they start to receive calls from the *private banking* team within the investment division of that local bank. "Hey, you have too much money sitting in cash and not working for you; you should come in and learn about our investment offerings." So now that the person has moved to the United States, they often still hold much of their investment savings at this foreign bank—even if they've already lived in the United States for 5 or 10 years.

Have You Earned Your Own Private Banker?

Most large international banks offer several different levels of relationship. For example, they might offer a "premier" banking relationship once you have the equivalent of about $50,000 invested or on deposit. Then, you graduate to a "private banker" relationship once you have even more money with the bank (perhaps $250,000). When you have over a million dollars, euros, or the equivalent on deposit with the bank, you are then often eligible for some type of "elite" banking relationship.

Not World-Class Investments

Unfortunately, the investment divisions of many of these large international retail banks often charge very high fees, and instead of being able to offer you an *open architecture*, they often recommend investing in their own proprietary investment products, that is, their own branded investment funds, which may or may not be good performers overall.

Additionally, at many foreign banks around the world, it has been common to guide investors into insurance-based investments or annuity-like products. These combine life insurance with an accumulating investment account, which, in turn, is then invested in a mix of investment funds exposed to the overall market. These insurance-based accounts generally carry very high expenses, and as a result they tend to be poor performers over time. Additionally, these *insurance wrappers* normally have onerous terms and conditions (like surrender fees and other penalties) that make closing or repositioning the accounts unduly expensive.

Not World-Class Advice

If you are looking for personalized financial advice and someone to help you make important decisions, you may have trouble finding a good partner at a big foreign bank, particularly if you are not an "elite" customer. When working with these large institutions, you are often restricted to working only with the investment personnel located in the specific branch where your account is based. This remains true at least until you graduate into the higher private-banking relationship levels. And in most cases, your advisor will be a commissioned salesperson with an incentive to sell you a profitable product rather than comprehensively review your situation and make recommendations that will truly serve you.

Tax Reporting and FATCA

Another problem for U.S. taxpayers is that those who have accounts at large retail banks located outside of the United States generally do not receive appropriate tax reporting for IRS purposes (such as a 1099 tax reporting document that provides all of the important data needed to file a U.S. tax return). So, if someone has moved to the United States and becomes a tax resident, they likely will not receive a 1099 tax report from the foreign bank where their accounts are located. This can lead to reporting hassles and punitive tax treatment in the United States.

Finally, most large international banks are now being forced to observe elements of the U.S.-led Foreign Account Tax Compliance

Act (FATCA), which is discussed in Chapters 1 and 10. This act requires all foreign financial institutions (FFIs) to interview their customers with respect to any and all U.S. connections, and to then report the identities of such customers and their assets to the U.S. Treasury. Given the tremendous cost and complexity of putting these reporting mechanisms into place, many of these FFIs have decided to simply cease serving both U.S. citizens abroad as well as those foreign people who have moved to the United States and become tax residents.

Of course, there are still many cross-border professionals who have moved to the United States but who have not been recognized by their foreign bank as being U.S. tax residents. For example, this can happen when a foreign-born individual still uses his or her original address—let's say his or her parents' address—on the home country bank account. But if an attempt is made to change contact information to a U.S. address or phone number, this can immediately lead to all accounts being restricted or even closed.

Large Offshore Private Banks

The second approach commonly used by cross-border families is to hold investments in accounts at the large international banks located in major offshore tax havens, such as Switzerland, Singapore, Lichtenstein, and the like. The institutions located in these well-established offshore tax havens have benefited greatly from the reputation these jurisdictions have long been known for: (1) secrecy, (2) asset protection, (3) stability, and (4) tax avoidance.

Private banking in many of these large offshore banks can be a very privileged affair. Many of these institutions will greet you for meetings in ornate offices with lavish décor; and you may even enjoy coffee or a meal served with expensive china and silver flatware. An impression of wealth, privilege, and exclusivity is projected—these are the kind of institutions that know how to handle "old money" and keep it safe—but such VIP treatment is pricey, and working with these firms can be quite expensive. Management fees and other expenses tend to be much higher at these firms. Moreover, while big offshore banks are known for protecting wealth once it has been accumulated, they have never been particularly good at growing wealth over the long term. That is, with their historical focus on secrecy and asset protection, these institutions tend to offer more conservative investment solutions with lower long-term growth and appreciation.

As discussed in Chapter 2, the traditional strengths of firms within the major offshore havens are now under attack. As one expert put it as early as 2007, there is an "unstoppable trend toward global transparency and the fast decline of offshore private banking."[4] These jurisdictions are now under a powerful microscope, and their future ability to provide secrecy and asset protection is in jeopardy. Their long-term focus on protecting wealth—as opposed to growing it—is a particularly notable additional downside in the current climate of low interest rates. Investors are now more focused on investment growth, and also on financial advice and retirement planning—services that have never been a real strength for offshore private bankers.

Additionally, like other foreign retail banks across Europe and Asia, these offshore private banks typically do not offer appropriate tax reporting for U.S. taxpayers. Some larger banks have addressed this by creating U.S./IRS-compliant divisions, but such services are generally only available to very wealthy clients.

Smaller Offshore Banks and Insurance Companies

Another approach we see is for globally mobile professionals to make use of smaller offshore banks and insurance companies for investment management and retirement planning. The number of these firms is huge, and their services are indeed vast—all manner of private banking, investment management, and insurance services are offered.

Historically, many cross-border professionals (expatriates) across Europe and Asia have bought into private pension insurance contracts and other offshore investment schemes that were touted as being independent from any employer or country. These offshore investment solutions have historically been sold throughout the global expatriate community by well-dressed—and often slick—salespeople promoting the benefits of holding assets offshore and out of the reach of any country. Such products and investment structures are offered from jurisdictions like Guernsey, Jersey, the Isle of Man, the Cayman Islands, the Bahamas, Bermuda, Cyprus, and other similar locales. These accounts look very similar to

---

[4]Philip Marcovici, "The Wealth Management Industry and Today's Wealth-Owning Families—From Chaos Comes Opportunity," *CFA Institute Conference Proceedings Quarterly* 24(4) (December 2007).

insurance-based investments sold throughout Europe, Asia, and the United States, with variable investment funds held inside of an insurance wrapper.

For some investors, these private pension fund schemes can actually work pretty well. For example, if you are a non-U.S. citizen living in another country, it is potentially possible for you to move wealth to an offshore destination that won't be reported to (or taxed by) either your home country or your country of residence. While this *may* work, once again it runs against the trend toward stricter reporting of worldwide assets and income to local tax authorities.

For U.S. citizens and tax residents, *these investments unequivocally do not work.* Not only will U.S. taxpayers—including resident aliens living in the United States and permanent residents living abroad—*not* receive the benefits being touted by the offshore pension salespeople, investing in this way can actually lead to tax penalties as a result of improper tax reporting (no 1099 tax reports) as well as the PFIC tax rules on foreign investments (see Part V for more details).

In our experience, these offshore pension schemes tend to be very poor performers as well. Their underlying investments are often extremely opaque and difficult to research, and they tend to have extremely high fees (at times approaching 10 percent a year). They also generally have very long surrender periods such that you may be obligated to continue contributing to the account for up to 20 years or longer. And, if you cease your contributions, you can be faced with a large penalty that would erode a substantial amount of the existing value of your account. Finally, these institutions have very little transparency, and sometimes have little to no regulatory oversight. Overall, despite how common these investment schemes are internationally, they are among the worst investment products we have seen, and we do not recommend them for U.S. citizens or tax residents (or for anyone else, for that matter).

U.S. Brokerage Accounts

The final location where many cross-border families invest is in U.S.-based brokerage accounts. We feel that regardless of where in the world you live, the United States can be a very good choice for where to hold a globally portable portfolio. In fact, the United States is now the fastest growing "offshore" investment jurisdiction in the world, as more international people seek to locate some of their wealth within U.S. borders.[5]

The United States has many rules that are meant to encourage and attract the investments of international families. The general benefits of the U.S. market include a transparent system with strong regulatory oversight. U.S. brokerage accounts generally have the lowest fees of anywhere in the world, and they offer significantly more investment alternatives than does any other country's investment market. Additionally, some U.S. brokerage houses now offer multicurrency accounts, which enable people to purchase foreign securities in the local currency and to also hold and exchange international currencies within an interest bearing account.

Should foreign people residing in the United States move away and give up their Green Card (becoming a nonresident for U.S. tax purposes), U.S. brokerage accounts remain an excellent place for them to hold their diversified investment capital. In general, there are no U.S. filing requirements and little to no taxes due to the United States. Put differently, foreign residents can continue to hold investments in the United States with only minimal income tax consequences and no filing requirements, yet they will continue to receive the many benefits associated with such accounts as already outlined. (See the Part V for more on the unique tax issues faced by foreign residents investing in the United States.)

Problems with Maintaining Accounts in the United States

There are, however, a few negatives for cross-border families investing in U.S-based brokerage accounts—in particular for families residing outside of the United States. First, in general, it has become very difficult to find a financial institution in the United States that will work with you if you are living *outside* of the United States (whether you are a U.S. citizen or not). That is, many U.S.-based banks and investment firms will refuse to provide service to someone who lives abroad out of concern for increased risk and reporting requirements.

Even if someone, who has been living in the United States and has developed a close relationship with a financial advisor working

---

[5]http://www.bloomberg.com/news/articles/2016-01-27/the-world-s-favorite -new-tax-haven-is-the-united-states.

for a large investment firm, would to Asia, for example, the firm will likely no longer allow the financial advisor to communicate with and advise the person (due, in part, to the risk of its advisor giving inappropriate advice). If it is a small client, the U.S.-based firm will often just try to terminate the relationship entirely. If the client is large enough, and the firm still wants them as a client, some firms have set up international account teams to take over or share the relationship with the old advisor. But these international teams are generally staffed with people who have been trained on how *not* to advise international people. That is, their special training is more grounded in teaching them what not to say (subjects to avoid discussing), rather than in any specialized knowledge or advice on cross-border issues.

It can also be challenging in other ways to manage your investments if you are living abroad. Even attempting to log into a U.S.-based account from a foreign location can raise flags and cause accounts to be restricted or frozen. Additionally, if you are labeled as living abroad, you can become ineligible to buy a whole segment of securities. For example, if someone is residing internationally, most brokerage houses will no longer allow them to purchase what are called open-ended mutual funds, even if they are a U.S. citizen. So, even if the client living abroad is able to log in and access his or her account, there are certain investment alternatives he or she will be prohibited from purchasing.

Foreign Residents with U.S. Accounts

Furthermore, upon the death of a foreign resident, his or her estate may incur an additional estate tax risk by holding investment assets or property in the United States. If you are a foreign resident living in a country that does not have a mitigating estate tax treaty with the United States, upon your death your estate may face a lowered estate tax exemption of $60,000 (compared to the current (2016) $5.45 million per person for U.S. citizens and tax residents). The value of any U.S. assets in excess of this significantly lowered exemption would then be subject to U.S. estate taxes. That means when compared to the assets of a U.S. citizen or tax resident, the U.S.-based assets of a foreign resident may be at risk of much higher U.S. estate taxes upon their death.

For foreign residents with accounts in the United States, then, there may not be many very good choices. One option is for the person who is about to become a foreign resident—the person who is moving away from the United States and giving up his or her Green Card—to simply sell everything he or she owns in U.S. accounts, and then take the proceeds home and then invest them there like any ordinary person living in that country would do. However, there are often qualified accounts, like 401(k) accounts, that cannot be withdrawn without incurring significant taxes and penalties for early withdrawal.

The Best Choice for Many People

To sum up, for cross-border families in the United States and abroad, locating investment accounts in a U.S.-brokerage account is a great choice and the option we generally recommend for all the reasons listed above. However, for those families who have left the United States—including U.S. citizens, permanent residents (Green Card holders), and foreign residents—while U.S.-brokerage accounts can still be an excellent place to hold investments, it can become increasingly difficult to properly manage those investments and obtain knowledgeable advice from a financial advisor.

PART III

401(k)s, IRAs, and Other Pensions and Savings Plans

5

A Global Approach to 401(k)s and IRAs

Cross-border professionals, especially those recently arrived in the United States, often have many questions about the retirement savings plans that are potentially available to them in the United States. Among the most common kinds of retirement plans include:

- 401(k) plans
- Other tax-qualified plans like individual retirement accounts (IRAs)
- Roth IRAs or Roth 401(k)s
- Employer-based pensions (defined benefit plans)

Likewise, most American citizens and tax residents are rather confused about how the IRS views foreign retirement plans, and whether they should participate in them when given the chance. Also, many people who are now in the United States own foreign retirement accounts of various types, which may not be viewed favorably by the IRS.

Investing Your Serious Money

Many international people are less accustomed than Americans to investing in stocks and bonds, and a 401(k) is often their first experience with public market investing. While this is changing—investing in the public markets is becoming more common in Asia and Europe—it is very important for those who are not familiar with this kind of investing to look at their 401(k) or IRA as an important long-term investment vehicle. Money in these accounts is serious money—a foundational element of one's retirement nest egg—and not some place to undertake speculative investing.

A prudent long-term diversified approach to investing is called for here, rather than concentrated bets on specific stocks with frequent portfolio changes. Generally speaking, the closer one gets to retirement—and the closer one is to needing to draw on the funds in these accounts to support themselves—the more conservative the investments in the account should be, but of course this depends on each individual's goals and financial situation.

401(k) Plan Basics

A 401(k) retirement plan is a long-term retirement savings plan that resides with your employer. Essentially, it is a salary-deferral savings program that allows tax-deferred contributions to be made from your salary—that is, directly from your paycheck before income taxes are levied. For 2016, the limit of how much of this pretax money you can contribute is $18,000 per year, or $24,000 if you are age 50 or older and make use of the $6,000 a year catch-up contribution.

Additionally, many employers offer a matching contribution benefit. That is, as part of their employee benefits package, many employers will match some of the contribution you make, usually based on a percentage of your contributions up to a set dollar amount. For some individuals, especially those over 50 who are using the catch-up provision, this can mean accumulating as much as $30,000 a year or more in total pretax investment savings.

There are many additional types of retirement accounts in the United States, and also more ways of making retirement plan contributions. The two most common methods of funding U.S. retirement accounts, after regular salary deferrals into a 401(k), include employer profit sharing programs and contributions to self-employed or small business plans.

Key Benefits of 401(k) Plans

The key benefits of contributing to your 401(k) savings plan include:

- *Pretax contributions:* You fund your 401(k) with pretax dollars—that is, from income before you have paid tax, thus avoiding U.S. federal and state income tax on the amount contributed.

- *Employer matching:* You also get the benefit of any employer match that is offered (when an employer contributes additional pretax funds on your behalf).
- *Tax-deferred investment growth:* You build an investment account that enjoys the benefits of tax-deferred growth, growth that can compound for many years until such time that you draw the funds in retirement.
- *Shifting taxable income to retirement years:* When you finally begin making withdrawals from the account, you will generally be taxed on the withdrawal as though it were ordinary income, but you will likely be in a lower income-tax bracket, assuming you are retired.

Given these benefits, it generally makes sense for individuals to fully participate in a 401(k) plan if their employer offers one.

Individual Retirement Accounts: A Good Start, But Not a Solution

As we have said before, there is a powerful trend around the world to push the responsibility for funding retirement down to the individual rather than having employers or the government do it for them (usually through the various forms of tax-advantaged salary deferral programs, or *defined-contribution* plans). Unfortunately, from our perspective, these kinds of plans are *not* a panacea and cannot be an effective replacement for the defined-benefit pension systems that have historically filled this role around the world.

Substantial research shows that the *majority* of people will not be successful under this system. First, we know that the average person will not save enough of their income every year to adequately fund retirement. Perhaps this can be partially solved by *requiring* that individuals and their employers make regular contributions to their plans, as is done in many other countries around the world. Second, research further shows that most people will poorly manage the funds that they've been able to save. On average, most individuals earn returns that are well below market averages, mainly as a result of poorly diversified portfolio construction and emotionally driven investment decisions (such as buying in when prices are high, and selling when markets are in correction).

Instead, we would like to see another solution that is obligatory yet takes some of the investment decision making and control out of the hands of individuals. Unfortunately, this may be too big of a challenge to solve easily. Perhaps the best we can hope for is to make incremental improvements to the current system to ensure at least a basic minimum retirement income for everyone.

Global Investing for a Global Retirement

As mentioned in Chapter 1, since international people have a more global lifestyle, it's important that their retirement assets match their retirement destination. The problem here, however, is that many cross-border professionals don't necessarily know where they will retire, or they may end up retiring in more than one country. For example, some people may want to retire to their country of origin, while some may want to retire in the United States, and still others may want to retire in a third country—or maybe they want to split their retirement between several locations. Likewise, American expatriates may plan to split time between the foreign country they now call home and a family vacation home they've visited on the East Coast since they were young. The ability to spend time in multiple places, of course, is highly dependent on the resources that are available when it comes time to actually retire.

What is most important here is that those who are likely to have a global lifestyle in retirement must make sure their investable retirement assets are properly exposed to the worldwide economic landscape. It's also important that they have exposure to a variety of different currencies, rather than having their investments all concentrated in one currency. Note, too, that if you are certain as to where you are going to retire, it might be wise to have a substantially higher concentration of the underlying investments in your retirement fund located in that country or currency, especially more conservative income-oriented assets like cash and bonds (however, this may not be possible, as we discuss later in this chapter).

A typical U.S. retirement account often has between just 10 percent and 20 percent of its total assets held in international investments, including both stocks and bonds. For most cross-border families, however, such a low exposure to international investments is inappropriate. Instead, they need a much more global exposure to match their more worldwide lifestyle.

The Location of Underlying Assets Is What Matters

It is both possible and desirable to build a global investment portfolio inside a 401(k) or IRA in the United States. But it is important to understand that even if you have a good worldwide distribution of investments reflective of where you are likely to retire, the investment holdings in your account may still be "presented" in just one country's currency—that is, in U.S. dollars. Importantly, the question of having good worldwide exposure is not about where your investment account is located (and the corresponding displayed currency), but rather, where the underlying assets that you own through the various stock and bond funds—the companies in which you own shares and debt obligations—are located. Having everything displayed in U.S. dollars does not necessarily reflect where the underlying assets in your account are located.

For example, you could buy a bond fund in the United States that holds nothing but high-quality Eurozone government bonds (which are all denominated in euros). Even if this is a highly safe and stable investment, if the dollar were to rise against the euro by 10 percent, everything else being equal, you might log into your 401(k) account and see a 10 percent drop in the value of that fund as it is presented in dollars. Or, in the reverse situation, suppose the euro appreciated by 25 percent against the dollar; in this case, all things being equal, the investment as displayed in dollars would show that it was worth 25 percent more than it had been worth.

The key here is that assuming you are retiring to someplace where the euro is the official currency, the real purchasing power of your particular investment fund will not have changed. It will still be worth the same in euros, whether euros have risen or fallen against the dollar. Substantial shifts in the euro value of that investment fund won't occur just because of currency fluctuations, since it is the location of the underlying investments that matters.

The Real Currency of Underlying Assets
Two Scenarios

Here is a two-part example to make this point even clearer.

Suppose you are originally from France, but have been working in the United States. You expect that you are likely to return to France, so as part of investing for a worldwide retirement in your U.S. account, you purchase a fund containing a portfolio of high-quality Eurozone government bonds worth €100,000, which at the current rate of $1.12/euro cost you $112,000, as shown in your online account summary. For simplicity's sake, let's now assume (1) some time has passed, (2) the underlying investment, ignoring dividends, is still worth €100,000, and (3) there has been a change in the exchange rate between dollars and euros. Consider two scenarios:

Fund Worth €100,000 on Purchase	Value Displayed Online on Purchase	Change in €/$ Exchange Rate	Current Value Displayed Online	% Gain or Loss Shown Online (in USD)	Actual Euro Value of Fund
Scenario 1	$112,000	Euro falls 10%	$100,800	−10%	Still €100,000
Scenario 2	$112,000	Euro rises 25%	$140,000	+25%	Still €100,000

In Scenario 1, when you look at your online account summary, you will see that the value of your fund, in dollars, is down to $100,800, a substantial 10 percent loss. But is this really a 10 percent loss? And if the euro is up 25 percent as in scenario 2, is that really a blockbuster gain for you? The answer is no in both cases, assuming you will return to France and are focused primarily on maintaining your purchasing power in euros.

The bottom line here is that if you are planning to retire to another country, you need to primarily focus on protecting and growing your purchasing power *in that country*.

401(k) Plans Lack a Global Perspective

Most 401(k) plans are not designed with cross-border people in mind. The investment offerings available tend to be very U.S.-centric, which poses distinct risks for someone with a more international retirement future. We are often asked to advise companies with a high percentage of international employees on how to structure their 401(k) plans. After researching their plans, we invariably find that they have a substantial lack of good international options as to stocks, bonds, real estate, and cash in foreign currencies.

Inherent Currency Risks

In addition to most 401(k) plans offering too few international investment alternatives, a particularly significant problem is a lack of "unhedged" international exposure. Even if foreign stock or bond fund choices are offered, the fund's managers will often utilize methods to lower exposure to currency fluctuations (called currency hedging). This is done with the goal of making the fund's performance (in U.S. dollars) more a result of security selection (which they can control) than of currency fluctuations.

This is a good thing for most people, as currencies can swing wildly and most American investors would be smart to limit those affects on their retirement savings. However, this is usually not good for those who have purposefully created more exposure to nondollar assets with the idea that in the long run they might be spending some or all of their retirement elsewhere. Unfortunately, it is often difficult to even find out whether an investment choice inside of a 401(k) plan is or is not currency hedged.

Over time, it has become easier to find 401(k) plans with a number of international and global investment alternatives. The biggest remaining challenge, however, is *the lack of foreign bond fund choices that are directly exposed to nondollar assets.* In particular, this amounts to a much higher risk for older individuals who are near retirement and who plan to retire outside of the United States.

These older people tend to have larger balances in their retirement accounts, and they also tend to be more conservative investors who focus on the safer offerings of cash and bonds inside of their 401(k) plans, offerings that are overwhelmingly concentrated in U.S. dollar-based assets. It's extremely important for such people, whenever possible, to also have nondollar exposure in conservative fixed income and bond investments in their 401(k) plans (or elsewhere if they cannot get that exposure within their 401(k) plans).

Example: The Danger of Not Owning Foreign Bonds

Suppose a cross-border couple nearing retirement has a 401(k) worth $1 million, which represents the majority of their retirement assets. Because they are near retirement, this account is invested completely in bond funds that are pretty conservative. Let's assume that this particular 401(k) plan does offer a foreign bond fund (most don't), and the family has 70 percent of the account invested there, with the remainder in several other U.S. bond funds. But unfortunately, the foreign bond fund is completely currency-hedged back to the dollar (something not made clear to them), and therefore the account is effectively invested all in bonds denominated in U.S. dollars.

Right before they retire and move back to Europe—where they will be paying their ongoing living expenses in euros—the euro rises 20 percent in value against the dollar. Will this hurt the couple? Yes, very much so. Although the 401(k) account is invested conservatively, it is still completely exposed to the fate of the dollar. In this example, the purchasing power of the $1 million in euro currency has effectively fallen by 20 percent, and the couple will effectively be 20 percent less well off as a result.

Target Date Funds: A Lot to Like and Dislike

The investment alternatives inside of most 401(k) plans tend to include stock funds, bond funds, real estate funds, and cash. A relatively new offering that has gained significant popularity is *target date funds* or *lifestyle funds*. These are bundles of individual stock and bond funds that, based on your age and expected retirement date, build a diversified portfolio that evolves over time to become more conservative. They do this by shifting your portfolio's asset allocation more toward bonds and away from stocks as you move closer to your expected retirement age. Essentially, these are managed asset allocation portfolios, which are personalized to you, but only in the sense that they know your birth year and can therefore estimate your retirement year. They have become the preferred "default option" in most 401(k) plans, and as such they tend to be by far the most common choice among participants (who generally don't switch away from the default option, which for most people is generally a good thing).

On the one hand, these one-stop investment solutions have a lot going for them, because for most people they take away the burden of selecting a mix of investment funds, and also remove the potential for making reactive emotional decisions with regard to investments.

On the other hand, these lifestyle funds are widely criticized for being far too conservative in their allocation to stocks, instead favoring bond investments. The managers of these funds routinely err on the side of caution, holding growth-oriented investments (stocks) for any given age group at a level that is below what is generally recommended. This can be especially problematic for retired people, who generally will need growth well into retirement in order to accomplish their spending goals.

Another problem with these funds is that they tend to be invested primarily in U.S.-based assets (often over 90 percent dollar based), which for someone aiming at a more global retirement future is often not the best alternative. Because of this lack of international exposure, these target date funds are generally not the best choice for people with an international retirement future.

IRA Rollovers

What should you do with a 401(k) account at a former employer? This question is especially common with those who have worked for multiple employers and have a number of 401(k) accounts. If you have an old 401(k) account, you have three options.

First, you can leave the account alone—that is, leave it in your former employer's 401(k) plan and make no changes to it. Second, you can do a tax-free rollover into your new employer's plan. Neither of these options is usually the best choice, because of the previously discussed lack of good international investment choices in most 401(k) plans.

The third—and usually recommended—alternative is to roll over one or more 401(k) accounts into an Individual Retirement Account (or IRA), that is, an individually directed account designed to maintain the tax advantaged properties of a 401(k). With the IRA, you will be able to take more control over the investment of your funds, which will be held at a U.S. brokerage institution where they can be managed with a more globally oriented perspective.

Also, transferring balances to an IRA can be less expensive, because 401(k) plans generally have a cost structure that includes paying for employee education and plan administration. Some employer-based retirement plans can be very expensive, but fortunately, the hidden fees charged within such plans have gotten a good deal of attention in the past few years. Because of this, the fees inside many 401(k) plans (and other similar employer-based plans) have quickly been falling to more acceptable levels.

Another advantage of an IRA is that it is easier to hire a financial advisor if you choose to, enabling you to have a much more personalized level of service than you will ever get through a 401(k) program.

IRAs Offer Distinct Advantages

In many ways, then, an IRA is a terrific choice as far as where to locate a globally portable portfolio because of the tremendous variety of investment offerings available at a brokerage firm here in the United States, and the overall stability of the U.S. capital market system, as discussed in Chapter 4. However, if you are planning to move away from the United States, you may encounter a more difficult time managing an IRA (as opposed to leaving the balance in the 401(k)) because of the complexities of dealing directly with financial institutions across borders. Overall, however, the benefits of an IRA in terms of lower costs and increased investor control outweigh these disadvantages, making the rollover of a 401(k) into an IRA an excellent decision in most cases.

Owning Real Estate Within an IRA

It is possible to purchase real estate and other alternative investments, such as art or precious metals, inside of an IRA. However, the process can be quite complicated, and is generally not recommended for most people. Investment real estate, in general, is a tax-sheltered asset because of the unique deductibility of noncash depreciation expenses. For that reason, it's often better to own it *outside* of an IRA, with regular after-tax investment capital. In general, an IRA is a better place to own more tax inefficient assets, which tend to be taxed at higher rates.

Still, many cross-border families—especially those who are uncomfortable or unfamiliar with public market investing—would prefer to own real estate within their IRAs. However, because the process needed to make a real estate investment through an IRA is complex, closely regulated, and fraught with additional costs and risks, it is quite uncommon for real estate to be purchased in this way. The process of purchasing real estate in an IRA is discussed in more detail in Part IV.

Leave It Alone and Let It Grow

Eventually, the distributions from a 401(k)—or from an IRA if you eventually roll over your 401(k) into an IRA—are taxable upon withdrawal. Ideally, however, those withdrawals will be very far in the future after you have benefited from many years of tax-deferred growth. Additionally, the expectation is that if you wait until after you retire to withdraw the funds, you will be subject to a lower tax rate because you will no longer be earning a salary. This further magnifies the value of making tax-deferred contributions while you are working. For high earners especially, the 401(k) can be a particularly effective method of saving, thanks to the ability to defer income tax at higher marginal tax rates.

Note, however, that there is a 10 percent penalty for early withdrawals from your 401(k) or IRA, defined as withdrawing funds before you are 59½ years old. That penalty will be in addition to whatever taxes are owed on the distribution, which will be taxed as ordinarily income (as if the money had come to you as part of your salary). It is possible to avoid the 10 percent penalty by following the substantially equal periodic payment (SEPP) rules, which involve making a calculation to withdrawal a set amount every year for at least five years, or until reaching age $59\frac{1}{2}$, whichever is longer. There are other exemptions to the early withdrawal penalty as well, based on individual circumstances.

On the other side of things, once you reach the age of $70\frac{1}{2}$, on a yearly basis you must make a required minimum distribution (RMD) of a small but increasing percentage of the account's value (approximately 3.5 percent of the account at age 70, rising to 10 percent by age 90, and higher thereafter). This creates taxable income, even if you don't need the money to spend. The penalty for not making your RMD is quite harsh—50 percent of the RMD amount!

As for how the funds in your 401(k) plan are actually invested, things are pretty straightforward. While you are still working at the company where the plan resides, you must leave the assets within the plan and choose from what is typically a limited menu of investment options. After separating from your employer, the balance can be rolled over into your new employer's 401(k) plan, or into an individual retirement account (IRA), where you can exercise significantly more control over the investment decisions.

CHAPTER 6

Unique Cross-Border 401(k) Issues

When we talk with international professionals who have recently arrived to the United States, one of the most common questions we hear is, "Should I participate in my employer's 401(k) plan, especially if I'm not sure that I'll be spending the rest of my life in the United States?" The answer to that question is generally, "Yes, for sure!" In most cases, foreign citizens working in the United States should participate in and maximize their 401(k) plans as they provide extremely valuable benefits and are among the best ways to build savings for retirement. As long as a foreign national is a tax resident of the United States, there are generally no foreign tax implications to their participation in a 401(k) plan; however, there are some special considerations for foreign citizens, which we'll shortly discuss.

Likewise, most American expatriates we meet already own various tax-qualified investments accounts in the United States, with 401(k) plans by far being the most common. In many ways, this makes sense, since many of the Americans who've ventured abroad are highly successful people whose professional competence has brought them opportunities internationally. Much like many of the foreign-born professionals moving into the United States, these Americans tend to be well-educated and high earners, and they intuitively are better savers than the typical American. The question of whether an American expatriate should participate in a foreign retirement plan is more complex, and will be discussed later in this chapter.

A Lack of International Tax Agreement

Throughout Part III, we seek to explain as well as possible the unique rules and regulations governing the cross-border retirement savings landscape. Unfortunately, this is an area fraught with uncertainty, stemming from a lack of coordinated international rules concerning the tax treatment by one country of the tax-advantaged savings programs of another. In fact, as we'll discuss, even many tax preparers are greatly confused as to exactly how they should be reporting various international retirement account structures.

As we've discussed, in today's world of growing longevity and increasing individual responsibility for one's retirement, it is vital for everyone to make saving for their future a high priority, as early in life as possible. Given the current environment of lower expected investment returns and rising taxes globally, tax-advantaged savings plans (also known as tax-deferred or tax-qualified, and generally allowing contributions with pretax income) are particularly valuable, and everyone should take full advantage of them whenever possible.

Most large nations have some type of tax-deferred savings vehicle, like a 401(k) or traditional IRA; however, the rules for these plans vary widely, as do the source of the contributions (the individual, employer, or government), and the various kinds of investments available. But in many cases, a 401(k) or other qualified retirement plan will be the very first place where people become investors in the public markets—within the options offered by their specific retirement plan—and have the chance to make their own investment choices and gain direct experience with stocks and bonds.

Throughout this chapter we will generally frame the discussion about U.S. retirement plans in terms of 401(k)s. However, many of the rules and benefits pertinent to 401(k)s also apply to other tax-qualified plans such as IRAs, SEP IRAs, 403(b)s, and 457 plans, as well as other programs that can be rolled over into a traditional IRA. Roth IRAs, however—which will be discussed in detail in Chapter 7—are quite different. In Chapter 7 we'll also discuss foreign retirement plans, which many cross-border professionals naturally tend to accumulate over time as they work in other parts of the world. However, because of the variety of these savings programs internationally, much of our discussion will relate to how the IRS treats existing accounts and new contributions by U.S. citizens and tax residents. Finally, for more general information about investing in 401(k)s and IRAs, please see Part II.

Do the Benefits of a 401(k) Follow You?

Our answer to this question is a resounding ... *probably*. For many years, we have informed people that the unique tax-deferred properties of a U.S. 401(k) account will generally move with them around the world no matter where they go in the future. By this we meant that most countries will honor the tax benefits of the account, even once you've returned home to your country of origin or have moved on to a third country. While it is mostly true that "in practice" the income and gains within your U.S. 401(k) or IRA will not be taxable in most foreign countries, this often isn't quite backed up by the letter of the law.

International Tax Law Is Unclear

Instead, the reality is that the international rules governing the taxation by one country of tax-advantaged retirement savings accounts in another country is very much a gray area. Most international tax treaties, which set the rules between two countries as to the taxation of cross-border income, were written a long time ago, and they rarely speak specifically on the subject of defined-contribution savings accounts (like a 401(k) or its international equivalents). Most tax treaties discuss retirement funds solely in terms of defined-benefit retirement plans (traditional pensions), which are really just a promise of future income, and the tax treatment of these is much more simple, as pension payments are generally taxed as ordinary income. Based on these treaties, the tax treatment of more modern cash-balance savings accounts (like 401(k)s) held across borders is, at best, an imperfect art.

The 401(k) Gets Respect

Given the uncertainty in this area, we felt that what would be most valuable here would be to convey to you the tax treatment that we *commonly see* happening for people living abroad who own 401(k) and IRA accounts, although in many cases this is not necessarily the proper tax treatment with the relevant international tax authorities.

In most cases, we have found that people living outside the United States who own 401(k)s are typically *not* taxed on the income generated inside these accounts in the foreign country where they reside. Generally, the accounts are *treated* as tax-deferred or are in essence not reportable on most foreign tax returns until distributed. Essentially, this means those accounts will generally be exempted from whatever tax structure would otherwise apply to a taxable investment account in that country. Thus, you'll likely be exempted from taxes on interest, dividends, and capital gains, or from other country-specific taxes on capital such as a percentage-based wealth tax.

With this being said, the tax treatment claimed in foreign countries is ultimately decided on by each independent tax advisor preparing the tax filing for the family who owns the 401(k) account (unless the family does its own tax preparation). What we've stated above is the most common treatment we see internationally; however, there will certainly be tax advisors who take a different position. Additionally, there are a few countries that have been more proactive and have expressly announced their position on the taxability of the U.S. 401(k) structure. Most of these have said that they will honor the structure; a few, however, have said they will not.

At this time, it would be fair to say that most foreign tax authorities have either independently (and unofficially) determined that they will respect the tax-deferred properties of a 401(k) account, or they have decided that for the time being they will not make looking for these accounts owned by their tax residents a priority.

Given the growing importance of the defined-contribution retirement plan (like the 401(k) and its international equivalents), and the rapid demise of traditional pensions, it is our opinion that international tax rules will evolve over time and the mutual respect among countries of the tax-advantaged retirement plans of other countries will become more codified and less ambiguous. Individual retirement savings has become too important an element of the retirement puzzle globally to be ignored.

Benefits May Travel with You, but Your Account Stays Put

Many international people ask us what happens to their 401(k) plan if they leave the United States and give up U.S. tax residency. While the benefits of owning the account may travel with you, the 401(k) or IRA account itself cannot. These accounts must continue to stay within the jurisdiction of the United States, even if you were to move away. While you may have heard that certain offshore structures allow you to take a 401(k) or IRA out of the United States, as far as we know, this information is incorrect. Note that many other countries have similar tax-qualified accounts, and the vast majority of those countries also require these accounts to stay within their jurisdiction, probably so that they can more easily enforce their right to tax distributions over time. There are, however, a few countries that have a process by which tax-advantaged retirement accounts, under certain circumstances, can be moved out of that country's jurisdiction.

Taking It with You

If you are leaving the United States, and you do not like the idea of your 401(k) plan continuing to be here, one option is to withdraw the funds (make a nonqualified distribution) and take them with you. You can absolutely do this, but *we strongly discourage it*, for three reasons. First, you will be taxed at your highest marginal tax rate, and if there's a large balance and you distribute it all at once, this can amount to quite a lot. Second, if you withdraw before age $59\,1/2$, in most cases there is a 10 percent penalty for early withdrawal. And third and most important, you will be losing the benefit of tax-deferred growth, a benefit that will likely persist in most parts of the world that you might choose to live in.

Must I File a U.S. Tax Return Because of a 401(k)?

We are often asked whether someone who moves away from the United States, but who still owns a 401(k) or IRA, must continue to file a U.S. tax return. The answer depends on your personal situation, but in many cases the answer is no.

As we've discussed elsewhere, the United States taxes all of its citizens and tax residents on their worldwide income no matter where in the world they live. So, as long as you keep your U.S. citizenship or permanent residency (Green Card), you must file a U.S. tax return no matter where in the world you live. Owning a 401(k) or IRA makes no difference. But if you move away and give up your U.S. residency—thereby becoming a nonresident for U.S. tax purposes—continuing to own a 401(k) or IRA account in the United States will not require you to file U.S. tax returns.

How Are Distributions Taxed?

There is often confusion about how distributions from 401(k)s and IRAs will be taxed. Of course, if you are making best use of your 401(k) or IRA account, you will leave the account intact and fully invested for many years, thus enjoying the power of tax-deferred compounding of returns far into the future. But eventually you will begin taking distributions from the account, either voluntarily or as a result of the required minimum distribution (RMD) rules, which were discussed in Chapter 5. When the time comes to draw funds out, there are a few different ways that the distribution can be taxed. In most situations, a 1099-R will be issued by the institution holding the account, which essentially notifies the IRS to expect a tax return to be filed. This is true even if there is ultimately no tax liability in the United States.

For U.S. citizens and tax residents living in the United States, the process is fairly straightforward. Distributions from qualified (tax-deferred) retirement accounts are taxed as ordinary income for federal and state purposes (assuming the state has an income tax, which not all do). These distributions are added to any earned income, investment income, and other taxable pension income when calculating your taxable income and ultimately your final taxes due.

What If You Are Living Abroad When You Draw Out Money?

If you live abroad when you eventually start to make withdrawals (or distributions), things can get much more complicated. Most countries have a tax treaty with the United States that governs who has the first right to tax pension payments and qualified account distributions (such as those from a 401(k) or IRA). Generally, the country in which you *reside* will have the first right to tax any pension distributions (although some treaties can give preference to the *originating* country). This is generally true both if you are a U.S. citizen or tax resident and if you are not a U.S. tax resident, although many tax treaties have special rules about this (in particular for short-term or part-time residents in their country). Also, lump-sum distributions can have special tax rules, so take care when considering withdrawing an entire account balance.

So, if you are a nonresident living outside of the United States, it's likely that you will be taxed on your withdrawals—on distributions from 401(k) and IRA accounts—in whatever country where you are currently living. However, it is also likely that whatever U.S. institution holding the account will withhold some tax to be forwarded to the IRS for "possible" taxes owed to the United States This is discussed in the next section.

Choosing Your Retirement Home Based on Tax Rates

At Worldview Wealth Advisors, when we help a client to plan for an international retirement, we often consider at length the tax rates charged by different countries on various sources of income, including taxable distributions from pretax retirement accounts. For both U.S. taxpayers and foreign residents, there may be a considerable advantage to retiring in a country that has a lower tax on pension income and retirement account distributions, especially if you expect to have very large distributions throughout retirement. Thus, you may originally be from a relatively high-tax country; however, you might decide to retire to a different country with a much lower effective tax rate. Because we work with so many unique cross-border situations, tax planning for retirement can take on a much more multinational view.

If the person living abroad is a U.S. citizen or tax resident, then the distributions must typically be reported as income in both the United States and the resident country. The person will receive an annual 1099-R tax report from the account custodian in the United States, and the IRS will be expecting your return to show that income. Any reporting of the taxable distribution to your foreign country of residence is up to you; there is no mechanism established to report that income otherwise. Assuming the foreign country asserts the first right to tax that distribution, then a foreign tax credit could be applied in the United States to ensure that the income is not taxed twice (once each by both countries). Also, most U.S. institutions will give you the option to withhold some of the distribution for possible U.S. tax purposes, which you may decline assuming that your ultimate tax will be payable to a foreign tax authority.

It's important that you seek expert advice within your resident country, or where you expect to be residing when you begin to take distributions, as the tax treaties between the United States and individual foreign countries are all unique, even though many follow a similar blueprint.

Tax Withholdings on Distributions to Nonresidents

If you are a nonresident living abroad when you begin to take distributions from your 401(k) or IRA in the United States, it's likely that the institution holding your account (the custodian) will withhold for "potential" taxes (in the United States) before they send you the funds. In fact, most types of U.S. source income paid to a foreign person are subject to a mandatory withholding tax of 30 percent (or lower per treaty). This withholding serves to insure that either an appropriate amount of taxes will ultimately be paid in the United States on this taxable distribution, or a suitable declaration will be made (via a nonresident U.S. tax return) to determine the appropriate amount owed to the IRS, frequently resulting in a refund.

Many U.S. Institutions Will Overwithhold Tax on Distributions

As we've discussed, the various rules and regulations regarding the taxation of pension distributions are detailed in each country's tax treaty with the United States. A significant amount of confusion is found throughout the world on this subject. Not only are individuals who do their own taxes confused, but professional tax advisors are confused as well. For that matter, the operations teams at most large U.S. financial institutions have tremendous difficulty interpreting all of the various rules surrounding the custody of accounts owned by individuals who are not U.S. citizens or tax residents.

It is because of this higher risk profile that many large U.S. financial firms will refuse to service accounts for nonresidents (even though there are no legal restrictions on serving clients in most foreign countries). Also, it is very common for large U.S. custodians to withhold tax from distributions at the highest 30 percent rate, even when presented with evidence that a particular country's treaty calls for a lower rate. (In 2016, one very large U.S. institution announced that it would only use the top 30 percent rate, and would no longer apply lower rates per treaty). There are big penalties levied against institutions who fail to withhold (or underwithhold) taxes, and most firms would much rather err on the side of caution.

How Are Foreign Residents Recovering U.S. Withholding Tax?

In response to this confusion about the proper withholding tax for payments to nonresidents, people in this situation are dealing with this cross-border tax conundrum in two different ways.

First, as we've said before, the most correct tax treatment (when a treaty exists) is typically for the foreign resident to report this "pension income" to their resident country, and then pay taxes on it. Then, this person can file a nonresident tax return in the United States in order to recover the taxes withheld. It should be noted that in practice many people living abroad do not voluntarily report this pension income to their local tax authority. This is usually not right, and the income should in fact be reported in the resident country; however, there is no real mechanism in place to notify foreign governments of pension payments received in the United States. Given the increasing environment of information sharing among governments (led most notably by FATCA), our expectation is that this will change, and that more such data will be shared in the future.

Unreported Income Isn't Right

The alternative scenario is perhaps the most common outcome, but that does not mean that it is correct. Here, foreign residents receiving 401(k) and IRA distributions from their accounts in the United States do not report this income to their resident country. Given that taxes were withheld upon distribution by the U.S. institution holding the account, the individual may believe that no further action is required related to the taxation of that income. It's very possible that their local tax advisor will also determine that no further reporting is required in the foreign country of residence. If no notice is ever made to the person's resident country tax authority, and no filing is made to the IRS to recover the funds withheld in the United States, it is possible that no further action would be required.

However, this is probably not the proper tax treatment, and in the long run it could prove problematic. Many foreign countries will go back several years when they discover improper reporting. For example, if it is determined by your country of residence that you should be paying taxes on that income, they might assess tax, interest, and penalties as far back as 10 years or more. You could then amend your U.S. returns and request a refund for incorrectly paying the tax to the IRS, but you would probably only be allowed a refund for the prior three tax years. For the years before that, you would effectively be paying double tax on that income.

This is a tricky issue, and we strongly advise that you get proper advice as to how to report this income, and to follow the tax rules of both the United States and your country of residence.

Contributions to IRA Accounts While Living Abroad—Be Careful

For U.S. citizens and tax residents living internationally, there can be significant confusion as to whether or not they should contribute to their pretax savings plans (like IRAs) in the United States (nonresidents would likely not be able to contribute to them). Very often, it is advisable to *avoid* making such contributions.

People who work abroad on short-term foreign assignments may have an expatriate agreement in place whereby they remain on the company's U.S. payroll and the employer then "insulates" them fully from the effects of foreign taxation (often called a *tax-equalized contract*, as discussed in Part V). In these cases, it is usually fine for the individual to continue to contribute to his or her 401(k) plan throughout the assignment period.

However, U.S. citizens and tax residents working abroad on a local contract (usually for an indefinite period) where they are on the local payroll system, or in a self-employed manner, will not have access to a 401(k) plan in the United States. These people should take great care when considering making pretax contributions to U.S. savings plans like an IRA. In most cases, they *should not* make them. They run the very real risk of first paying tax in the foreign country on the amount contributed to the IRA account, and then later in life, when they then withdraw those funds from their (pretax) IRA, they would again pay tax on that same income.

As an example, imagine if a U.S. taxpayer spent a decade living in Australia. During those years, he or she contributed $5,000 per year to an IRA account in the United States. Even though these annual contributions were of a pretax nature for U.S. tax purposes, this person lives in Australia and pays taxes there on his or her income at a rate of approximately 50 percent, with no deduction for the IRA contributions since it is not a "qualified" plan for Australian tax purposes. And because foreign tax credits fully offset any tax in the United States, there really are no effective tax savings in the United States, either. So, over the 10-year period, he or she would have paid the Australian equivalent of $25,000 in local taxes on the $50,000 of income that was contributed to his or her IRA account (even though they were pretax contributions in the United States).

Let's assume another decade goes by, and now this person has retired and returned to the United States. He or she has decided that that the IRA money is needed and withdraws the full $50,000. (Let's assume this person wasn't much of an investor, which is why the account never grew beyond the original $50,000.) Well, that distribution is now taxable in the United States at an assumed 40 percent tax rate. In this situation, he or she would now be paying a 90 percent effective income tax rate (first the Australian income tax, then the U.S. tax)—which looks a lot like double-taxation.

The moral here is that there can be strange outcomes when making pretax (deductible) contributions to United States retirement accounts when living abroad. Take great care to ensure that any such contributions will actually work for you in the big picture when considering both the IRS and your foreign tax liabilities (a knowledgeable cross-border tax advisor should be able to help). There are certain rare situations where it can still make sense to make pretax contributions—for example, when someone has U.S.-sourced income that is exempt from local taxation in his or her foreign resident country.

It should be said that it could still make sense to make after-tax (nondeductible) IRA contributions in the United States, even when living abroad on a local employment contract. However, the specific mechanics are likewise very complex, and given the generally low contribution limits, one may question whether it is worth the effort to do so.

7

Foreign Retirement Plans, Pensions, and Other Savings Accounts

The two primary types of retirement savings accounts we've discussed are 401(k)s and IRAs. But cross-border professionals often have additional types of savings accounts available and it can be challenging to navigate the options. This chapter covers some of those other retirement options—foreign retirement plans, Roth IRAs and Roth 401(k)s, and traditional pensions—as well as 529 plans for educational savings.

Foreign Retirement Plans

Many types of retirement savings plans are found in different countries throughout the world. Some of these are primarily funded by contributions from the foreign government, but more often these plans are funded through a combination of employer and employee contributions made through a salary deferral mechanism, much like the way a 401(k) plan works in the United States.

Ultimately, tax-advantaged salary deferral programs that are meant for retirement savings are here to stay. As discussed elsewhere, they have supplanted the defined-benefit pension programs that used to be the primary fulcrum of most countries' retirement solutions for their citizens, in part because they shift the risk from either the government or the private employer onto individuals themselves.

Most successful foreign professionals will fully participate in these programs when available; they are generally smart to utilize, because they offer tax savings and other incentives to encourage individual saving. Many U.S. citizens and tax residents working abroad similarly face the question of whether or not to participate. Given the many benefits of tax-deferred retirement savings (investing with pretax money), most U.S. taxpayers living abroad also participate in foreign retirement plans when given the opportunity.

This, of course, brings up the question as to how the IRS views both the tax-advantaged contributions to these plans for U.S. taxpayers, as well as the existing balances in the plans (both for U.S. taxpayers and for foreign nationals who later become U.S. tax residents). We will now try to provide some clarity and guidance to these important but difficult to answer questions.

U.S. Tax Treatment of Foreign Retirement Plans Is Often Unclear

The United States does not unilaterally accept the qualified (tax-advantaged) status of most foreign retirement plans. U.S. tax laws are very rigid as to the rules making a retirement plan qualify for special tax treatment, and few foreign plans meet these tests. Some foreign retirement plans are specifically considered in their country's tax treaty with the United States, but not many. In most cases, even when the foreign retirement plan is substantially similar to a U.S. plan, you are required to get "corresponding approval" from the IRS if you want to treat the plan in the same way as a U.S. plan. Corresponding approval is obtained through a Private Letter Ruling with the IRS, which is done on an individual taxpayer basis, and is an expensive and time-consuming (as well as very rare) process. Even when these plans are defined by treaty or have corresponding approval, they may not be recognized by individual U.S. states, whose tax laws often do not follow federal tax treaties.

What Is Really Happening Now?

Most tax treaties are simply not clear as to how various foreign pension programs and employer-based retirement plans will be viewed from a U.S. tax perspective. As a result, professional tax advisors, both in the United States and abroad, will often *assume* that these retirement plans *are* tax deferred and they will then treat them similar to qualified U.S. plans when U.S. tax returns are filed. This tax treatment is usually incorrect, but tax advisors who are not experienced in working with cross-border taxation often don't realize it.

And even when they do recognize that foreign retirement accounts should not be treated as qualified for U.S. tax purposes, the tax treatment required to properly handle the accounts is so complex and specialized that one can't expect most tax advisors to be familiar with it.

While the tax-advantaged (or not) status of foreign retirement programs remains a gray area for now—often even for professional tax preparers—this situation will likely receive increasing attention in the future, particularly as more cross-border information sharing happens between different countries and their tax authorities. We can expect, then, that over time there will indeed be an increasing number of ever-clearer bilateral agreements addressing this subject.

Contributions by U.S. Citizens and Residents to Foreign Plans

For American citizens and tax residents who are working abroad, and who are able to participate in a voluntary employer-based savings plan, we generally recommend that they do indeed participate, as long as they plan to be abroad for at least a few years and are fine with the increased complexity that comes along with such participation. Indeed, in our experience the vast majority of people are doing just that. However, there is a trade-off between the immediate benefits of participation and the longer-term risks and complexity that come from owning a foreign retirement plan.

Of course, a person must normally be a localized employee in the foreign country to even be eligible for a plan. If they are employed with a large American company on a short-term expatriate assignment, they will generally remain on U.S. payroll and not be eligible for a foreign plan.

For U.S. Taxpayers: Foreign Contributions Typically Do Lower Taxes

New contributions made to foreign retirement plans by U.S. taxpayers are almost never tax deductible with the IRS. However, there are still reasons to participate, especially if you are working in a country with tax rates that are at or above U.S. tax rates. This is because contributions to the plan will usually save taxes in the host country, and may also benefit from some sort of matching component from the employer. And because of foreign tax credits and exclusions from U.S. taxation, like the foreign earned income exclusion (which is discussed in Part V), the foreign retirement contribution will effectively not be taxed in the United States, either, even though it is reportable as income on the U.S. tax return. Said another way, making pretax contributions to the foreign retirement plan generally does result in an overall net tax savings for the taxpayer.

It Is Likely Not Being Reported to the IRS at All

Most U.S. tax preparers really don't know how to report these contributions (mainly because it is so complicated), and in our experience they generally avoid the issue entirely. This is not necessarily their fault, as it is often difficult or impossible for them to become informed enough to do more. Given the difficulties in determining the exact terms of the foreign retirement plan, and of assessing how that corresponds to and works with the U.S. tax treaty (if any) with that country, it is hard to blame these preparers for not doing more.

In most cases, the U.S. tax preparer simply reports the taxable income amount from the foreign wage statement (similar to a W-2, but generally in a foreign language) on the U.S. return, and that number is usually net of any pretax retirement plan contributions in that country (as is the W-2 in the United States). And even if the preparer were to inquire deeper into the retirement plan contributions for that year (something we rarely see), and increase the reportable income to the IRS accordingly, it is unlikely that that would increase the person's total tax liability, due to foreign tax credits and exclusions.

Best Planning of All—Save Now and Save Later

When an individual is living in a foreign country and contributing to a foreign pension plan, but *not* taking a deduction for U.S. tax purposes (reporting the contribution as income to the IRS), it is important that he or she keep careful track of these nondeductible contributions. When the retirement funds are eventually distributed, he or she will only pay U.S. tax on the growth in the account, not on the original contributions (similar to how things work with a nondeductible IRA). This can actually be very smart planning, since the individual will take the deduction at the higher tax rate in a foreign country (lowering his or her foreign taxes), and not pay any "net" U.S. tax at the time because it is covered by foreign tax credits. He or she can then distribute the money later in retirement (assuming he or she has returned to living in the United States) and pay no tax on the original contributions, because those were after-tax (nonde-ductible) for U.S. purposes.

Existing Foreign Retirement Accounts: The Real World

What about the situation in which a U.S. citizen or tax resident has one or more foreign retirement plans from the time they spent work-ing outside the United States? For those who worked abroad and accumulated assets in these accounts, a certain amount of complexity cannot be avoided.

As we have said before, there is a tremendous amount of confusion surrounding how to report an existing foreign retire-ment account in the United States. Many foreign plans are not technically "qualified" for U.S. tax purposes (they are not eligible for tax deferral); likewise, most foreign nations do not specifically accept the tax-deferred qualities of a 401(k) plan or IRA account. Also, reporting foreign investment funds inside of most foreign retirement plans to the IRS—which can be very cumbersome and lead to negative tax treatment—is something most tax preparers would rather avoid (accounting for a Passive Foreign Investment Company, or PFIC, can be very difficult and problematic; please see Chapter 12.)

How Are People Reporting Existing Balances in Foreign Plans?

How are most foreign retirement accounts reported to the IRS? In our experience at Worldview, the vast majority of tax preparers in the United States will treat a foreign retirement account as though it were a qualified 401(k) or IRA for U.S. tax purposes. That is to say, even if most people report distributions as income, they will omit any reporting on the income and gains within the account on the individual's U.S. return. In doing so, they will sidestep altogether the onerous reporting requirements of PFIC (as discussed in Chapter 12).

In most cases, this is not the proper tax treatment according to the IRS. But in some ways, it seems quite reasonable: The accounts generally qualify as tax-deferred in the country where they are located, and they typically do not generate any annual tax reporting documentation (like a 1099 in the United States) that summarizes taxable dividends, interest income, or capital gains. So without any direct tax reporting for the tax preparer to work from, in some respects there really isn't anything for them to report on a tax return—unless, of course, the tax preparer wants to go looking for it, which is almost never the case. The reverse situation with foreign tax preparers is very similar, as they will generally disregard balances in a U.S. 401(k) or IRA account for purposes of calculating foreign taxes.

Better International Reporting and Coordination Is Needed

So, what are we all to do with these plans, which are so common and have essentially replaced the traditional defined-benefit pension? In our opinion, in the future we will begin to see greater mutual acceptance of foreign retirement plans among different nations, and the rules regarding cross-border reporting and tax treatment for these accounts should likewise become better codified. The highest likelihood is that the larger and more developed nations of the world will develop a system such that individual retirement accounts—which were accumulated in a qualified pretax manner in another country—will continue to be viewed as tax-advantaged should the owner relocate to another country. There are, however, no guarantees, and things may simply continue on as they are, with many gray areas remaining.

Investing Inside a Foreign Retirement Account

In our experience, from an investment perspective, many international retirement plans are inefficient and poorly performing. Often these plans are built within an insurance company's infrastructure, which can dramatically increase the expenses of the plan. Furthermore, the investment options offered within foreign plans are often poorly performing proprietary funds that are closely associated with the plan administrator or insurance company hosting the plan. In contrast, far more desirable is a more modern *open architecture* plan where high-quality investments from different investment managers are offered primarily based on the merits of the investments themselves and not on who is providing them.

High Fees and Poor Investments: A Headwind Against Growth

As a result of these drawbacks related to cost and investment performance, we have seen that the overall performance of many foreign retirement plans has been poor—often over very long periods of time spanning decades. Also, many of the investment programs associated with these plans are structured to be much more conservative than is typically recommended here in the United States, meaning that they have a much higher percentage of cash and bond investment alternatives compared to more growth-oriented investments like stocks. With an overly conservative allocation, little growth, and high costs, these plans have been a disappointment for many of the investors that we meet or work with. It stands to reason that if you have a conservative allocation within an already inefficient and high cost plan, you are likely to see little growth or even a decline in the account's value over time.

One way to address this situation is for owners of these plans to elect to invest them more aggressively, when possible, as a way to off-set these inefficiencies and attempt to create more growth. If a more aggressive allocation is possible and is chosen, it may then make sense to offset this with a somewhat more conservative approach in the individual's other retirement accounts (such as another 401(k), IRA, or other more efficient account). In this way, the combination of the foreign retirement accounts and other investment accounts can reflect a risk profile that matches the investor's overall long-term goals.

> Fortunately, we have seen considerable improvement in many foreign retirement plans over the past five to seven years, with more of these being structured like 401(k)s to include a number of highly rated investment fund choices. Also, many foreign plans are adding index-based investment offerings, which offer the potential for lower management expenses and better long-term performance.

Roth IRAs and Roth 401(k)s

Roth IRAs and Roth 401(k)s are extremely valuable retirement savings structures here in the United States. They essentially allow you to make contributions to an account with money on which you have already paid taxes, and then the funds in the account can grow tax-free for your lifetime, and very often into the lifetime of your heirs.

Suppose you put $100,000 of after-tax dollars—money you've already paid taxes on—into one of these plans, and that money grows to $400,000 over 20 years. If you then needed that money for retirement and withdrew all of it, there would be no tax on the $100,000 you already put in, nor would there be any tax on the $300,000 gain over that time. Compared to the tax-deferred growth offered by traditional 401(k)s and IRAs, this kind of long-term tax-free growth, which can take full advantage of the power of tax-free compounding, can be much more valuable. In some cases, however, those with a very high income might find that the immediate tax benefits of investing in a regular 401(k) or traditional IRA outweigh the long-term tax-free growth provided by a Roth structure.

How to Get Money In

There are a number of ways to get investment funds into a Roth structure. The most common method is by contributing annually to a Roth IRA. However, the amounts that can be contributed every year are relatively small, and people with higher income—who stand to benefit the most from this structure—are prohibited from contributing at all.

A relatively new structure is the Roth 401(k), which may be available in lieu of the regular 401(k) offered by an employer. Here, the contributions can be fairly large, as they roughly match the limits for regular 401(k) contributions. But remember, these contributions are after-tax, as opposed to the pretax nature of a regular 401(k) contribution. Thus, for people with very high income, contributing to a Roth 401(k) in lieu of a regular 401(k) means they are electing to pay a fee of as much as 50 percent (in terms of the income taxes they otherwise would be deferring) in exchange for the promise of tax-free growth for life. Of course the longer these Roth accounts are left to grow tax-free, the more valuable they will be. However, for someone with a very high tax rate now, who may later in retirement have a much lower tax rate, the immediate tax deferral of a 401(k) could be more advantageous.

Finally, one can elect to "convert" other tax-deferred IRA accounts into Roth IRAs, paying the income tax now in exchange for tax-free growth in the future. For some people, this is a hard thing to pass up. We have seen investors pay hundreds of thousands of dollars to convert regular IRAs to Roth IRAs. Of course, the "fee" (i.e., the tax bill) being paid here in order to enjoy tax-free grow forever can be quite high. There has been talk that the U.S. government, out of a desire to increase tax revenue, could somehow reduce or eliminate this promised tax-free status (like, for example, by rescinding the promise of tax-free growth for higher income families). This would certainly be upsetting for anyone who had made a high priority of investing through a Roth structure.

Foreign Implications of Roth IRAs and Roth 401(k)s

Even though the benefits of these plans are significant, we often question whether it makes sense for cross-border families to participate in them. This is especially true if a family currently living in the U.S. expects that they will one day move away for good. Why? Roth plans are relatively new, and their promise of tax-free growth for one's lifetime is a very expensive promise for any government to make. There are those who believe that these benefits could somehow be rescinded or eroded in the future by the United States—particularly for higher-income families—and we think it is possible that this could indeed occur one day.

Moreover, from an international perspective, things may be even riskier. While the basic 401(k) structure (tax-deferred salary deferral) is well known and understood throughout the world, the Roth structure is relatively new to the international table. As such, very few, if any, foreign governments have yet agreed to reciprocally honor this very generous tax-free account structure.

Roth Accounts Don't Speak Foreign Languages

So, then, if you plan on living in another country later in life, there is substantial risk as to whether most foreign countries would recognize the tax-free properties of a Roth account. We have already seen situations where these Roth structures have not worked out well for international people. For example, we've met someone who made it a top priority to make large contributions to a Roth IRA by converting from a regular IRA, paying substantial taxes upfront for the right to enjoy tax-free growth forever. Then, the person moved to a foreign country that did not recognize the Roth structure (their tax preparer required that the account be treated as taxable), and they were subject to a great deal of additional taxation on what was supposed to be a tax-free account. Even though such a conversion is expensive, it might have paid off had the foreign country recognized the Roth structure and its tax-free growth nature, but unfortunately, it did not.

These problems can occur even when the person who has moved abroad is a U.S. citizen or tax resident. Even if the United States continues to honor the tax benefits that a Roth plan provides, the foreign country where they are living, which will become their primary taxing authority, may not recognize these benefits, resulting in a complicated situation as well as additional taxation.

However, for a foreign citizen who comes to the United States and plans to stay for life, the risks associated with a Roth structure are far lower. Generally, these people will not be taxed by their country of origin after they come to the United States. For these families, the significant benefits of the Roth structure will often make a great deal of sense in the long run, as they do for most regular Americans.

Traditional Pension Income

As previously discussed, traditional defined-benefit pensions offered by employers are becoming more and more rare. With a defined-benefit pension, benefits are accrued over many years of service at an employer until such time that the employee has earned a certain annual income for life upon retirement. These pension payments are generally equal to some percentage of the employee's final income, and are partly based on the number of years of service.

The defined benefit pension is becoming extremely rare in the United States, and is also on the decline in Europe and Asia. There appears to be an irreversible trend toward the responsibility for one's retirement being placed firmly on the shoulders of each individual (as opposed to employer or government taking it). Over time, then, due to the rising cost of these plans—and as result of longer lifespans and relatively lower investment returns—they are likely to continue to decline and will perhaps go away entirely for younger workers. Still, many people have earned some pension benefits, so we will briefly consider them here.

Pensions Paid Across Borders

Pension income is generally taxable in a manner similar to how a distribution from a 401(k) plan or an IRA is taxed, that is, it is taxed like ordinary income in most cases. For cross-border families, tax treaties with the United States specifically consider what qualifies as pension income and how that income should be taxed, depending on where the payment originates and where the recipient resides. Typically, under most tax treaties, pension income is taxable where the person resides, although this is not always the case. Thus, if you earned a pension in a foreign country and now live in the United States, your foreign pension would likely be taxable in the United States, and vice versa—that is, if you live in a foreign country now, your U.S. pension will likely be taxed there.

U.S. Taxpayers Abroad with U.S. Pension Income

If you are a U.S. citizen or tax resident, you can usually elect to receive pension payments from within the United States either with or without estimated taxes withheld. Most people will choose to have some taxes withheld, just so that they don't risk incurring penalties for underpayment of estimated tax. But if you have retired abroad, you may be required to report any such income to your resident country and pay taxes there. So, it might not be necessary to have any tax withheld in the United States, because the application of certain treaty benefits may reduce U.S. taxation on pension income, and foreign tax credits might otherwise offset any U.S. tax liabilities.

Not Reporting to Foreign Authorities Is Risky

It's also possible—and quite common—for people to either knowingly or unknowingly fail to report their U.S. pension income to the foreign tax authority where they reside. In this case, the individual would still owe the U.S. taxes on that income. This can happen either because the individual receiving the pension income didn't realize that it's taxable in the country where they now reside, or it may be that their local tax preparer simply didn't know about the income or the local reporting requirements.

As discussed earlier, this can be very problematic. If the foreign tax authorities discover that you haven't been reporting this income properly, they may require you to amend many prior years of returns and pay the unpaid taxes. You can then amend prior U.S. tax returns in order to claim a refund for those foreign taxes paid, but generally you are limited to going back only three years. It is our advice that you seek professional tax advice in your country of residence, such that you are properly following both the United States and local tax laws.

U.S. Taxpayers Abroad with Foreign Pension Income

It is common for U.S. citizens or tax residents living abroad to have pension income from a country other than the United States. Let's assume for a moment that a U.S. taxpayer is receiving a pension from the foreign country where he or she is living. This could easily happen if a foreign individual worked in his or her home country for a long time (say, 20 years), before then moving to the United States and working another 10 or 20 years (long enough to secure citizenship or permanent residency). Now, that individual has returned to his or her home country in retirement, but still maintains U.S. tax residency. Likewise, the reverse could also happen, where a U.S. citizen moves to a foreign country early in life, and ends up staying there for good.

In these situations, foreign pension income is usually taxable within the country where the individual is living. But then, of course, all U.S. taxpayers must report their worldwide income back to the IRS. It's likely that, due to foreign tax credits and other exclusions, there will be no additional income taxes owed to the United States on that foreign pension income, depending on the local income tax rates and other factors. But unique situations sometimes arise where additional taxes are owed to the United States over and above the local foreign income taxes that are paid.

Let's not forget the scenario where pension income is paid to a U.S. taxpayer living abroad and the payments originate from within a third country. Actually, these situations are quite common. Depending on the individual's tax status in the foreign country of residence, he or she may or may not be taxed on worldwide income (probably yes), as is the case for their obligations to the United States. So, that pension income originating in a third country is likely reportable to both the foreign country of residence and the United States, and the resident country would usually have the first priority. This assumes that the third country where the pension payments originated does not seek to tax them, which would only complicate things further.

Nonresidents Living Abroad with U.S. Pension Income

There are situations where a foreign person formerly worked in the United States and earned a pension there. That person may be a U.S. taxpayer (Green Card holder), or he or she may be a nonresident for U.S. tax purposes. If that person is a nonresident (he or she gave up his or her Green Card), he or she may experience some strange tax outcomes as a result. Generally, the payer of the pension in the United States (a corporation or financial institution) will want to know the recipient's U.S. tax status. Once it learns that he or she is a nonresident living abroad, the payer will be required to document the recipient's resident country and then make a mandatory tax withholding of 30 percent (or lower rate per treaty) from each payment.

Don't Claim to Be a U.S. Tax Resident When You Are Not

Don't try to trick the institution paying the pension by claiming to be a U.S. tax resident. If you do so, an annual tax document called a 1099-R will be generated in your name and passed on to the IRS. That document basically tells the IRS that you have been paid taxable income, and that it should expect to hear from you via a tax return. When you fail to file that return, it creates a red flag, and could lead to problems down the road.

Proper Tax Treatment

The ultimate taxation of this kind of U.S.-sourced pension income very much follows the treatment of qualified distributions from 401(k) and IRA accounts.

First, as we've previously said, we believe the most likely tax treatment—depending on the tax treaty in place—is for U.S.-sourced pension income to be primarily taxable in the foreign person's country of residence. In that case, taxes on that pension income would be paid in the foreign country. If mandatory tax withholdings were made in the United States on behalf of a nonresident, that person would need to file a nonresident tax return in the United States in order to recover the taxes withheld.

Another common scenario is for foreign residents receiving U.S. pension income to not report that income to their resident country (this is similar to what we see with 401(k) or IRA distributions). Because taxes were withheld on the payments in the United States, the individual may believe that no further action is required. If no notice is ever made to the person's resident country tax authority, and no filing is made to the IRS to recover the funds withheld in the

United States, it is possible that they would never hear from either tax authority.

Of course, this is likely *not* the proper tax treatment, so it still may cause difficulties in the long run. Suppose that in fact the pension income was taxable in the foreign resident country, and the tax authority there eventually found out about it. They would likely assess tax for all prior years; however, it may then be too late to obtain a refund for the excess taxes withheld in the United States for some of those years.

Educational Savings: 529 Plans

U.S. 529 plans are similar to a Roth IRA in many ways because they generally allow after-tax contributions to be made into an account structure that then offers tax-free growth as long as the eventual distributions are used for qualified education purposes at an accredited university in the United States (as well as a small number of institutions abroad). The rules of these plans are pretty broad, and allow wide latitude in terms of what are considered qualified education expenses. Funds can be used for the beneficiary named on the account, but the beneficiary can also be easily changed from one child to another. For this reason, we often suggest families open just one 529 account for convenience reasons—assuming the main goal is just college savings, and not to specifically allocate money between different children (in which case, opening separate accounts makes sense). You can even change the beneficiary to an adult—even yourself—and then use distributions for things like professional cooking school or other legitimate adult education programs.

If funds are withdrawn from the plan to use at an ineligible institution, or for ineligible expenses, the account owner must pay income tax along with a 10 percent penalty on any gains in the account. When making nonqualified withdrawals, it is important to know that distributions are allocated pro-rata between principal (original investment) and earnings, and only the earnings are subject to income tax and the 10 percent penalty.

Although there are some older education savings structures in existence, the 529 plan is the most modern and efficient version. There is a certain level of complexity in setting up these plans and choosing among the specific investments they offer. Moreover, different plans are offered by different states, and some state plans are better than others in terms of their cost structure and the availability of investment options. A few states provide a state tax deduction on contributions to these plans, but generally, the current income tax savings are small. The real value is in the tax-free growth.

To Maximize Benefit, Start Very Young

If you are going to make use of a 529 plan, you should set the plan up and start making contributions when your children are very young. This will enable you to maximize the time benefit of having your investment funds grow tax-free before you end up using them, for example, when your children reach age 18 or so and are ready for college. If you wait until your children are 14 or 15 to put a plan like this in motion, you may not experience significant tax-free growth in the value of the fund over just a few years (because the investments ought to be fairly conservative), yet you will have gone through the hassle of setting it up and following the special rules related to qualified withdrawals.

Foreign Residents Beware

We often question whether it makes sense for cross-border families to participate in these plans, especially those who plan to leave the United States before their children reach university age. Echoing the earlier discussed concerns we have with Roth plans, these tax-free education savings programs (like 529s) are generally not recognized by other countries. Therefore, you might end up with an account that you had prioritized making contributions to, thinking it would provide a valuable tax-free growth vehicle, and then eventually find out that it did not provide the expected tax benefits.

Moreover, international people planning to leave the United States must consider that it is quite possible that their child or children could one day decide to attend a foreign university. Unfortunately, however, in order for distributions for qualified education expenses to be tax-free, they must be used at an accredited university in the United States (or a foreign affiliate of an accredited U.S. university). In that case, funds left in the account would need to be withdrawn and would be subject to taxes and penalties. This risk makes 529 plans somewhat less attractive for international families.

So, if you are an international person, and you haven't started contributing to such a fund when your children are very young, or if you think you might leave the United States in time for your children to go to high school and then on to a foreign university, you should carefully consider whether the benefits of this kind of plan are worth the added complexity. Of course, specifically saving funds for your children's education is always a smart move, but this can be accomplished in other ways as well.

Finding Good Advice Is a Challenge

Knowledgeable advice is important, but hard to find. It's important that you seek expert advice within your resident country (or where you will be residing when you start to take distributions), as the tax treaties between the United States and individual countries are all unique, even though many follow a similar blueprint. Furthermore, the interpretation of these rules varies significantly among different professional tax advisors. Some professionals and large accounting organizations have different interpretations of the various tax laws, and thus it can be very hard to fully make sense of things.

PART IV

Real Estate

CHAPTER 8

Renting, Owning, and Investing

Crazy for Real Estate

Experience shows that there is no asset that international families are fonder of than real estate. Successful families everywhere generally consider real estate ownership to be a smart and stable asset in which to hold one's wealth, and foreign citizens in particular seem to have a cultural predisposition to owning property. In most foreign countries, wealthy families frequently maintain a large majority of their wealth (outside of business assets) in property.

We understand and agree with this attitude, and view real estate ownership as a fundamental long-term objective for most families. And, in fact, the vast majority of the international families with whom we work—including both foreign-born families and Americans citizens who live abroad—own both the home they live in and at least one other property.

Real Estate Appreciation Likely to Slow in Future

Overall, real estate has proven to be a wonderful long-term investment over the past several decades. However, given the already high price of real estate and the current environment of exceptionally low interest rates in which we find ourselves as this book is being written, it seems likely that real estate values will rise more slowly in the future. This view partly reflects the already high prices in most markets around the world, and also results from the likelihood that interest rates will begin to rise from current levels. (Rising interest rates often prove to be a significant headwind against rising real estate prices.)

Nonetheless, real estate ownership still makes sense for most cross-border families, both because it serves as a tool for wealth creation, and because this asset class represents a core cultural value for many international people. This chapter will consider important information both with regard to residences (including primary residences and vacation homes) as well as rental and other investment properties.

Primary Residences and Vacation Homes

One of the biggest initial decisions that must be made by cross-border families moving to a new location—whether that location is in the United States or in a foreign country—is whether to purchase or rent the home they will be living in.

Obviously, the duration of time a globally mobile family plans to spend at the new location is a big factor in the decision to buy or rent. We believe that other than in the case of a fairly short-term stay, it's generally a good idea for people to purchase the home they will be living in, assuming it is within their budget and otherwise feasible. But the decision of whether to buy or rent will ultimately depend on each individual family's goals and financial situation.

Advantages to Owning Your Home

There are three core advantages to owning your own home:

1. Capital appreciation
2. Tax-deductible expenses
3. Pride of ownership

First, while home values are likely to rise at a slower pace than in recent decades, they are still likely to go up, especially in more desirable urban and suburban areas. Combining this general upward price trend with the fact that most people amortize (or pay down) a small portion of their mortgage debt every month, over time there can be significant wealth created in the net equity value of the property.

Second, some countries around the world (including the United States) offer valuable tax deductions for various types of home ownership-related expenses. The deduction of mortgage interest and property taxes are among the most common. The deduction for mortgage interest in the United States is currently limited to interest paid on a maximum loan of $1,000,000 (plus $100,000 on a second mortgage loan), which can be the loan against your primary residence and/or one additional vacation home. These deductions can be especially valuable to higher-income families, who generally find themselves in a higher tax bracket, although there are rules in place to limit these deductions for very high-income families. The United Kingdom famously ended its mortgage interest deduction for good in 2000, in part to cool a red-hot housing market. A growing faction within the United States is also calling for the elimination or significant reduction of this tax benefit. But we don't expect this to change anytime soon.

And third, there are significant other nonfinancial benefits that come from owning one's own home in terms of pride of ownership, having a sense of belonging, and becoming a permanent member of the local community.

Owning a Vacation Home

Given the overall value that international families place on owning real estate, it's not surprising that some also consider purchasing a *second* residence—often also known as a *vacation* home. Many families view this as something that is both an asset for their personal use as well as an investment. Given the steep price increase of most vacation homes over the past few decades, families have mostly been rewarded for this perspective. Many vacation homes can indeed serve as good long-term investments, and can even provide a source of ongoing rental income if desired.

But a vacation home should be viewed primarily as a second home that provides a vacation getaway for the family, and that may eventually serve as somewhere where the family and extended family members can reside and visit in retirement. We generally recommend that our clients approach a vacation home not so much for its investment value, but more because they would personally value owning it and plan to use it with their family for years to come. Why? Simply, there is no guarantee that vacation properties will keep going up in value over time, particularly if interest rates begin to move higher.

The Process of Buying a Home in the United States

Among the most common questions asked by those newly arrived in the United States is how the process of purchasing a home here works. Most commonly, homes in the United States are purchased with a 20 percent down payment and a mortgage loan covering the remaining 80 percent of the purchase price. By far the most common mortgage type is a 30-year fixed-rate mortgage. This loan carries an interest rate that is fixed for the entire 30-year term of the loan, and a specified monthly mortgage payment that does not change. These loans are fully amortizing, which means that the monthly mortgage payment includes both interest expense and an amount that goes toward principal reduction, such that on the last month of the 30-year period, the mortgage will be paid off in full. One feature of this structure is that interest expense (which is the tax deductible element) makes up a relatively high portion of the total mortgage payment in the early years of the loan, with the amount of the payment going toward principal reduction being a somewhat smaller portion of the payment. In later years, as the principal amount of the loan is reduced, interest expense becomes a smaller portion of the monthly payment and principal reduction picks up speed.

Other types of mortgages also exist. Some allow a down payment of less than 20 percent, some have a 15-year term or other time periods, and some are interest-only for a fixed period of time. Additionally, it's possible to add a second mortgage on top of a first mortgage through a home-equity line of credit (HELOC), which can also be tax deductible for balances of up to $100,000. These credit lines can be drawn on when needed, and are often used to fund home improvements or to pay other personal expenses as needed.

Building up Credit Rating

Since most homes will be purchased with the help of a mortgage, it is important for newly arrived international families to rapidly establish a favorable credit status with the major credit rating companies in the United States. This can be accomplished in a number of ways, but we've found that two effective ways to establish credit include purchasing a new car with a car loan and utilizing a prepaid or secured credit card.

Selling Expenses and Property Taxes

In the United States, the seller of a home typically pays most of the costs associated with marketing and selling a property, including the cost of using real estate agents (typically between 5 and 6 percent of the selling price). This is quite different from what happens in many other countries, where the buyer often pays the selling expenses or the expenses are shared between buyer and seller.

Many countries outside the United States have large transfer taxes that are generally paid by the buyer. This tax can often amount to as much as 10 percent or more of the purchase price—quite a substantial amount! This transfer tax arguably leads to less trading among different homes in many other countries compared to here in the United States, given the significantly higher transaction costs.

While there is generally no equivalent transfer tax paid by the buyer in the United States (although there are often smaller recording fees of various kinds), there are ongoing annual property taxes in the United States, and these serve the similar purpose of providing a revenue source for local governments. Property taxes vary by state, but are usually between 1 percent and 1.25 percent of the assessed value of the home (which is usually approximated by the home's purchase price). Many states have enacted limits on the annual increase of property taxes, often linking them to the general rate of inflation. However, the sale of a property generally leads to a reset of this *taxable value,* which often leads to a significant increase in annual property tax assessments.

Although some foreign countries do have annual property tax assessments, the amount is generally much smaller, and many newly arrived foreign citizens are quite surprised when they learn about the ongoing liability for property tax in the United States. (Note, again, that the assessment of annual property taxes in the United States can, in some ways, be seen as making up for the lack of a large transfer tax.)

Buy or Rent upon Arrival?

We often see globally mobile families struggle with the decision of whether to buy or rent upon arrival in a new country. As previously discussed, many people (especially foreign-born individuals) place a very high value on owning property, and their first inclination is nearly always to want to immediately purchase a residence.

In many cases, however, renting can make more sense, especially in situations where the family members may only live in that location for a few years (e.g., in the case of being sent abroad on an assignment for a defined period of time, like two or three years). But the desire to own is often quite strong, driven both by the general culturally embedded desire to own property, as well as—especially for high-income families—the powerful tax benefits that are inherent in home ownership. For these reasons, it is still quite common for globally mobile professionals to purchase property as soon as possible upon arrival in a new country.

Another factor that has driven international families to decide to purchase rather than rent is the seemingly unstoppable rise in real estate values around the world over the past several decades. Notwithstanding the housing crisis and Great Recession between 2007 and 2009, there has been an extraordinary surge in home values over time. This increase in prices is in large part a response to the incredible drop in interest rates globally (rates in the United States have been steadily falling since the early 1980s—over 35 years), and today we have perhaps the lowest interest rates in recorded history. This history has led to a feeling among many that "you cannot go wrong" by owning real estate. Of course this is not true, and perhaps now is indeed the time to become a bit more cautious about real estate investment in general. In fact, studies have shown that the historical inflation-adjusted return on U.S. home prices was less than 1 percent per year from 1890 to 2005, so it may make sense for everyone to lower their expectations for the future.

Going forward, we can expect to see a more normalized increase in real estate appreciation that is more in line with the general inflation rate, if not even a period of below-normal growth or even declines in value (assuming interest rates begin to climb higher, as has been expected for some time). If this does happen, then perhaps some of the old "break-even rules" of home ownership may once again be useful. It has long been thought, for example, that before you decide to buy a home you should plan to live there for between 7 and 10 years. That way, if you had to sell it, it would have appreciated such that at least you could break even on the sale.

Ultimately, then, as a cross-border family, the big question comes down to how long you expect to be in the home. Given that you already have an internationally mobile lifestyle, you should recognize that there is a good chance you likely won't be in the home for that traditional 7- to 10-year minimum period.

When You Should Probably Own

Our general recommendation is that if a cross-border family (a) feels it is likely they will stay in the area for at least five to seven years (this is somewhat shorter than the old rule of thumb), and (b) they can afford it, then they should probably go ahead and purchase a home, particularly when tax deductions give ownership strong advantages over renting. But they should not necessarily feel like they are missing something by taking some time to rent and get to know the area. In the end, there is value to maintaining flexibility, to being able to relocate to another area within town, or to pursue another opportunity in a different city or country whenever you like. Globally mobile families, perhaps, should place a higher value on keeping their options open.

Real Estate as an Investment

As previously said, many international families place great value on the ownership of real estate: it's tangible (i.e., by definition it is "real" property), it's easy to understand, and throughout most of the world over time it's been a good long-term investment (although this has been argued by some researchers). In addition to purchasing residential real estate, then, it's not surprising that many cross-border families are also interested in other types of investment property. This remains true even though current prices are high (party because interest rates are low), making it more likely that future returns on real estate investments of all types will be lower than what we have seen in the recent past.

Before Even Considering an Investment

Among our clients, many of whom are originally from a foreign country, we have seen a strong interest in purchasing investment properties. This usually comes at a point when (a) the family has already purchased the primary residence they live in, and (b) they have accumulated additional after-tax savings that they desire to invest in a long-term income-producing asset. We should point out that before considering purchasing an investment property, we believe that most people should first have accomplished the following:

1. Already own their primary residence (unless their personal situation makes renting a better choice);
2. Be already fully maximizing their 401(k)s, IRAs, and any other tax-advantaged retirement savings programs available to them; and
3. Have accumulated a solid cash reserve for emergencies (usually recommended to be at least 6 to 12 months of living expenses).

Benefits (and Some Negatives) to Investing in Real Estate

Real estate investment has long been viewed as perhaps the most stable and tangible asset class throughout history. It isn't ever going to go missing, and can't easily be stolen. It can be seen and touched at any moment, which is a very comforting thing for many people. There are many other advantages to investing in property in addition to your primary residence. These advantages include:

- *Preservation of capital and appreciation:* Real estate values rarely fluctuate wildly and they usually trend higher over time, generally at least keeping pace with the rate of inflation.
- *Reliable income:* Real estate can provide a durable source of income that rises over time.
- *Tax-shelter benefits:* Real estate income enjoys a tax shelter benefit in the United States related to the deduction of non-cash depreciation expense. This is one of the few remaining viable tax shelters available to high-income investors.
- *Direct ownership:* Property is usually owned directly, without the need to invest alongside other investors or pay investment management fees (although it is common to hire professional property management).
- *Inefficient market:* It is possible to uncover opportunity in the real estate market through hard work and by gaining a special understanding of a certain geographical area or class of investment.

However, there are also certain disadvantages, and these include:

- *Illiquidity:* Property cannot be easily sold or exchanged for other property.
- *Management time:* Depending on the type of property, proper management can require a great deal of time.
- *Lack of diversification:* It is very difficult to diversify one's exposure across multiple properties, regions, or property types.
- *Repairs and maintenance:* Most properties require a significant amount of ongoing repairs and maintenance to keep them in good condition. Some of these expenses are often disregarded when investors calculate their total return on a property.

Property Types: Single-Family Homes Versus Commercial

By far, the most popular type of investment property that we see among individual investors is a single-family home that can be reliably rented to one family.[1] As we've said, in many cases our clients have simply moved on to another place, and then put their former home on the market as a rental. This usually works quite well, although these specific properties may not always be particularly well suited to be a rental. For example, it may not be in the ideal location to attract rental demand, or perhaps the condition of the property is such that it requires constant maintenance.

Types of Commercial Real Estate Assets

Some cross-border families, however, are able to look at real estate more broadly, and they see the potential in other types of commercial real estate. Commercial real estate is commonly divided into the following five categories:

1. *Multifamily apartments:* These units typically house multiple families in a single building or group of buildings.
2. *Office buildings:* These properties provide long-term office space for businesses.

---

[1] There is also an emerging trend for people to rent out either a primary or vacation home to short-term visitors through websites like Airbnb and VRBO. However, such short-term renting can produce taxable income as well as give rise to other local occupancy taxes. The laws governing this activity are only now being developed, and it is certain to receive much more focus in the future by local governments and tax authorities.

3. *Industrial buildings:* Warehouses, factories, and other more industrial uses.
4. *Retail buildings:* These are typically found in more visible locations, often in areas of high pedestrian or automobile traffic, where other retail shopping and restaurants are located.
5. *Raw land and other:* Undeveloped land and other specialized uses such as self-storage, hotels, and so on.

Commercial real estate can offer many special benefits to an investor, such as higher investment returns, greater tenant stability, and potentially lower management involvement. However, these various types of commercial real estate investments often have very different characteristics unique to the specific type of use, and they generally require specialized knowledge about that particular asset type and the specific market in which the property is located. For these reasons, commercial real estate can be difficult for many individual investors to properly evaluate and manage, especially for those who are not already experienced in that area.

This discussion is focused on developed real estate assets, which are already established and usually have existing tenants. There is another investment category altogether known as real estate development (or redevelopment), which generally involves making improvements to raw land or to an existing building in order to reposition it for a different, and often more profitable, use. An example of this would be buying a vacant parcel of land, and then constructing a building that is then leased to a large corporate user. This type of project can deliver significantly higher investment returns, but as you can imagine, the risks are of course far greater. For this reason, real estate development is usually best left to professionals who are completely focused on this market.

A Love Affair with Apartment Buildings

For many of our clients at Worldview, multifamily apartment properties are by far the most appealing type of commercial real estate. This is due to the inherent simplicity and lower risk of the business model, which is to offer residential units to multiple families in one property. But, multifamily real estate also tends to be the most management intensive type of commercial property, particularly for smaller buildings that do not have full-time property managers. The large majority of our clients, who have made property investments in something other than single-family homes, have done so in the multifamily apartment area.

Owning Property: Directly or with Other Investors

There are different ways of owning investment properties, the most common of which is simply to purchase a property directly in your own name. As already said, many of our clients have converted their former homes into rental properties, while others have purchased a home with the specific intention of having it serve as an investment. This approach is simple and easy to understand, and it gives you, the owner, full control over the property in addition to all of the investment risk and return (that is, the income and any associated tax advantages). There are some negatives, however, including lack of diversification (you only own one thing), property management hassles, and higher risk generally (tenant problems, unusually high repair costs, persistent vacancies, etc.).

Even though many investors would like to diversify their real estate assets by investing in other types of commercial projects, often the scope, size, and value of many commercial properties tend to make direct ownership less feasible except for those who are quite wealthy.

Real Estate Partnerships

Another way to gain access to commercial real estate is by investing alongside other people, often through a real estate fund or private partnership. These structures can be created among friends, or more commonly, they are offered by professional real estate investment managers. These arrangements allow you, the investor, to own a fractional share of a much larger and higher quality asset, and often because the individual investment size is much smaller, you can build a much more diversified real estate portfolio. Additional benefits include minimal management responsibility, limited risk (usually only up to the amount you have invested), and often higher upside potential on the investment.

There are also some negatives to owning property in this way. These include a lack of control, illiquidity, and the fact that you have to pay additional fees to the professional managers of the project. Still, for many busy cross-border professionals who already own one or more rental properties directly, this way of investing in property—all things considered—is a desirable and generally recommended solution.

To Rent Out or Sell a Former Home

The decision to sell or rent a former residence is a quite common dilemma among cross-border families, who more often have professional opportunities that take them from one country to another. This question arises for both foreign nationals moving to the United States, and Americans either being sent abroad or returning home from a foreign assignment. All of these people face similar challenges here, and because foreign nationals coming to the United States will generally become U.S. tax residents, those people have very much the same tax considerations as internationally mobile Americans.

Of the international families that we work with, a clear majority prefers to hold onto and rent out their former residences, whether they are left behind in the United States or in a foreign country. American citizens returning home from an extended foreign assignment may be the one exception; if they are returning permanently to the United States, they are more likely to consider selling a foreign residence. But in all of these situations, there are many important tax and other ramifications that should be considered as part of the decision.

Why Turn Your Old Home into a Rental Property?

The decision to convert your former residence into a rental property is ultimately a very personal one. Of course, it can at times be a great income-generating investment, but it also involves a fundamental shift in how the asset is viewed by the IRS.

The primary advantages of renting out your old home include having a stable asset that is likely to grow over time, along with generating a consistent rental income. Often, people who decide to keep their old home are expecting its value to rise in the future. Of course, given the already high prices of real estate at this time, future expectations for appreciation should perhaps be lowered.

There are a number of disadvantages to keeping a former home as a rental property. First, families very often hold a large share of their total net worth in their home. This can cause problems, particularly if money is needed to buy another home somewhere else. Also, it is not uncommon for families to experience negative cash flow when renting their home, especially if they have a large mortgage on the property. Furthermore, many people underestimate the time required to manage a rental property, as well as the repairs and maintenance expenses that inevitably arise. When owners hire a local property management company to oversee the property—which is very common—the expense of doing so further reduces the property's income potential.

Do You Like Fixing Toilets?

Ultimately, those who are in this situation must ask themselves one very important question: "Do I want to be a landlord?" That is, are they willing to commit to all of the time and energy demands that come with being an absentee landlord?

In our experience, the vast majority of foreign nationals who come into the United States have kept and rented out their former residences abroad. Because of the significant increase in real estate prices in the past 10 to 20 years, most have done quite well and are very happy with their decision. We have also seen people who have experienced challenges, either due to declining assets values, persistent negative cash flow, unusually large and unrelenting repair expenses, high vacancy rates, or bad tenant experiences.

Ultimately, the decision really comes down to three things: whether or not (1) you can afford to leave your net investment equity locked up in the property, (2) the opportunity cost of leaving your money in the property compares well with putting it into other investment opportunities, and (3) you are willing to accept the ongoing management requirements and maintenance expenses that always come along with being a landlord.

You Have Three Years to Decide

So suppose someone who is a U.S. tax resident is about to move, and that person owns a residence that has appreciated greatly in value since it was originally purchased. Not sure if his family will move back into the property later on, this person decides to rent it out, and then doesn't make the final decision to sell the property until after more than three years has gone by. In this case, the person would lose the ability to claim the gain exemption discussed earlier, and would have to pay taxes on the gain. For a property that has greatly appreciated, this can come to a substantial amount. Alternatively, if you do decide to sell the property, you have some time before you lose the tax-free exemption on a gain (up to $500,000 for married filing jointly, or $250,000 for single filers). That's because to qualify, the rule says that it must have been used as your primary residence for two out of the last five years. Also, you don't have to be living in the house at the time that you sell it. That is, your two years of ownership—and use as a primary residence—may occur any time during the five years before the day the home is sold.

So, for example, you can live in the house for two years, and then move out of the house and rent it for up to just short of three years and still qualify for the gain exclusion. So decide if you really want to keep the house within those three years. This is especially true if the property has appreciated significantly, because the ability to avoid tax on up to a $500,000 gain is extremely valuable. For example, if the value of your house has increased by exactly $500,000 and you are subject to U.S. state and federal capital gains tax at 32.8 percent (assuming 23.8 percent federal plus 9 percent state tax rates), your total tax savings from using the exclusion could be as much as $164,000 ($500,000 gain × 32.8 percent).

Cross-Border Situations Where a Home Is Left Behind

Next we will discuss some unique situations for U.S. taxpayers who are going through a cross-border relocation, based on the types of clients we frequently see.

Americans on the Move

We often see situations where an American is being sent abroad or is relocating back to the United States. Many times when they are being sent abroad, Americans will keep and rent out their former residence in the United States, partly due to uncertainty about whether they will like living abroad or will otherwise be returning home fairly quickly. Americans who live abroad and who own their foreign home may be a bit more likely to sell it when returning to the United States. In either case, U.S. tax rules are a primary consideration.

However, those who own a foreign property must recognize that it is possible that the foreign country may seek to tax any gain on the home sale. In our experience, fewer foreign countries will attempt to tax gains on the sale of primary residences—most have some type of gain exclusion like the United States does.

Foreign Nationals with U.S. Residency

Many international families living in the U.S. eventually move abroad for a variety of reasons (either personal or professional). There is still a strong cultural belief among these people to hold on to their former home back in the United States, and many of them do.

But these international families must think hard about what their future plans are regarding their U.S. residency (their Green Card), especially when they own a home that has appreciated significantly. If they plan to keep the home indefinitely, and will likely return to the United States within a few years, then they can treat this decision similar to how a U.S. citizen might. However, if they expect in the future to give up their Green Card and become a non-resident for U.S. tax purposes, they may want to reconsider holding on to the property.

As long as they are U.S. tax residents, they can claim the home sale gain exemption (up to $500,000 for those married filing jointly). There is, however, some confusion and doubt about whether a non-resident, who was formerly a Green Card holder and otherwise meets all the tests, would qualify for the home sale gain exclusion. It seems likely that they would qualify. One important exception to this is that the gain exclusion is not available to *covered expatriates* (certain individuals who have given up their Green Card or citizenship and are subject to the Expatriation Tax).

Homeowners expecting to give up U.S. tax residency should strongly consider whether to sell their former residence in the United States while they are still able to benefit from the gain exclusion, even if that means purchasing another property for investment immediately after. However, they would be wise to further research the unique tax rules for nonresidents owning investment property in the United States.

Foreigners Might Sell Before Becoming a U.S. Tax Resident

If you are a cross-border professional who has not yet established U.S. tax residency—you do not yet have a Green Card and you have not yet met the substantial presence test—it's important to consider the information here very carefully.

Many foreign nationals who are becoming U.S. tax residents already own highly appreciated residential property abroad, and often that appreciation has occurred many years before they came to the United States. The home sale gain exclusion rules will work for them after they become U.S. tax residents, so it is very important for them to decide within the three-year period whether they really want to own this property for the long-term. If not, it probably makes sense to sell the property before losing the home sale gain exclusion.

Even if they want to keep their former residence as a long-term investment property, it still might make sense to sell that property and then buy a similar property to hold as an investment, especially if the current property has gone up significantly in value before they moved to the United States. This is even more important if the original property is located in a country that does not tax gains on the sale of a residence. By swapping one property for another, they would effectively be raising the tax basis for IRS purposes, thus ensuring that they would never be taxed on that prior gain in the United States. Otherwise, were they to one day in the future decide to sell the rental property (their former home), they would owe taxes on the entire gain of the property going all the way back to their original purchase date.

Selling Before Entering the United States, When Gains Are Very Large

Consider another situation where you own a home with a gain in value significantly above the $500,000 maximum gain exclusion amount (for married filing jointly). In this instance, you would likely owe significant taxes on the sale of your former home, even if you were able to qualify for the gain exclusion. Assuming you live in a country that does not tax residential home appreciation, you would be wise to sell this property before becoming a U.S. tax resident. Assuming you stay a U.S. taxpayer from then on, you would never be able to escape paying taxes on the gain from a sale. If you really wanted to keep that property as a long-term rental, you would be wise to still sell it prior to entering the United States (tax free), and then purchase another similar property (how about the house next door?) to hold as a rental. This may sound like a substantial effort, but don't underestimate the value of raising your tax basis and avoiding future taxes on a large preexisting property gain.

Sale and Lease Back

Some of our clients who would prefer to sell their property before becoming U.S. tax residents have complained about wanting to stay in their foreign residence all the way up until when they move, so as to not upset their family. This is fine, but why not consider selling your home with a required leaseback clause? This would allow you and your family to sell a property but stay in the home—effectively as renters—until it is time to actually move.

CHAPTER 9

Real Estate Taxation and Other Considerations

Basic Tax Treatment of Real Estate

We will now consider the taxation of real estate by the IRS, starting with the basic treatment of real estate and moving on to some more complex situations. Most of what will be covered here applies to all U.S. citizens and tax residents, whether or not they reside in the United States. Later, we will briefly discuss some unique considerations for nonresidents who own property in the United States.

Taxation of Primary Residences

Broadly speaking, owning your own home is a smart financial move because you receive the tax benefit of deducting certain types of property expenses. These tax benefits are particularly valuable for high-income people who typically pay income tax at the highest marginal tax brackets (as explained in Part V). Generally speaking, both the mortgage interest paid on a home and the property taxes are tax deductible as an itemized deduction on the owner's federal tax return.

There are, however, some limitations to deductions for high-income people. The mortgage interest deduction is only available for up to $1.1 million in total aggregate mortgage debt (including first mortgages up to a combined $1 million, and home equity debt up to another $100,000). Additionally, for very-high-income families, there are several other ways that these deductions can be limited or phased-out. The amount of itemized deductions (which includes property related deductions like mortgage interest and taxes) begins to be phased-out at a certain level of income, progressively reducing the amount of the deduction the higher the taxpayers' income. Also, the alternative minimum tax (AMT) is a supplemental income tax on high earners that can further limit itemized deductions by removing the deduction of property taxes entirely.

Tax-Free Gain on Sale of a Primary Residence

If you sell your primary residence, the gain on the sale is generally tax free up to a $500,000 gain if you are married and filing jointly ($250,000 for single filers). To qualify for this exclusion, you need to have owned and used this property as your principal residence for two out of the past five years. You do not need to be living in the home at the time of the sale, so it is possible to still enjoy this tax-free gain if you have moved out and rented the home, as long as it has not been rented for more than three years consecutively at the time of the sale. This is particularly important for families who have moved across borders (into or out of the United States) and rented their former home while they try out a new location. For foreign families coming into the United States, consider carefully whether to sell a former residence before this three-year anniversary; otherwise, any gains on the former home going back to the original date of purchase (in U.S. dollar terms) will be taxable in the United States. This exclusion can be very valuable, sometimes changing the investment equation significantly.

Another rule is that you can't have used the gain exclusion for another home sale during any time in the previous two years—that is, the exclusion is available for use only every two years. There are, however, some exceptions to this two-year rule that allow for a partial gain exclusion even when failing to meet the two-year rule, generally as a result of changes of employment, health issues, or other unforeseen circumstances. In these situations, the gain exclusion is ordinarily limited to the percentage of the two years—up to the date of the sale—that you owned and occupied the home as your principal residence.

For U.S. taxpayers living abroad, it is important to know that this exclusion does not require that the property be located in the United States; that is, the exclusion also applies to foreign property as long as it was your primary residence. However, the exclusion does not apply to any gain on the repayment of a foreign currency-denominated mortgage, a unique currency risk when owning foreign real estate with a mortgage (a topic that we will consider later in this chapter). The exclusion also does not work for former U.S. citizens and former Green Card holders who have expatriated (given up U.S. citizenship or tax resident status) and fall under the "covered expatriate" rules, and are therefore subject to a different set of nonresident tax rules. Covered expatriates will be discussed in more detail in Chapter 12.

The Treatment of Vacation Homes

The taxation of vacation homes is very similar to that of a primary residence, but there are some important differences. Current tax laws do offer certain tax breaks that can make owning a second home more affordable, as long as you do indeed use the property as a vacation home and not as a rental property. Importantly, you can deduct mortgage interest and property taxes in the same way that you do for your primary home. However, the amount of tax-deductible interest is limited to interest paid on a combined debt of $1.1 million of indebtedness on both your primary and second home. No additional debt beyond this limitation qualifies for the interest deduction.

Note, however, that the home sale gain exclusion available on your primary residence does not apply when you sell a vacation home. Since it's not your primary residence, you may have to pay the usual capital gains tax just as you would with any investment property. However, if you make the second home your primary residence for at least two years before you sell it, you may be able to avoid some tax on the gain. The rules around converting an appreciated property to a primary residence are strict and somewhat complex, and you may still owe tax on some gains from the period when it was not your primary residence.

Taxation of Rentals and Other Investment Property

Owning investment property offers a number of distinct advantages. In particular, this is an investment class that offers stable income and appreciation, along with significant tax benefits (particularly for higher income families). To better understand how all of this works, we'll consider how U.S. taxpayers are taxed on both the ongoing income from real estate as well as on gains from the sale of appreciated investment property.

Reducing Income Tax—A Shelter from the Tax Man

To better understand how all this works, let's begin by considering how the tax is calculated on real estate income. From a U.S. perspective, the taxation of real estate income can be very beneficial because it offers one of the few real tax shelters left in the U.S. tax code, as a result of how non-cash depreciation expenses are treated. This can make income property especially valuable to higher income families who are already being taxed at the highest marginal tax rates.

To understand how real estate income is taxed, you first must determine the total amount of gross income (e.g., rental income) from the property. From there, you are allowed to subtract standard operating expenses including things like property taxes, insurance, utilities, repairs and maintenance, leasing expenses, and property management expenses. After deducting these operating expenses, you are left with the net cash income from rental activities, also known as net operating income (NOI). From there, you may also deduct any financing costs, like mortgage interest expense, to arrive at a final net income. Professional real estate investors often evaluate properties using NOI, which excludes financing costs, because it better reflects the true earnings power of the individual property regardless of the indebtedness employed by the owner or investor.

After calculating an investment's net income, in most situations the owner can then also deduct for tax purposes a noncash depreciation expense related to any buildings, machinery, or equipment on the property. This depreciation is in theory an allocation of the cost of a depreciating asset over that asset's useful life—essentially claiming an expense equal to the reduction in the value of the structure over time. This depreciation expense is noncash (essentially, not a real cost in any given year); however, it is tax-deductible, and therefore, it provides a reduction to taxable income without anything having been actually spent (i.e., it is a tax shelter).

After taking all of these deductions, including depreciation expense, the investor ends up with the final taxable income. Primarily as a result of depreciation, it is actually possible to have a tax loss in a given year even if the property had a positive cash flow. It is also possible to offset other income with the tax loss on the rental properly, although the owner has to follow complicated *passive activity loss* rules that can delay the ability to deduct certain losses into the future.

Selling Investment Property—Calculating Taxable Gains

Much like with any other investment asset, gains on the sale of an investment property are subject to capital gains tax. Unlike with the sale of a primary residence, however, there is no gain exemption at all on the sale of an investment property. But, property that is held for more than one year is taxed at more favorable long-term capital gain tax rates (usually 15 percent, or for high earners 20 percent plus the 3.8 percent net investment income tax) plus state taxes, if applicable.

When an investor sells an investment property, the taxable gain is calculated based on the net sales price received minus the tax basis. The tax basis equals the original purchase price plus any capital improvements that have been made (excluding repairs and maintenance), minus any accumulated depreciation deducted over the life of the property.

Tax Basis and Accumulated Depreciation—Shifting Income Down

Depreciation expense is valuable because it effectively shelters current income from taxation; however, that income does eventually get taxed. As discussed earlier, depreciation expense does indeed lower your current year taxable income. However, the accumulated depreciation that is recorded every year does progressively lower the tax basis of the property. In turn, this means that depreciation ends up increasing the taxable gain on the property if and when it is sold in the future.

Therefore, in many ways, the depreciation rules act as a method of deferring income tax into the future by sheltering current income and converting that amount into a potential future gain on the eventual sale of the property. We say that the income tax is deferred into the future, but of course it is also possible that the property will never be sold, and as such the tax may be avoided altogether. Alternatively, were a property to be sold at a loss, accumulated depreciation would effectively reduce any tax-deductible loss.

Assuming a property is purchased and then sold some years in the future, in addition to delaying the payment of taxes, depreciation will have lowered the effective tax rate by shifting income from current ordinary tax rates to long-term capital gains tax rates.

As a quick example, suppose you own an investment property for which you paid $200,000, and every year you deduct $5,000 in depreciation from taxable income. If 10 years go by and you have made no improvements to the property (which would increase the tax basis), then at the end of the 10 years your tax basis will have been reduced to $150,000. If you then sell the property for $300,000, instead of having a $100,000 taxable gain (without depreciation), you would have a $150,000 gain. Fortunately, that gain will be taxed at the more favorable long-term capital gains tax rates. And, very importantly, all throughout that 10-year period, depreciation expense was lowering your tax liability by deferring the taxation of income into the future.

Foreign Properties Often Not Reported to the IRS

Foreign nationals who come to the United States very often still own real estate abroad, which is often their former residence. We have observed that in many cases these people fail to report the ownership of this property, and any income derived from it, to the IRS. (Note that if they own a vacation home abroad that is not an income-producing property, there may be no general requirement to report it.) It is easy to understand and appreciate the dilemma many international people face with regard to reporting their foreign properties and rental income to the IRS.

Often, upon first arriving in the United States, they are completely unaware of the reporting rules for foreign rental income. And in many cases, their foreign property was not yet rented when they first arrived in the United States. In these situations, the foreign residence in question may not have even been reportable for U.S. tax purposes (although as soon as it was rented out, it became so). But after some time, perhaps after a year or two of filing taxes in the United States, most foreign residents become aware of the requirement to report foreign assets and income to the IRS—these days, it is becoming increasingly difficult to avoid hearing about foreign asset reporting.

At this point, many foreign residents begin to worry that revealing their foreign property to the IRS could somehow make that property—and therefore make them personally—forever taxable in the United States, even if they were to one day move back abroad and give up their U.S. tax residency. Quite often, once people fully realize the reporting requirements surrounding their foreign real estate assets, they become troubled and uncertain as to how to move forward. This uncertainty is especially hard for those who like living in the United States and have decided to stay here indefinitely.

Go Ahead, It Won't Hurt Too Much

We generally advise cross-border families in this situation to begin reporting their foreign rental income right away, especially given that the ramifications of doing so are probably much less onerous than they expect. Often, when beginning to report income from a foreign investment property that was previously unreported, professional tax preparers will go back and restate as many as six years of their clients' U.S. tax returns. In many cases, however, it's likely that doing so would not create significant additional tax obligations to the IRS.

This is especially true if the owner is already paying foreign tax on the property's income in the country where it is located. Why? Most countries tax rental income from real estate in some way, so whatever tax has been paid locally becomes a credit against tax that would be due to the IRS. Furthermore, the way the IRS taxes investment property—where a noncash depreciation expense is utilized to shelter a portion of a property's income from current income tax—leads to a fairly low taxable income for U.S. purposes, and perhaps even a tax-deductible loss, when compared to many other countries.

As a result of the depreciation rules, the IRS often taxes rental income at lower rates than other countries do, and so the resulting U.S. tax on that income could be fully offset by credits for foreign taxes paid. It's even possible that by going back and reporting prior years of rental activity, the taxpayer might have actually accumulated a deductible tax loss, or "excess" foreign tax credits that can be applied against other income. Imagine that someone could have waited and worried all these years, yet in the end, the reporting of the foreign rental income will have resulted in a tax benefit!

It's Not Really "Forever"—But It Might Be

Moreover, fears that the United States will continue to tax the foreign investment property forever are generally ungrounded. An international professional who leaves the United States and gives up his or her tax residency is no longer required to file U.S. tax returns with regard to any foreign rental income (this person would, however, need to continue to file if he or she kept a rental property in the United States). Alternatively, if U.S. tax residency is retained, then he or she will indeed always need to report the foreign investment property and any income from it on his or her U.S. tax returns.

Global Transparency Is Coming

Another thing to consider is that we're in a world with FATCA and other growing international information sharing agreements among governments. Right now, most efforts are primarily focused on bank accounts, investment accounts, and other financial assets. But over time, it's very likely that these efforts will evolve to also include foreign property ownership. That is, in the long run, it won't be possible to get away with not disclosing foreign investment properties or reporting the income they generate. In general, then, it's better to come into alignment now with the way the world is already moving and thereby avoid any possibility of penalties or punitive treatment by fully and immediately reporting everything that is required.

Foreign Property Gifted by Family Members

Family members gifting property to U.S. tax residents—or those who are likely to become U.S. tax residents—can result in interesting tax complexities. In many countries, especially in Europe and Asia, it's very common for individuals to inherit property from their parents, often at a young age, as a means of avoiding the eventual estate tax levied by that foreign country upon the death of the parents.

Very often, this property is used as a rent-free residence by the parents (who have already given the property to the child or children), and from a U.S. tax perspective it is treated like a second home in which the owner allows his or her parents to live rent-free. In other situations, the gifted property generates rental income that goes to the parents, as opposed to going to the legal owner of the property, that is, the child or children. This can create some U.S. tax complexity, but generally, there is a way for the actual property owner—who is a U.S. taxpayer—to claim a credit for the foreign taxes paid by the parent on this rental income, thus avoiding double taxation.

It is important to note that property received as a gift retains the cost basis of the person who gave the gift. For example, consider a property purchased by your grandfather in 1940 for the equivalent of $5,000, which was gifted to you some time ago and now has a current value of $1,000,000. This property would, for you, have a basis of $5,000 when you received it. If you sold the property the day after receiving it as a gift, you would have a taxable gain of $995,000.

Property received by inheritance, on the other hand, gets a "step up" in its basis to its current value on the date of the owner's death. In both cases, it is important to file Form 3520 for any year when you receive a gift (or combined gifts) or inheritance with a current value exceeding $100,000 from a foreign person or foreign estate (or more than $15,601 from a foreign corporation or partnership).

Owning Property Inside of an IRA

As previously noted, many cross-border families have a strong preference to own real estate as an investment, as opposed to other types of investments like stocks and bonds. In general, they are more comfortable with the stability of real estate, which tends to experience far fewer ups and downs than more volatile public market investments.

Many people don't know that it is possible to also buy real estate—and many other alternative assets—*inside* of an IRA, although the process is complicated, and usually not recommended for most people. Investors typically own traditional investments inside of IRAs—assets that are generally easily liquid or marketable—like stocks, bonds, and cash, primarily because the process of investing in these liquid assets is much easier and better suited for an IRA account. Alternative assets, like real estate, tend to be less liquid, unregulated, and more complex in nature, so owning them inside of an IRA creates a number of other issues, which we will now discuss.

In general, investment property is not well suited to be held inside of an IRA. One big reason for this is that rental income is normally tax sheltered as a result of the unique noncash depreciation rules, as explained earlier. These benefits are lost inside of a tax-deferred account like an IRA.

Rules to Be Carefully Followed

Nonetheless, for those who strongly prefer real estate to other more traditional investments, owning property within an IRA can be an option. For this reason, we will now briefly explain how the process works.

First, the IRA must be located at a special self-directed trust company that takes a role in approving the investments and annually filing certain forms with the IRS. The need to use this kind of a special account custodian does add additional cost and complexity.

Be Careful to Read the Fine Print

It's also easy to get in trouble here. There are a long-list of prohibited transactions and a strict set of related rules that need to be followed. Failing to follow these rules can lead the IRS to invalidate your entire IRA! This means potentially risking the loss of the tax-deferred status of the account, as well as incurring taxable income on a deemed distribution of the entire account, plus a 10 percent penalty for those under the age of 59.5.

Some of the most important rules include:

1. *No co-mingling of funds:* You cannot utilize both IRA and other after-tax (non-IRA) accounts in any way connected to the investment. This means you can't combine funds to purchase a property, nor can you utilize after-tax funds for ongoing improvements or maintenance of the property. In short, you need to have enough additional cash in your IRA for any repairs, maintenance, or other cash-dependent needs that result from owning the property.

2. *No personal use:* There is also a strict prohibition on any personal use of a property owned by the IRA, that is, you are barred from personally using or occupying it in any way. This applies both to you and to any member of your family.

3. *Professional contractors only:* You are also generally barred from working on the property personally, that is, you may only use professional contractors and property managers for any repairs or other needs related to the property.

It can also be difficult to obtain a mortgage, given the complexities and legal structures involved when the owner of the property is an IRA. Moreover, there is a possibility of receiving some taxable income from the investment, even though the property is located inside of a tax-deferred IRA account. This occurs in situations where the asset produces *unrelated business taxable income* (or UBIG). This can happen when either (a) the income is earned from real estate held inside of a limited partnership or an LLC (limited liability corporation), or (b) where the property incurs debt financing, as when a mortgage is used to partially fund the purchase.

Finally, once you are over the age of 70 1/2 years, you are under the obligation to begin required minimum distributions (RMD) from your IRA. In this case, you need to be very careful that you have sufficient cash reserves within the IRA to meet these minimum distribution requirements, which generally rise every year.

Overall, then, if you do decide you want to own property within your IRA, you have to make sure that you understand and follow all of the rules and requirements, or things can go quite badly. It is, however, possible to find a self-directed trust company that will help guide you through the entire process.

Other Cross-Border Considerations

In this section, we discuss a number of interesting considerations and planning ideas related to real estate for cross-border families and foreign citizens.

Tax-Free Exchange of Investment Property—Doesn't Travel Well

A tax-free like-kind exchange (a 1031 Exchange in the U.S. tax code) is a very popular strategy for those looking to sell appreciated investment property while deferring any tax into the future. This strategy works very well for those who want to sell an investment property and then immediately buy another investment property while also postponing any tax on the gain. Reasons for doing this may include:

1. Selling a property that has already greatly appreciated in order to purchase one that may have better upside investment potential;
2. Selling a property that requires a lot of ongoing management, and exchanging it for one with less ongoing management; and
3. Diversifying from one larger property into several smaller ones.

To qualify, the replacement property must be "like" property, which, according to the U.S. tax code, means that just like the old property, it must be for an investment use or be a property that is used in the regular course of business. Many people confuse the term *like-kind* as meaning that the two properties must be equivalent for this to work, but this is not true. In fact you can exchange one *type* of investment property for a different *type*—you could sell an office building and buy an apartment building—but *since both the old property and the new property have an investment use,* they are both considered to be "like" properties.

There are very strict rules that state that you must identify the new replacement property within 45 days of selling the old property. Additionally, you must complete the purchase within 180 days of the sale of the former property. Other rules also apply that are essentially meant to link together the exchange of the old property with the new purchase transaction. It's important to ensure that all of the transactions are properly executed, and that all of the rules and timelines are meticulously adhered to, to avoid losing the gain deferral.

Sorry, This Only Works for U.S. Properties

They are many U.S. taxpayers who own appreciated foreign investment property and who would very much like to be able to exchange that foreign property for a U.S. property that would be both closer to them and easier to manage. Unfortunately, tax-free like-kind exchanges are only allowed on the exchange of one U.S. property for another U.S. property; therefore, it cannot be applied to foreign investment property. This rule is somewhat unusual, as most U.S. tax laws related to real estate investments do not change depending on where the property is located.

Avoid Owning Foreign Real Estate Through a Foreign Corporation

Anyone who decides to buy property must first decide how to actually own or hold legal title to the property. Real estate can usually be owned by the individual in his or her own name, or through some type of intermediary holding entity, which is actually very common outside of the United States. Indeed, wealthy people throughout the world often hold personal assets like real property inside of various foreign corporations and trust structures.

However, the use by U.S. taxpayers of foreign entities to acquire foreign assets typically requires special and sometimes burdensome reporting to the IRS. Given their history of use in tax evasion and otherwise hiding assets, the rules governing foreign entities owned by U.S tax residents are vast and complex. So, if you have an ownership interest in a foreign entity that owns real estate, and then you come to the United States and become a tax resident, you are subject to all of these rules. So, for example, if you own an apartment building in

Spain through your Luxembourg trust, you are going to potentially face some substantial tax challenges upon becoming a U.S. taxpayer.

In certain situations, when a U.S. tax resident holds property through a foreign entity, the property can be subject to what is called *controlled foreign corporations,* or CFC, tax rules. These rules can result in much greater tax complexity and potentially higher U.S. income tax upon the sale of the foreign property.

Our basic recommendation here is that it is best to avoid owning property through foreign entities because the IRS simply does not like it and will make things difficult for you. If you come to the U.S. and already own property through such a foreign entity, it is best to get professional advice as soon as possible, ideally before becoming a U.S. tax resident.

Unique Currency Risk When Owning Property Abroad

Certain unique currency-related issues arise when owning property located abroad, where the purchase amount is denominated in a foreign currency. When purchasing property outside of the United States, you must establish the tax basis of the investment in U.S. dollars at the time of the transaction. This is true even when the original purchase was before the owner became a U.S. tax resident. The full gain on the sale of foreign property is likewise based on the net sale proceeds converted into U.S. dollars, at the current exchange rate on the day of the sale. This can lead to unusual results, where large swings in the foreign exchange rates can substantially affect the final taxable gain or loss amount for U.S. tax purposes.

For investment properties, it is possible to make a special election to have a property classified as a qualified business unit (QBU), which effectively allows all transactions to be left in local currency until they are earned, and then the net income or gain is converted into dollars on the effective date. This can help alleviate some of the strange currency effects discussed above—although depending on exchange rate movements, making this election can either help or hurt the final taxable result.

Strange Gains and Losses on the Retirement of Debt on Personal Residence

U.S. citizens and tax residents can experience very unusual tax treatment when utilizing mortgage debt denominated in a foreign currency to purchase personal residences. As we know, selling a property at a gain generally is a taxable event here in the United States (notwithstanding the gain exclusion for a primary residence), and that gain can be enhanced or reduced as a result of currency fluctuations between the time of purchase and sale. However, the IRS also considers it a taxable gain when personal debt is retired at an amount that benefited from currency movements (although it is interesting to note there is no provision to claim a tax-deductible loss when the opposite occurs).

This rule is rather obscure, and we very rarely see it come into play. In fact, we speculate that many professional tax advisors are unaware of it. Furthermore, it is hard to imagine how the IRS would ever really know about it, unless it was self-reported by the taxpayer. Nonetheless, we thought we should offer a quick example of when and how this gain or loss on the retirement of debt can go badly.

Let's suppose someone purchases a foreign property for a total purchase price in euros that was equivalent to $1 million at the time, and he or she finances 100 percent of the purchase with an interest-only mortgage (no principal reduction over time). Several years later, after the euro has risen 20 percent against the dollar, the owner sells the property for a final net sales price exactly equal to the price originally paid in euros. Of course, the full proceeds of the sale would go to pay off the local mortgage, also denominated in euros, and then the transaction is done. It's simple: no gain, no loss, right?

But, in fact, it is not that simple. Because the sale price is converted into dollars at a 20 percent higher rate, there is actually a $200,000 taxable gain. But of course, there actually was no "cash" gain, since the full proceeds were used to pay off the mortgage. So then the owner effectively had an equal and offsetting $200,000 loss on the retirement of debt, because in dollar terms it cost 20 percent more to pay off the mortgage. Unfortunately, losses on the repayment of "personal" debts are not deductible (even though gains are taxable).

The reason for this is that financing transactions for personal property that result in currency losses are considered to be a separate and discrete event from the purchase of the underlying asset. And as per relevant IRS rules, since the mortgage transaction was not entered into in the normal course of a trade or business, the currency loss is not deductible and cannot be used to offset the gain realized on the sale.

Now let's change the situation around and assume the dollar weakened by 20 percent. The property would then have a $200,000 loss on the sale (a net sale price in dollars of $800,000). Unfortunately, you cannot deduct a loss from the sale of a personal residence. Now it also cost 20 percent less to repay the mortgage, meaning that in dollar terms the person had a "gain" of $200,000 on the repayment of the mortgage, which is taxable as ordinary income. Basically in this case, the IRS gets to have its cake and eat it, too!

The moral of the story is, be very careful when financing large personal real estate purchases abroad, because there can be strange and costly outcomes when things are translated back to dollars for U.S. tax purposes.

Nonresident Aliens: Investing in the United States and the EB-5 Program

There has been an increasing trend for very wealthy international families to make investments in the United States, whether they are in real estate, financial assets (stocks and bonds), or even operating businesses. Often, these investors have goals that go beyond simple investment: They are often looking to move money out of their country and into the United States and the dollar, which are considered to be more stable. There's also often a desire for anonymity, which can mean the use of various trusts and legal entities to execute these investments. Below are a few situations that we often see along these lines.

Nonresident Aliens Investing in U.S. Real Estate

Wealthy international families frequently purchase real estate in the United States, even when they have no other connection to this country. The news often contains stories about wealthy Chinese investors who show up and offer to buy properties for cash, but there are also similar investors from Russia, Latin America, and many other places around the world who are eager to purchase U.S. properties.

When foreign residents purchase property in the United States, this generally creates significant legal and tax complexities. For example, the income tax treatment for nonresident owners of U.S. income property can be very complex, and there is also a mandatory tax withholding on the gross rental income and the gross proceeds of a sale. This and other unique tax provisions were put in place by FIRPTA (the Foreign Investment In Real Property Tax Act of 1980).

See Part V for a more detailed discussion of the unique tax rules for nonresidents who own assets within the United States.

Becoming a U.S. Resident—EB-5 Visas

Many foreign nationals have taken advantage of the EB-5 program, which provides a method for them to obtain permanent U.S. residency (Green Card) by investing money in the United States. To obtain this visa, individuals must invest at least $1,000,000 (or at least $500,000 in a high unemployment area) into a business or project that creates at least 10 jobs in the United States, not including jobs for the investor and his or her immediate family. Wealthy international families are doing this for themselves, and often for their children (who may even move here and live in the home they've recently purchased). Unfortunately, many of these wealthy foreign families fail to fully appreciate the tax complexities they are buying into when obtaining U.S. residency, where their worldwide assets and income have now become reportable and taxable here in the United States.

Estate Taxes on U.S. Property Owned by Nonresidents

There are also unique estate tax rules related to the foreign ownership of U.S. property as well as other assets. The most important of these rules is the lower estate tax exemption of just $60,000 for U.S.-based assets owned by nonresidents. This means that upon the death of the nonresident owners, the value of any U.S.-based property above $60,000 is taxable at regular estate tax rates. It's possible to mitigate this estate tax by purchasing the property through offshore entities, but this, in turn, adds significant complications. See Part V for a more detailed discussion of the unique tax rules for nonresidents who own assets within the United States.

Risk of Estate Taxes with Foreign Property

Anyone who owns property in more than one country should be aware that most countries levy an estate tax on real and personal property located within their borders. This can create significant complexities for the heirs of an estate, because they will often need to deal individually with each and every country where the estate's property is located.

Depending on each countries unique estate tax rules, there may be an estate tax liability or transfer fee. Often, foreign countries will levy estate taxes on the net equity value of property owned by foreign owners (with *foreign* meaning not a citizen or legal resident of that country). Because most countries tax the net equity of a property (fair value minus any debt), owners of foreign properties may, for estate planning purposes, benefit by adjusting the mortgage levels on various properties in different places.

As an example, someone who owns two properties in different foreign countries may learn that one of the countries has a high tax on the net equity of property owned by foreigners, while the other has no such tax. In that case, the owner could reconfigure his or her debt levels (assume they both had mortgages equal to 50 percent of their fair value) by refinancing the debt to 100 percent of the fair value in the country with a high estate tax, and, in turn, pay off the mortgage in full for the other property. In this way, the owner will have substantially lowered the potential estate taxes for his or her heirs.

P A R T

V

Cross-Border Taxation

CHAPTER 10

Understanding the Three Types of Cross-Border Families

The Unique Complexities of Cross-Border Taxation

Cross-border professionals face a highly complex tax situation, particularly when their financial affairs touch the United States. Very often, these people have income, assets, and other financial connections in multiple countries. This can make things extremely complicated because they must then generally interact with two or more national tax authorities. Unfortunately, for those whose financial affairs are indeed connected to the United States, one of those tax authorities will be the Internal Revenue Service (or IRS), and this often changes things dramatically. As discussed in Chapter 2, the United States is the only major nation to *tax all of its citizens and tax residents on their worldwide income and assets regardless of whether they currently reside in the United States.* This overlapping worldwide reach brings an overriding complexity to any cross-border family's tax picture.

In addition, as we discussed in Chapter 2, we find ourselves today in an environment of rapidly evolving tax laws and ever-greater aggressiveness on the part of tax authorities in various countries to gather information about their citizens' worldwide income, assets, and financial affairs (such as with FATCA[1]). Not only the United States but many other countries have also imposed a wide variety of rules, regulations, and requirements as to foreign asset reporting, disclosure requirements, and money restrictions. All this—on top of dealing with multiple tax authorities and the worldwide reach of

---

[1]Foreign Account Tax Compliance Act. See Chapter 2 for more about FATCA.

the IRS—really does make for a very complex and often difficult tax situation.

Given this complexity, the mechanics of the tax reporting process and optimal tax planning are naturally a big part of the challenge for international families with regard to personal wealth management and retirement planning. There are also many tax-related questions concerning investment structures, asset location, investment management, retirement savings plans, and more. That is, taxes touch nearly everything of financial significance in an international family's life, so dealing with the tax ramifications of these many related questions—on top of the increasing reporting and filing requirements imposed by multiple jurisdictions—is indeed a very tall order.

The Lack of Available Information and Help

Even with perfect information and easily accessible advice, it can often be a daunting challenge for cross-border professionals to optimize everything related to taxation. In the course of our work with clients at Worldview, we have unfortunately found that there is a tremendous lack of accessible and affordable help with regard to both international taxation and the many other wealth planning strategies found throughout this book. While very wealthy families can afford to build their own team of cross-border experts in the areas of tax, law, investment, banking, and so on, the majority of cross-border families cannot. This book aims to serve those people.

Among younger and less wealthy families, there is a tremendous information gap caused by a paucity of readily available, cost accessible, and easy-to-digest assistance. That is, for the vast majority of families who may not be wealthy but nevertheless are successful and have high incomes, there is a real lack of accessible, usable, and low-cost information. Our overarching purpose is to break things down, summarize them, and make them understandable, approachable, and useful so that cross-border families can make smart decisions about the entirety of their financial situation, both in the short run and in the long run.

It is not our goal here to teach people how to do their own taxes. Rather, we've tried to illuminate many of the tax-related issues affecting cross-border families. Our hope is that this will lead to improved understanding and will enable better decision making, or just help families to identify important questions or areas of concern that may require further investigation. This is a lofty goal, as each personal situation is unique, and it is not possible to address all of the significant or important elements for everyone in this book. We have done our best to discuss the most common questions and challenges that apply to the vast majority of cross-border families. Ultimately, we remain strong proponents of seeking personalized advice and guidance from an experienced and qualified professional.

Tax Profiles: Three Types of Cross-Border Families

In the "Who's Who" section in Chapter 1 (please see Figure 1.1), we distinguished between three main kinds of cross-border individuals and families according to their U.S. tax status:

1. Foreign nationals living and working in the United States (i.e., resident aliens according to the IRS, or permanent residents if they hold a Green Card)
2. Americans citizens (expatriates) and permanent residents living abroad
3. Foreign nationals living outside of the United States with assets in the United States (i.e., nonresident aliens according to the IRS)

It's critically important to understand the unique status and attributes of each group so that you know which profile you fall into and what the likely tax ramifications (and necessary planning steps) will be for you. Following, we further define these profiles and provide some of their unique tax planning considerations.

Type 1: Foreign Nationals in the United States

Foreign nationals living in the United States are the first group we'll consider. They are technically referred to as *resident aliens* by the IRS, but they can also be known as *tax residents,* U.S. residents, or permanent residents (if they hold a Green Card). They represent a growing segment of foreign workers, those who are born outside the United States and then come here in a professional capacity. They tend to be successful people who are well educated and have a high income. It is important to understand that while they are here in the United States, they will generally be taxed the same as any other American, except with the added complexity that they often own assets located outside of the United States and otherwise have additional foreign connections in their lives.

With the ongoing globalization of business and the growth of our interconnected global economy, increasing numbers of foreign nationals are coming into the United States. They tend to be accomplished professionals who save at a much higher rate than their American peers. However, they also have far more complicated financial affairs than a typical American, and both their financial planning and investing needs can be quite different indeed.

Learning the U.S. Tax System

Foreign nationals often struggle with understanding the U.S. tax code, including its general level of complexity and its worldwide reach. For those who are used to a simplistic or "flat" tax system, the U.S. tax code and its requirements can be truly mind-boggling. Similarly, foreign nationals are often faced with making decisions as to various retirement and investment options that are completely unfamiliar to them.

Additionally, many foreign nationals who work for large corporations come to the United States on short-term work visas or temporary assignments, where they are somewhat insulated from the full ramifications of becoming a U.S. tax resident. However, it is common for many of these short-term workers to eventually choose to stay in the United States more permanently. When this occurs, they must then become better informed about what becoming a U.S. tax resident—a Green Card holder or someone who passes the substantial presence test—will mean to their personal finances, even if this takes place several years after they first arrived in the United States.

While some cross-border professionals come into the United States at a relatively young age, others come here later on in their careers. Most of those who have already worked abroad have already accumulated assets such as cash, real estate, investment portfolios, and retirement savings accounts. These foreign assets are immediately subjected to U.S. taxation, which often comes as a big and unwelcome surprise. For that reason, correctly planning a move to the United States is extremely important, and will be discussed later in this chapter.

Type 2: American Citizens and Permanent Residents Living Abroad

Today's global economy is leading to more and more opportunities for professional growth and advancement all around the world. Many American citizens are moving abroad for work reasons. Additionally, foreign nationals who come to the United States and establish permanent tax residency here are occasionally later sent abroad on work assignments. Importantly, in both of these cases, those U.S. citizens and permanent tax residents who are living abroad are essentially treated the same by the IRS.

There is a considerable amount of confusion surrounding personal finances and retirement planning for this group. Much of that confusion revolves around how they integrate U.S. taxes with whatever foreign taxes they are paying in the country where they are working and residing.

Those in this group are generally taxed on their foreign income first by the foreign country where they are working. In addition, both U.S. citizens and permanent tax residents living abroad must continue to file U.S. tax returns and report all of their worldwide income. In some cases, they will owe U.S. tax on their income during their time working abroad; however, there are special tax provisions in place to avoid double taxation in this situation. We'll cover this in some detail later in the chapter.

U.S. taxpayers who are living and working in a foreign country will usually not owe any *state* tax on their foreign income, because U.S. states generally base their taxation on an individual's residency or intent to be domiciled within the state. However, many U.S. states are rather aggressive in pursuing former state residents in an effort to tax them, so be careful to follow your state's rules to officially terminate residency when you move abroad, or you may find that you still owe state taxes.

Foreign Citizens Leaving the United States for Short-Term Assignments

Occasionally, foreign citizens who are permanent tax residents of the United States will pursue an opportunity abroad without necessarily planning to stay away from the United States forever. For that reason, many of them do not give up their Green Card just because they've left the United States. The downside to holding onto their Green Card, however, is that they continue to be viewed—and taxed—by the IRS in the exact same way that a regular American citizen is taxed for as long as they retain their permanent tax residency. Of course, this also applies to foreign nationals who have become U.S. citizens or dual citizens. The key point here is that even people who have the ability to sever their tax reporting requirement with the United States often choose to remain connected in order to preserve their right to return here whenever they wish.

Expatriate Assignments and Tax-Equalized Employment Packages

Often, American citizens and tax residents are initially sent abroad on a short-term assignment with their employer, usually for three years or less. In these cases, it is common for the employee to be offered a *tax-equalized* contract, which means two things. First, the employer will insulate them from most of the tax and administrative complexity of their foreign assignment, and will completely handle their tax preparation needs. Second, the employer will also see to it that the employee is effectively taxed at the same rate as he or she would have been taxed at had he or she still been living in the United States, thereby removing the effect of different tax rates from the overseas assignment.

For example, suppose the employee lives in California and has been sent to work in Hong Kong. The employer will have an accountant prepare hypothetical federal and state tax returns as if the employee was still living in California and being taxed there on his or her gross income. Then the employer handles all of the true complexities of preparing and filing the employee's local tax return in Hong Kong, as well as filing the employee's U.S. federal tax return and claiming any available credits for foreign taxes paid. At the end of the day, the employer basically ensures that the employee is "equalized" and made whole on a net after-tax basis. The employer will either pay the extra tax owed over and above the employee's "equalized" tax liability or will keep any net tax advantage in situations where the employee's effective net tax liability would have been lower while on assignment.

In either case, tax-equalized assignments are expensive and complicated for the employer. The employer takes on much or all of the responsibility not only for preparing and filing taxes in multiple jurisdictions, but also for paying any necessary equalizing taxes to either the United States or foreign tax authority. In some cases, however, as mentioned previously, tax-equalized contracts will work out to the benefit of the employer when the employee is sent to a lower tax environment. That is, it is very possible that if the employee were not tax-equalized back to his or her original place of U.S. residency, say California, he or she might actually pay a much lower effective tax rate.

In general, tax-equalized assignments to higher-tax countries (like many in Europe) are often much more costly to the employer, while assignments to lower-tax countries (like many in parts of Asia and elsewhere) can result in a net tax benefit to the employer. This can incentivize employers to offer different types of overseas assignment packages depending on the tax policies of the various countries they are sending their employees to.

In either case—whether it benefits the employer or the employee—tax-equalized contracts are becoming increasingly less common (except among senior-level executives). In part, this is so because they are difficult to manage and inherently expensive and complicated. Additionally, there's been a general shift in business attitudes with regard to overseas assignments. Such assignments used to be seen as a significant hardship, and therefore the employee had to be enticed to agree to the move. This attitude has changed in recent years, with overseas assignments increasingly being seen as an important opportunity for global experience and career advancement.

"Localized" Employment Contracts in Another Country

Ultimately, far fewer tax-equalized contracts are being offered by employers, and instead employees are often from the start considered to be "localized" in whatever country they are sent. Additionally, it is becoming more common for individuals who are sent abroad on a tax-equalized contract to then choose to stay put and become a localized employee after the initial term of their original assignment ends. In either case, localized employees are pretty much on their own. The responsibility for properly filing income tax returns shifts to them, and it is likely that a localized employee will end up paying either a higher or lower effective tax rate than they would have had they still been living and working in the United States.

Whether there is a favorable or an unfavorable difference depends on the tax rates of the individual country where the employee is working and living, and whether there are any special foreign worker tax holidays that lower the employee's effective tax rate. Many foreign countries have special tax incentives to attract foreign workers, such as a window of time—often as long as 10 years— where an individual will experience a lower effective tax rate than would a typical citizen of that country, and where the individual's foreign assets and income are also not taxed.

The bottom line is that if an American citizen or permanent tax resident who is living abroad is localized in a foreign country, things will be substantially different for that individual. He or she will bear the full responsibility of filing tax returns and paying taxes in the local country, and of preparing U.S. tax returns (which in turn may claim credits for whatever taxes have been paid in the foreign country). Essentially, a localized employee is responsible either for making sense of the way the two countries' tax authorities speak to each other or for hiring a tax advisor to do this work for them. In situations where there is a good deal of income or net worth, this situation can become extremely complicated.

Reducing U.S. Tax for Taxpayers Living Abroad

U.S. taxpayers living abroad will often find that they owe little to no additional U.S taxes on their foreign income. This is usually the result of two unique tax provisions that benefit those living abroad: (1) foreign income exclusions, and (2) foreign tax credits (FTC). The foreign income exclusions—including both the Foreign Earned Income Exclusion (FEIE) and the Foreign Housing Exclusion—are the tools used most often to reduce or eliminate U.S. tax liabilities for taxpayers living abroad. If a taxpayer continues to owe U.S. tax after applying these income exclusions, FTCs will often further reduce or eliminate that tax liability. What follows is a discussion of how these tools work together.

Foreign Earned Income Exclusion

For many people, the FEIE is an effective tool for ensuring that their foreign earned income (foreign salary and wages) is essentially taxed only by their country of residence, and not also by the IRS. The FEIE allows U.S. citizens and tax residents to exclude a certain amount of their foreign earned income for U.S. tax purposes every year, which in 2016 was $101,300 (adjusted annually for inflation). So while those living abroad are still taxed on their worldwide income, the amount that is considered taxable in the United States is reduced by a significant portion every year.

Foreign Housing Exclusion

In addition to the FEIE, there is a related Foreign Housing Exclusion for foreign housing expenses such as rent and utilities. This exclusion enables U.S. taxpayers abroad to exclude from their U.S. taxable income a portion of their compensation that goes toward overseas lodging. Typically, the maximum allowable excluded amount is roughly 30 percent of the amount of the FEIE ($30,390 for 2016). However, in many higher-cost housing areas, it can be a higher amount (this includes most major international cities). There is also a base floor amount that you are not allowed to deduct, which is 16 percent of the maximum FEIE amount ($16,208 for 2016). This is subtracted from the taxpayer's total housing expenses for purposes of calculating the housing exclusion.

Foreign Tax Credits

In situations where a U.S. taxpayer still owes tax after taking advantage of the FEIE and Foreign Housing Exclusion, he or she still has the option of applying foreign tax credits (FTCs) to reduce or eliminate any U.S. tax liability.

FTCs allow U.S. taxpayers to claim a dollar-for-dollar credit for taxes paid in a foreign country or countries against any U.S. tax that is due on their foreign-sourced income. Consider, for example, those with high incomes who work in a relatively high-tax location, such as many Western European countries. If the effective tax rate that they pay in a place like the United Kingdom is higher than their tax liability to the IRS, by applying a credit to their U.S. tax liability for the foreign taxes that have already been paid, they would not have to pay any additional U.S. tax. They may even accumulate a foreign tax credit carry forward, which can be used at a later date to reduce U.S. tax—generally, if after returning to the United States, they continue to have foreign earned income.

However, there is another element to this called the *scale-down rules*, which effectively limit the use of certain foreign tax credits when you also use the FEIE and/or housing exclusions. Essentially, U.S. taxpayers may not claim a credit for foreign taxes that relate to income that was already excluded for U.S. purposes via the FEIE and/or housing exclusion. Put another way, the IRS lowers the amount of foreign tax that can be credited against your U.S. tax liability by excluding the foreign tax paid on income that was excluded from U.S. taxation.

Revoking the Foreign Earned Income Exclusion

When living in a country with a higher tax rate than the United States, you are likely to have sufficient foreign tax credits to offset the U.S. tax on foreign income items, making the Foreign Earned Income and Foreign Housing Exclusions unnecessary. Surprisingly, utilizing these exclusions can result in a higher U.S. tax than if you didn't use them (or significantly reduce foreign tax credits that carry over and can potentially be used in the future). The reason for this is complex, but essentially there are *stacking rules* when using the FEIE that cause all of your nonexcluded income to be taxed at higher tax rates. (Stacking rules require excluded income to be added back for purposes of calculating tax rates.)

This means that if you have income that is not eligible for foreign tax credits, it will be taxed at a higher average rate. Fortunately, you are allowed to revoke the FEIE and/or the Foreign Housing Exclusion. But be careful: Once you revoke, you generally cannot elect to use them again for five tax years! This is a fairly complex issue; you would be strongly advised to discuss this with a qualified tax advisor before making a decision.

Likely U.S. Tax Liabilities for U.S. Taxpayers Abroad

It should be said that for a significant number of U.S. taxpayers living abroad, there will be no additional income tax owed in the United States. For both anyone earning below the Foreign Earned Income Exclusion ($101,300 in 2016), and anyone who lives in a country that taxes income at a higher rate than the U.S. federal government, will generally not owe additional income taxes to the United States on their foreign income.

U.S. taxpayers with higher levels of income, who are living in countries with a lower tax environment than the United States has, potentially face significant additional U.S. taxes on their foreign income. Foreign countries with a lower effective tax rate (and ultimate tax liability) will create a smaller foreign tax credit for U.S. purposes. Likewise, taxpayers with higher income levels will ultimately be taxed at the highest U.S. marginal tax rate (39.6 percent for 2016). As taxable income rises, the importance of the FEIE falls, and the differential in marginal tax rates between the foreign country and the United States ultimately becomes the most important factor in determining additional taxes owed here.

However, many high earners living abroad will continue to be exposed to the net investment income tax (NIIT), which potentially levies an additional 3.8 percent Medicare supplemental tax on all net investment income (not earned income) above certain thresholds. For some, this may essentially be a completely new tax owed to the United States, when before no taxes were owed to the United States. This tax is discussed in detail in Chapter 12.

Type 3: Foreign Nationals with Assets in the United States

The final profile to consider is foreign citizens who live outside the United States, but who still have assets in the United States. We are talking now about nonresident aliens—individuals who are neither U.S. citizens nor U.S. tax residents—who generally have no immigration status in the United States as well as no obligation to file tax returns here. For purposes of our discussion related to U.S. residency and tax obligations, we will refer to these individuals simply as nonresidents.

The most typical situation we see is a foreign professional who came to the United States to live and work for a period of time. The individual may have been here on a work visa for just a year or two, or perhaps they secured a Green Card and stayed in the United States for 10 to 20 years or more (individuals giving up a Green Card after more than 7 years may potentially be subject to the expatriation tax, which is discussed later in this chapter). Even though working in the United States can lead to significant opportunity, many people do decide to move away, often to return to their home country to be near family, or to pursue another opportunity that takes them to an entirely different third country.

In these situations, it is common for people to continue to own certain types of assets in the United States, even after they've moved on. The most typical assets we see this group continuing to own in the United States include:

- Bank accounts
- Retirement savings accounts—like 401(k)s from former employers, IRAs, and other tax-advantaged structures
- Other investment portfolios—held in regular taxable accounts
- Former residences from when they lived here—which are often converted to rental properties

Often, when foreign citizens permanently leave the United States, they will liquidate their regular taxable investments and wire the resulting cash, along with their other savings, on to their next destination, whether that's their country of origin or a third country. They might need that money to get established in their new home, or perhaps they just don't feel comfortable leaving it behind. But it is very common to leave behind 401(k)s, IRAs, and other tax-advantaged accounts because of unique benefits of those structures, and the substantial taxes and penalties that are incurred if they are liquidated. Departing families will frequently hold on to property when they leave, as a result of their natural predisposition to hold real estate as a long-term investment.

We have also seen situations where a foreign national inherits U.S.-based assets. We have even met people who own substantial assets in the United States, even though they are not U.S. citizens and have never even visited this country. These individuals are often surprised by the unique tax reporting requirements that come along with their inheritance in the United States.

Another common situation is when very wealthy international families, such as Latin American or Chinese families, seek to shift a portion of their wealth into the United States for a variety of reasons. This is frequently done in an effort to protect certain assets from another country's legal or tax system. International families often appreciate the relative safety of the U.S. dollar compared to their local currency, and they value the safety and transparency of the U.S. capital system—which is generally viewed as a safe and well-regulated system that is far less prone to corruption and governmental intervention.

Taxation by the IRS—On Passive U.S. Investments

The tax implications for these people are complex, but in general the individual owners of U.S.-based assets are required to pay taxes on the income they generate, unless that income is protected from taxation by an international tax treaty. For this discussion, we'll focus on the taxation of "passive income," which generally includes interest, dividends, rents, royalties, and certain capital gains. According to the U.S. tax code, this U.S.-sourced passive income is generally taxed at a flat tax rate of 30 percent on a gross basis (before any deductions). However, this amount can be reduced, and in some cases entirely eliminated, depending on the type of income and tax treaty in place.

If a nonresident's only U.S.-sourced income is passive income, then the nonresident is generally not required to file a U.S. tax return. Instead, the 30 percent flat tax rate (or a lower treaty rate) is collected through a mandatory withholding, which is implemented by the payer of the income to a nonresident—typically, a corporation paying a dividend or a U.S. financial institution effecting a distribution of income.

The most common U.S. assets we see owned by nonresidents are cash, real estate, and investment accounts, so we will focus our attention on how these are taxed. Note that it is common for nonresidents to own 401(k)s, IRAs, and other tax-deferred investment accounts in the United States. Because the income from inside these accounts is tax-deferred, there is no tax reporting (nor any withholding tax) required for nonresident owners. There are, however, significant tax consequences when nonresidents make distributions from these accounts. See Part III for more on how distributions from these accounts are taxed.

Interest Income, Dividends, and Capital Gains

There are special tax rules that exempt certain types of passive income from U.S. taxation when the person receiving the income is a nonresident, regardless of whether there is a tax treaty available. Interest earned from debt instruments issued by U.S. entities is not taxable; this includes interest on bank deposits as well as interest from bonds and bonds funds.

Additionally, capital gains on most types of passive investments, such as stocks and stock funds, are generally not taxable in the United States to a nonresident, unless the capital assets are U.S. business assets or U.S. real property interests.

However, U.S.-sourced dividends are not exempt for nonresidents, and are subject to U.S. tax at a flat 30 percent withholding rate (or lower treaty rate). To take advantage of a lower treaty, it is important to provide your account custodian with a copy of Form W-8BEN so that the correct amount can be withheld. If your account custodian incorrectly withholds a higher amount than the applicable treaty rate, you can get a refund by filing a U.S. tax return for that year. However, having the correct tax held at source often means you do not need to file a U.S. tax return for that year.

Rental Real Estate Property In the United States

Many nonresidents own U.S. rental properties whether they are former residences or were purchased with the original intention to be an investment property.[2] This type of income is usually classified as passive income, with gross rental income subject to the 30 percent withholding tax (or a lower tax treaty rate)—without the benefit of any expense deductions. Because this form of taxation could result in a significant burden and discourage foreign investment in U.S. real property, nonresidents can, and nearly always do (when properly advised), elect to treat any rental activity as business income by attaching a special statement to the first tax return that includes the rental property. This allows the nonresident landlord to be taxed on a net basis using graduated tax rates. Because the landlord is taxed on a net basis (gross rental income less associated deductible expenses), this will often result in a significantly lower U.S. tax liability.

When a nonresident sells a U.S. property, any gain is taxed in the same manner as if the property had been sold by a U.S. citizen or resident. Therefore, a gain may qualify for lower long-term capital gain tax treatment, provided it meets the test and has been owned for more than 12 months. Even though the gain or loss is ultimately taxed on a net basis through the filing of a tax return, a severe 15 percent nonresident withholding tax is still levied on the gross receipts (sale proceeds) of the transaction unless you have received a specific exemption from this withholding (which can be difficult to obtain). A lower rate of 10 percent applies to dispositions under $1 million for U.S. property that was acquired as a personal residence.

The taxation of rental properties owned by nonresidents is very complex, and is subject to very specific rules. We recommend foreign residents take great care to ensure that they fully understand these rules, which often can mean seeking out professional guidance and assistance.

Overwithholding Tax on Bond Interest Inside a Fund

We have observed that many large U.S. financial institutions are overwithholding tax for nonresidents who own investment funds,

---

[2]Wealthy international people also often choose to purchase residential real estate in the United States that does not necessarily generate income. They often purchase it as a store of value, a way to hold and maintain their wealth in what's perceived to be a more stable and safe environment.

holding bonds (bond funds) in their accounts, thus creating the potential for double taxation. The rules about mandatory tax withholdings are meant to apply only to the dividends of U.S. companies. As stated before, interest earned from debt instruments (bonds) issued by U.S. entities is not subject to tax withholding. However, we've found that many U.S. financial institutions routinely withhold tax at the 30 percent rate (or lower treaty rate) on the dividends from bond funds, even though those "dividends" are actually just the pass-through of interest income paid from the various underlying bonds within the fund. Because of this, nonresidents may be wise to avoid investing large amounts of money into bond funds registered in the United States.

Estate Tax Exemptions for Nonresidents

A final area of importance for nonresidents holding U.S.-based assets concerns a lower estate tax exemption than U.S. citizens and permanent residents receive. When a nonresident, or any non-U.S. domiciled person passes away (some U.S. tax residents may not be considered domiciled in the United States for estate and gift tax purposes, and thus could also be included here), instead of receiving an exemption from the U.S. estate tax of approximately $5.4 million per person (for 2016), nonresidents with U.S. assets only receive a $60,000 exemption, after which they owe U.S. estate tax on their assets here. Obviously, the difference between these exemptions is very large, and nonresidents in this situation may potentially face high U.S. estate tax liabilities. There are also, however, a very small number of countries that exempt their residents from U.S. estate tax on certain types of assets here through their estate tax treaty with the United States.

Becoming a U.S. Resident for Tax Purposes

For a foreign national coming to work in the United States, among the most important things to understand is whether he or she will be classified as a U.S. resident for tax purposes, also simply referred to as a tax resident. Foreign citizens who are newly arrived in the United States often misunderstand both whether they will be classified as a tax resident as well as what it means to be so classified (i.e., what the bottom-line economic and tax implications will be). While the book has discussed this to some degree in Chapter 2, it is vital information that bears more in-depth discussion here.

As has been pointed out throughout the book, U.S. tax residents are taxed on their worldwide income. However, there are situations where a visiting worker can remain a nonresident for tax purposes, and will only be taxed on his or her U.S.-sourced income. But someone who does become a tax resident has opened up his or her entire worldwide income to U.S. taxation. For example, consider someone who owns a foreign business and comes to the United States for a short time to launch a subsidiary, and then ends up staying here longer than originally planned. This person could end up being classified as a U.S. tax resident, which could potentially expose the entire worldwide business operation to U.S. taxation. That would come as quite a nasty surprise to someone who did not realize they had become a U.S. tax resident.

Two Tests to Determine U.S. Residency

There are two tests used to determine whether a foreign person has become a U.S. tax resident. If you meet the requirements of either of these two tests, you will be treated as a U.S. tax resident, with all that follows from such treatment:

1. The lawful permanent resident test
2. The substantial presence test

Lawful Permanent Resident Test (the Green Card Test)

The first of the two tests for determining whether someone is a U.S. tax resident is called the *permanent resident test*. A foreign national is considered a U.S. permanent resident if he or she has been issued a Green Card granting the privilege of residing permanently in the United States. One important feature of a Green Card is that it can be surrendered by its holder, and, of course, it can also be revoked by the U.S. immigration authorities. (The U.S. Citizenship and Immigrations Services is a component of the U.S. Department of Homeland Security.) In general, though, a Green Card equates to permanent tax residency in the United States, and the tax status and treatment of a Green Card holder is, for almost all purposes, exactly the same as that of a regular U.S. citizen.

Substantial Presence Test

The second test, known as the *substantial presence test,* is more complicated and relies on the number of days you have been physically present in the United States for the current year plus the two prior years. You pass this test if you have been physically present in the United States for at least 31 days during the current calendar year and a total of 183 days—as per the formula below—for the entire three-year period including the current year (being present here for 183 days in the current year means you have already met the test). According to the IRS:[3]

> You will be considered a United States resident for tax purposes if you meet the substantial presence test for the calendar year. To meet this test, you must be physically present in the United States on at least:
>
> 1. 31 days during the current year, and
> 2. 183 days during the 3-year period that includes the current year and the 2 years immediately before that, counting:
>
>   • All the days you were present in the current year, and
>   • 1/3 of the days you were present in the first year before the current year, and
>   • 1/6 of the days you were present in the second year before the current year.

It's important to count *only* one-third of the days in the year before the current year, and one-sixth of the days in the year that is two years before the current year. So, if you were here 110 days in the current year, 120 days during the year before the current year, and 180 days for the year before that, you would get a total of 110 + 40 + 30, or just 180 days, and you would not meet the test. However,

---

[3]https://www.irs.gov/Individuals/International-Taxpayers/Substantial -Presence-Test.

if it had been 110 days this year, 180 days the year before that, and 120 days the year before that, you would get 110 + 60 + 20, which is 190 days, and you would meet the test.

There are certain exceptions to the substantial presence test. For example, any days spent in the United States as an exempt person—such as a government official here on business, or a traveling teacher, student, or athlete—will not count as part of your total number of days. And, according to the formula, if you spent less than 31 days in the current year, you do not meet the test. Another exception is called the *closer connection exception*. Here, even if you meet the substantial presence test according to the previous formula, you can argue that you have maintained a taxable residence in another country and have a closer connection to that country than you do to the United States. This exception, however, is pretty rare. Finally, if you have remained a tax resident in your home country, you may be able to use an international treaty—if there is one—to avoid being considered a U.S. resident even if you meet the substantial presence test.

Situations When Taxed Only on U.S.-Sourced Income

As previously discussed, by becoming a U.S. tax resident, you open up your worldwide income to U.S. taxation. All of your global income is reportable and taxable here, unless by treaty another country has the right to tax certain income first, which then creates a tax credit against U.S. taxes (you may still owe additional tax to the IRS if the effective tax rate on your foreign income is below the U.S. rate).

Alternatively, if you are not a U.S. tax resident (you are not a U.S. citizen or Green Card holder, and do not meet the substantial presence test) and you are here to work on a short-term basis, you will be required to file a U.S. tax return and will be taxed on your U.S.-sourced income but not on any foreign-sourced income. One example of this would be someone who is in the United States on a short-term work assignment and has received income here, but who hasn't passed the substantial presence test. Another situation where this could apply is in the case of a nonresident living abroad who has certain income sourced in the United States. Different types of U.S. income have different sourcing rules, and these rules quickly become very complicated. For example, capital gains on financial assets in the United States, such as those from stocks or bonds, are typically not taxed in the United States, as is the case with most interest income from bank accounts and time deposits (CDs). One notable exception to this is that individuals who were present for more then 183 days in the current year are subject to U.S. tax on their capital gains from the sale of U.S. stock, even if they are not considered to be residents of the United States, using a tax treaty or other exception to the substantial presence test.

However, dividends from U.S.-sourced companies are generally taxable to a nonresident through a mandatory tax withholding of 30 percent (or lower per treaty) by the payer of that income. In this situation, you are not required to file a U.S. tax return. Finally, real estate income and capital gains from the sale of a real property owned by a nonresident are usually taxable in the United States. The taxation of U.S. real property owned by foreign citizens is primarily governed by the Foreign Investment in Real Property Tax Act of 1980 (FIRPTA), which requires various mandatory tax withholdings, depending on the situation.

Tax Treaty Basics

The United States has entered into income tax treaties with most major countries around the world. The goal of these treaties is to eliminate the kind of double taxation of income that can occur when people are subjected to taxation by more than one country. This is accomplished by creating a system of exemptions and foreign tax credits that essentially offset the need to pay taxes in one country when corresponding taxes have already been paid to another country that has priority. This foreign tax credit mechanism generally works well to alleviate most double taxation burden, but it doesn't always work perfectly and there are situations where double taxation can and does occur.

One of the most important elements of the tax treaty system is the guidelines to determine which country has the first right to tax various sources of income. Priority is usually accorded based on tax residency of the owner, although certain income is always sourced to the location where it was generated (like rental income, which is taxable where the property is located). That is, the treaties provide mutually agreed upon guidelines to determine which country or tax authority has the first right to tax certain sources of income, and those guidelines are usually based on where someone resides.

Regardless of where someone resides, the United States still claims ultimate authority to tax the worldwide income of all U.S. citizens and tax residents.

Another important element of most tax treaties is the treatment of passive income or investment income. Very often, tax treaties will specify a reduced withholding tax on certain types of passive investment income earnings by a resident of the treaty country. If you are a citizen of or resident in a country that has a tax treaty with the United States, you should probably seek advice from a professional tax advisor to determine whether that treaty can benefit you given your particular situation. Most tax treaties are very similar in structure, but they often have specific terms unique to that treaty or the countries involved.

CHAPTER

11

U.S. Tax Overview: Federal and State

Taxing Worldwide Income: The IRS Is Different

As a U.S. resident taxpayer—such as a foreign national with a Green Card—you will be taxed in the United States in the same way as a regular U.S. citizen. This means that you will be taxed on all of the worldwide income that you earn during the time you are a resident.

Compared to many other countries in the world, the way the U.S. taxes income is very complex, in part because of the unique worldwide nature of the U.S. tax system. In addition, the U.S. tax code is very intricate, with large numbers of exceptions and exemptions, many of which are designed either to increase the tax burden on higher income people, or to achieve some other sort of social goal such as home ownership or charitable giving. In contrast, many foreign countries have a much simpler system, with many having a flat or nearly flat tax, which greatly simplifies everything. However, many foreign countries also levy various forms of value-added tax (VAT)—a national consumption tax (like state sales tax here in the United States) based on the purchase of goods and services—to raise additional government revenue over and above income tax.

The U.S. tax system also differs from the tax systems in many other countries because it is generally based on the family unit. Many foreign tax systems are based only on an individual and his or her earnings. But in the United States, most married couples file under a married filing jointly status, but this rarely results in lower tax than does the married filing separately status. Another possibility is to file as head of household—that is, an unmarried individual who has dependent children. If you are married to a nonresident and also have children, you may be able to choose to be "considered unmarried" for U.S. tax purposes and file as head of household, which is usually more favorable than married filing separately.

Filing Deadlines

If you are a full-year resident, you'll be required to file Form 1040, along with any taxes that are due, by April 15th of the year after the reporting year. However, if you are living outside of the United States on April 15th, you are given an automatic two-month extension to file your U.S. tax return, but you need to attach a statement to your tax return indicating that you have used this extension. If you are not able to submit your tax return by April 15th (or June 15th if living outside of the United States), you can file Form 4868 to get an automatic extension to October 15th. Even if you've filed for an extension, you are still required to estimate and pay your taxes by the April 15th deadline or you will be charged interest and potentially late-payment penalties.

If you are a U.S. citizen or resident living outside the United States, and are still unable to file your tax return by October 15th, you can request an extension to December 15th by writing a letter to the IRS. Finally, if you are unable to file your tax return until after December 15th because you are waiting to qualify for the Foreign Earned Income Exclusion, you can request a special extension until up to January 30th of the following year using Form 2350. Note that some states will accept federal extensions, but many will not, so it is important that you also check the rules for extensions for any required state income tax returns. The penalties for late filing (or even late payment) for states can be severe, sometimes as high as 25 percent of the tax due (plus interest), even with a valid extension.

Nonresidents living outside of the United States who have wages that are subject to United States withholding must file a return with the IRS by April 15th of the following year. All other nonresident returns have a June 15th initial tax return due date. It is also possible for nonresidents to request various extensions of these due dates.

Income Tax Overview

Figure 11.1 outlines the primary elements used to calculate U.S. federal income tax liabilities. An explanation of each of these primary elements follows.

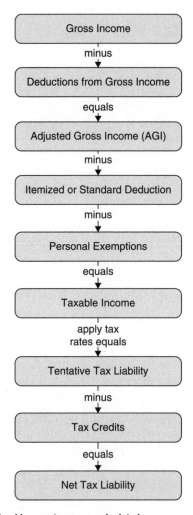

Figure 11.1   How U.S. federal income taxes are calculated

Gross Income

The computation of U.S. tax always starts with your gross income from all sources, including wages, salaries, and other compensation (including income from a business or partnership, royalties, or alimony), as well as investment income such as interest, dividends, and capital gains. For business owners, gross income includes the net profit result of their business, which should be supported by a statement of profit and loss that includes all revenue minus any qualified business expenses. For nonresidents, only U.S.-sourced income must be reported.

Deductions from Gross Income

From here, deductions are then taken from gross income, and various adjustments are made to arrive at your adjusted gross income or AGI. Your AGI is important, as it is the figure used to calculate various phase-out calculations for higher earners. These pre-AGI deductions include such things as contributions to various retirement plans, contributions to medical and health savings accounts, tuition deductions, and alimony. For self-employed individuals, there are deductions for self-employed health insurance and one-half of the self-employment tax. For most people, retirement plan contributions make up the majority of these deductions, which is why it's so important for most people to maximize any tax-advantaged retirement savings programs (like a 401(k) or IRA). These contributions are often the easiest to reduce taxable income.

Itemized or Standard Deductions from AGI

Once you arrive at your AGI, a number of additional deductions are available. These are generally grouped into either an *itemized* deduction or *standard* deductions. The standard deduction is a general deduction to AGI based on your filing status, and you are not required to provide any detail as to your actual deductions (the standard deduction is not available to nonresidents).

Instead of the standard deduction, many people will choose itemized deductions because these allow for a larger amount to be deducted from their AGI. That is, if the sum of your itemized deductions is greater than the standard deduction, it probably makes sense to itemize. The most common things that qualify as itemized deductions are deductions of state and local income tax (or sales tax), real and personal property taxes, home mortgage interest, and charitable contributions. There are also a number of other income-limited deductions (typically based on AGI) that in some cases can materially increase total itemized deductions; these include things like investment interest, investment advisory fees, tax return preparation fees, out-of-pocket medical expenses, and unreimbursed employee expenses.

For most high-income people, particularly those who own a home with a mortgage, it's very common for the total of their itemized deductions to be far greater than their standard deduction.

At a certain point, however, the amount of allowable itemized deductions is phased out for those with very high incomes.

Personal Exemptions

Finally, after the standard or itemized deductions are subtracted, there is an additional exemption that is taken, which is essentially a set reduction to taxable income for each individual and dependent within a family. For example, a family with two parents and two children would have a total of four individual exemptions. Personal exemptions are also phased out for higher-income taxpayers.

Final Taxable Income

Once you have taken all of your deductions and exemptions, and made any other adjustments, you arrive at your taxable income. This amount is then applied to a graduated table of tax brackets to reach the amount of tax you owe or the amount of refund you are owed based on how much you already paid into the system in estimated tax (e.g., through employer withholdings) during the year in question. Note that there are many details surrounding tax returns that can be highly complex and that deserve specialized treatment by an expert, and for this reason, those who have any complexity to their financial lives should hire a professional tax preparer.

Understanding Marginal Tax Rates

For planning purposes, it's important to have a solid understanding of the concept of what's called *marginal tax rates* or *marginal tax brackets*. A marginal tax rate is the rate of tax assessed on an additional dollar of income. The marginal tax rate for a taxpayer will increase as income rises, until such point that they reach the highest marginal tax rate.

That is, when your taxable income reaches a certain threshold, you then move up into the next higher tax bracket, and every dollar of taxable income that you earn above that threshold is taxed at the higher "marginal" rate associated with that next tax bracket. For example, for 2016 a single taxpayer reaches the highest tax bracket once their taxable income exceeds $415,050, at which point they will owe tax of $120,529.75 plus 39.6 percent of everything over $415,050 (any state, city, or other local tax is in addition). For a married couple filing jointly, the highest tax bracket of 39.6 percent starts at $466,950.

Note also that you will often hear the term *effective tax rate,* which is the average tax rate calculated when dividing your total tax liability by your total gross income before any deductions. In the previous example, if we assume the single taxpayer who had taxable income of $415,050 had a gross income of $500,000, then he or she would have an effective tax rate of 24 percent ($120,529/$500,000).

Depending on your level of income, you keep moving up, or *graduating* into higher tax brackets until you reach the highest marginal tax rate. This can be important when you have the opportunity to reduce your total income (e.g., when making retirement plan contributions). Let's suppose that you are a single taxpayer with taxable income of $150,000 in 2016. In this year, single individuals whose taxable income is between $91,151 and $190,150 will owe tax of $18,558.75 plus 28 percent of the amount over $91,150; in other words, they are in the 28 percent marginal tax bracket. Now, if the individual in this case contributes $18,000 into his or her 401(k), and all of that money would have been taxed at this 28 percent marginal tax rate, then the individual is reducing federal income tax owed by $5,040 (28 percent of $18,000). A similar calculation could be done for any state income taxes saved. Put differently, anything you can do to reduce your taxable income lowers your tax liability at your highest marginal tax rate.

One common misunderstanding is that by earning more income and moving into a higher marginal tax bracket, you can somehow end up with a lower net income, because your income is taxed at a higher rate. This is incorrect, because while any additional income you make will indeed be taxed at the highest applicable marginal rate, everything under that tax bracket threshold will still be taxed at the rate for the previous bracket. So it's always best to maximize your income to the highest possible level, and you will never end up with a lower net income just because you have moved into a higher tax bracket. With that said, it is also possible to lower one's net tax liability by timing the receipt of income from one year to the next in order to lower the income taxed at higher tax rates.

Lower Tax Rates on Capital Gains and Dividends

The IRS has designated two fundamentally different types of income in order to tax them at different tax rates. These are (1) ordinary income, and (2) qualified investment income (including long-term capital gains and qualified dividends). Ordinary income is commonly thought of as salaried income, or income from a business where the income is actively generated through your personal time and effort, but it can also include income from pensions, alimony, state income tax refunds, etc. Ordinary income is generally taxed at normal graduated tax rates.

It's long been a feature of the U.S. tax system to have a lower tax rate for certain types of investment income. For example, capital gains on the sale of an investment asset may be taxed at a lower tax rate, often referred to as the long-term capital gains tax rate (which for 2016 can be either 0 percent, 15 percent, or 20 percent, depending on your overall income—with 15 percent being most common). To receive the long-term capital gains tax rate, you must have owned the asset in question for at least one year. If you own it for less than a year, the gain is classified as short-term, and it is taxed at graduated rates like other ordinary income.

Qualified dividends paid by corporations are also taxed at the lower long-term capital gains tax rate—this includes qualified dividends from both U.S. and foreign companies. In general, qualified dividends are dividends paid out of profits that have already been taxed at the corporate level. For dividends paid via a U.S. brokerage firm, it is easy to differentiate between qualified and nonqualified dividends because this is indicated on the tax form you received (called a 1099-DIV). For dividends paid by a company located in a foreign country, it can be more difficult to make this determination, but in general, if the dividends come from a large corporation within a major country, then they are probably qualified.

Real Estate Rental Income

It is common for foreign nationals to rent their foreign residence while on assignment in the United States. Similarly, many families living abroad continue to own a residence in the United States, which is rented out while they are away.

Real estate rental income is taxed in a unique way that often confuses people not originally from the United States. The net income from rental properties is taxed as ordinary income. However, the taxable income associated with rental properties is calculated by starting with the gross rental income, and then subtracting ordinary and necessary expenses incurred. These expenses include property tax, mortgage interest, repairs and maintenance expenses, leasing expenses, property management expenses, and so on. It is worth mentioning again here that nonresidents must make a special election to treat their rental property as "effectively connected" U.S. income, or their tax will be 30 percent of the gross income, without taking into account any expenses.

That net income is then further reduced for tax purposes by depreciation. Deprecation is a noncash expense—meaning that you haven't actually spent anything on it—and it is calculated by taking a percentage of the property's purchase price associated with the structure (and not the land), and then dividing that amount over a period of what is usually between 27.5 and 40 years, depending on the type of property. On a yearly basis, this depreciation amount then further reduces the taxable income from the property for that tax year. However, it also lowers the cost basis on the property, so that when the property is eventually sold—presumably at a gain many years in the future—there will be a gain calculation based on the period of ownership whereby the cost basis will likely be lower than the original purchase price due to deprecation.

Essentially, then, such deductible annual depreciation amounts to a kind of tax shelter against current income tax. For this reason, income-generating real estate can be very valuable, especially for those in higher tax brackets. And while it is also true that the deducted depreciation lowers the cost basis on the property, thus creating a larger capital gain when the property is eventually sold, such a capital gain will generally be taxed at a lower long-term capital gain tax rate. In summary, then, the ability to deduct depreciation is quite valuable because it effectively shelters current income from tax at ordinary rates and converts that income to long-term capital gain, while also deferring the tax until the property's eventual sale in the future.

The rental of a residence outside of the United States is considered foreign-sourced income. However, this income is still subject to U.S. tax while the owner is a U.S. tax resident. The rental of a U.S. property will always be taxed in the United States, regardless of whether the owner is a resident or a nonresident, because this is considered U.S.-sourced income.

Stock-Based Compensation: Options

Many employees receive a substantial percentage of their total remuneration through stock-based compensation, which is a unique kind of compensation that is different from their regular salary and bonuses, and is intended as an incentive for the employee to remain with the company for an extended period of time. While there are a number of different types of stock-based compensation, one of the most common are *nonqualified* stock option grants, where a company gives the employee the right to purchase shares at a fixed price per share, which is usually the fair market value at the time the options were granted. Such options usually vest over a number of years and expire after a fixed period of time, often as long as 10 years or until such time as the employee is no longer associated with the company.

Let's assume an employee is granted options to buy 1,000 shares of the company's stock at $10 a share. Now suppose the value of the stock goes up to $20. In this case, the difference between the "strike" price of $10 that the individual can exercise the option for, and the current market price, is the intrinsic value of the options. If the employee then exercises the option at the $10 a share "strike price," he effectively buys 1,000 shares worth $20,000 for only $10,000, resulting in a profit of $10,000.

Upon the exercise of the stock options, the employee is treated as receiving taxable compensation measured by the excess of the fair market value of the stock received over its purchase price. The subsequent sale of the option stock acquired will result in a capital gain or loss. In determining gain or loss, the basis of the option stock is the purchase price plus the compensation recognized at exercise, and the holding period to determine if the ultimate sale qualifies as a long-term gain or loss begins on the date of option exercise.

Stock-Based Compensation: Stock Grants and RSUs

Stock grants are another form of stock-based compensation in which the employer grants shares of stock to the employee, which vest over a period of years. One common way to implement this is with RSUs, or restricted stock units, which are shares that the employee will receive (generally at no cost to them) when all of the restrictions have lapsed (generally a certain number of years after they are granted).

Note that the value of the RSUs that vest in a given year is considered taxable compensation for that year. In this sense, whenever RSUs vest, they should be looked upon as a bonus that has just been paid to the employee in the form of shares, not simply as the receipt of shares. In other words, you can think of the vesting of stock grants as if you had been paid a cash bonus and then invested that entire amount into shares of company stock without any taxes having first been withheld. Most companies, however, will automatically sell a certain percentage of the shares and withhold that amount for taxes.

Overexposure to Your Company's Stock

Most people already have significant exposure or risk associated with their employer, both because of their employment and also their exposure to the company's stock through vested and unvested options and stock grants. Most employees tend to have an emotional attachment to their company, and its stock, and end up owning too much of that stock as a percentage of their overall net worth.

In fact, studies have shown that employees view company stock as an unrealistically low-risk investment—they naturally want to believe that the prospects for their company are better than for competitors—and thereby often end up owning much more of the stock than is prudent. For this reason, following basic principles of diversification and asset allocation, we recommend that people regularly sell down stock and exercise options, particularly if they already have large exposure to the company's shares.

Exchange Rate Issues When Taxing Foreign Income

It is very important for international families who are U.S. taxpayers to understand the unique way that the IRS views investments and other transactions that occur in a foreign currency. Whenever someone prepares a U.S. tax return, the income and expenses that are reported on that return must always be converted into U.S. dollars regardless of whatever currency any underlying transactions may have occurred in. Because of this, it is possible to see strange effects, whereby either a significant loss or gain seems to have occurred (in U.S. dollars) even when there was no actual gain or loss in the local currency. Such gain or loss will be completely attributable to the change in foreign exchange values that occurred. A good example of how this works can be seen in Chapter 9 on real estate taxes.

Put differently, it is possible to see a gain or loss for U.S. tax purposes that is very different from the gain or loss in local currency terms (where the transaction actually took place), purely as a result of the fluctuation of the dollar against the local currency. Since you are required to report the U.S. dollar equivalent of the purchase and sale price on the date of the respective transaction, we recommend keeping careful records of the amounts paid and date, as well as what the then-current U.S. dollar equivalent amount was. This will greatly assist you when it is time to report that transaction on your U.S. tax return.

These rules also come into play when borrowing funds in a currency other than U.S. dollars. It is quite possible to have either taxable gains or taxable losses from the retirement of foreign denominated debt. However, while currency-related gains on the retirement of debt are taxable, currency-related losses on the retirement of foreign denominated debt are generally not deductible for U.S. tax purposes.

Thus, if you borrow the equivalent of $1 million in euros, and two years later you retire that debt at a cost of $900,000 (because of a stronger dollar), you would have a taxable gain to report. However, if you had borrowed $1 million and one year later paid that back, but to do so cost you $1.1 million, you would have a loss of $100,000 due to exchange rate fluctuations, but that loss would not be deductible. This lack of deductibility on a currency loss related to debt can be a big problem when there is an equal and offsetting gain on the corresponding asset that was purchased with the loan. The example in Chapter 9 illustrates this.

It should be noted that foreign currency transactions entered into for trade or business purposes are subject to different rules entirely. This is a complex area of tax law, and you should always consult with a knowledgeable tax advisor whenever you enter into large transactions that are denominated in a foreign currency. Most commonly, this occurs with the purchase and financing of real property, but there are many other situations where this can also occur.

State Income Taxes

In addition to federal income and social security taxes, foreign nationals who are working and/or living in the United States also have to contend with state income taxes and possibly local city or county taxes. Most U.S. states have a state income tax that applies to the residents, and often nonresidents, of that state. There are, however, nine states that have no income tax, including Alaska, Florida, Nevada, New Hampshire, South Dakota, Tennessee, Texas, Washington, and Wyoming (New Hampshire and Tennessee do levy a tax on certain kinds of investment income).

Some U.S. cities, as well as some U.S. counties, also levy an income tax on their residents. New York City is the most well known of these cities, so if you live there you will have to file a separate New York City income tax return and pay any taxes owed. By working with an accountant or tax preparer familiar with the local state, county, and city laws, you will ensure that you do not fall short in your tax preparation and filing.

State Tax Returns Often Based on Federal Returns

Most state income tax returns follow a structure that is very similar to the federal tax return. A separate state return must usually be filed at the same time that the federal return is filed. Very often, state returns are somewhat more simplistic in their structure, and they often begin with either adjusted gross income or taxable income from the federal return. They will then add back certain items that, for state purposes, do not qualify for deductions, and then subtract certain items that qualify as special deductions in that state. The income tax rates for most states range from 5 to 10 percent.

Different Treatments of Long-Term Capital Gains and Qualified Dividends

While the U.S. federal government taxes long-term capital gains and qualified dividends at a lower tax rate than ordinary income, most states tax these types of gains and income at the same rate as ordinary income. This can prove frustrating to taxpayers in some states, who end up paying the state taxing authority nearly as much as they pay to the federal government for certain types of investment income.

State Tax Residency: Requirements and Termination

U.S. states generally do not follow the same rules as the federal government for establishing tax residency, such as the substantial presence test described in Chapter 10. Instead, most follow their own rules, which can be much more subjective and open to interpretation by the state's tax authority. For this reason, state residency must always be evaluated independently of federal residency rules, or you could end up being surprised to find that you've been deemed a resident of one but not the other.

Many states, including California, establish residency rules based mostly on intent and domicile, that is, on the location that the person intends to make his or her permanent home (or to where he or she would likely return should another more short-term residency end). Many states are known as being quite aggressive in arguing someone's intent to make a permanent home (their domicile) in that state.

It is important to understand that an individual can only have one domicile, and once he or she has acquired that domicile, it cannot be changed unless another is acquired. To change domiciles, one must physically leave the old home and move to the new home with the specific intention to stay there permanently or indefinitely. Some states look at certain overseas assignments that are for a specified period of time (like for two to three years) as a temporary move and not as a change in domicile.

It's also very important that if you are leaving the United States, you effectively terminate your state residency. You generally cannot just submit a written notification to end your state tax residency, but must instead carefully understand the state's residency rules and do whatever is necessary to successfully terminate it. In fact, in some states when you file a part-year resident tax return—essentially announcing that you are no longer a resident of that state—you are required to indicate your new state of residence. But if you are moving abroad, there is no new state of residence to select. The state and federal tax systems are not always easy on people who move abroad.

For example, suppose you are leaving the United States (as either a U.S. citizen or Green Card holder), but expect that in the future you will likely permanently return to the United States to live—although not necessarily return to the state where you currently live. In this case, you would still need to be careful about deliberately terminating your state residency so that your current state can't come back and claim that you never actually gave up your state residency. Factors involved might include the number of days spent in the state, whether you have kept a home in the state, whether you have kept a car registered in the state, whether you have maintained your driver's license, and whether your family still resides in the state. All of these factors can be considered by state authorities to determine whether you have successfully terminated your state residency.

When States Come Looking for You

In practice, it is fairly unusual for a state to claim you were a tax resident for a period when you lived outside the country, since most state tax authorities do not track the specific activities of all current and former tax residents. Generally, if you have not earned income within a certain state, and you cease to file state tax returns, then you likely won't hear from them again. Then again, it is also true that taxpayers with higher levels of income generally get more attention from tax authorities. I think this is pretty obvious to most of us.

There are two situations when this issue of state domicile can come up. The first is when a taxpayer continues to have income sourced from that state, but the taxpayer begins to file the state return as a nonresident. This frequently will lead to state to inquire further.

The second instance is when a person who was a resident of a certain state ceases all filings in that state, and then at some point in the future again begins to file as a resident of that state. The state authority may see that the person was a tax resident for some time, then took a break (maybe even for many years) from filing in the state, before again returning. At that point, the state authority may review the federal tax returns for those intervening years and make a determination that the person retained their state residency during that time and should have filed state returns. This could obviously result in some very surprising and costly tax bills. This often happens to professionals who have taken an overseas work assignment, so again, take great care to engineer your overseas experience to be more indefinite if possible.

U.S. Tax Residents Living Abroad with State Tax Liabilities

There can be some confusing outcomes when a U.S. citizen or permanent resident leaves on a foreign assignment without terminating his or her state residency. In these situations, it is possible to have foreign earned income that is still taxable by a U.S. state. Many states follow different rules than the U.S. federal government does, and they frequently do not grant the same international treaty protection as the federal government. There are also many states, including California, that in certain situations do not allow the Foreign Earned Income and Foreign Housing Exclusions, nor do they offer a credit for foreign taxes paid. This can lead to the payment of taxes on foreign income, with additional taxes then also due to a U.S. state, with the end result being a form of double taxation—effectively paying more in total tax than would have been owed to either country individually.

For example, suppose you paid a 40 percent income tax in Europe on income generated there, and assume that the U.S. tax would have also totaled 40 percent, a combination of a 30 percent federal tax and 10 percent state tax. The 40 percent paid internationally creates a foreign tax credit that should fully offset the federal tax liability. However, most states do not follow the federal tax treaties and do not allow a credit for foreign taxes paid, so you are liable for the full amount of state tax on this income, if you are still a resident of that state. In this example, then, since you paid 40 percent abroad and then another 10 percent to the state, you would in effect end up paying 50 percent in total tax.

Avoiding Unnecessarily Becoming a State Resident in the First Place

U.S. state tax issues can create a great deal of complexity and confusion for globally mobile professionals. For this reason, it's very important to avoid becoming a state tax resident in situations when you are on a short-term assignment. If, then, you are going to be on a short-term assignment, you should structure the time you spend within any particular state to avoid becoming a tax resident of that state.

Suppose you have a six-month assignment in a given state. It may be that if you went back to your original home, or to an office outside of that state, and worked there for one month, you would avoid being classified as a state resident. Of course, if you are tax equalized to another location entirely, as explained earlier in this chapter, it might not matter to you because your employer would be covering all of the extra costs associated with filing and paying any state tax.

Many states can be very aggressive when significant amounts of cross-border income and assets are involved. For this reason, *it's always wise to consult with a knowledgeable tax advisor,* ideally one who lives in the state or who is very familiar with the residency tests of the state in question.

12

Additional Tax-Planning Considerations

Investing Outside of the United States—Avoiding PFIC Rules

U.S. citizens and tax residents must be very careful about holding certain kinds of passive investments outside of the United States. The IRS has developed a system of rules whereby holding investment assets outside of the United States generally creates a significant amount of additional tax complexity, and in many cases leads to higher taxes than if the investments were located in the United States.

When investments are held at U.S. financial institutions, those firms will issue you a 1099 tax report every year with a detailed summary of your interest income, dividends, and capital gains from the prior tax year. Keep in mind that long-term capital gains and *qualified dividends* qualify for a lower tax rates, usually 0 percent, 15 percent, or 20 percent (15 percent for most people), while all other investment income is taxed at higher ordinary income tax rates. However, when investment accounts are held outside of the United States at a foreign institution, those institutions generally *do not* provide a 1099 tax statement every year, often making it difficult to properly report that income to the IRS.

Passive Foreign Investment Corporations (PFICs) Explained

A passive foreign investment corporation (PFIC) is a non-U.S. company that derives income from investments (passive income). The official definition of a PFIC is any foreign company where 75 percent or more of the company's income is passive, or at least 50 percent of the company's assets produce passive income (i.e., from interest income, dividends, capital gains, etc.).

Originally, the rules relating to PFICs were designed to create a disincentive for U.S. citizens to utilize foreign corporations to hold passive investments, a strategy that had long been employed by wealthy families around the world to both hide assets and evade taxes. These rules have largely worked to halt the use of foreign structures by most wealthy American families. Unfortunately, these PFIC rules were written in such a broad way that today the most commonly seen PFICs are non-U.S. based investment funds (i.e., pooled funds, like mutual funds). Foreign securities owned directly, like stocks and bonds of individual corporations or governments, are generally not considered PFICs and are most often treated the same as if they were located in the United States (except for certain unique exchange rate issues, which are discussed in detail in Chapter 11 under the Exchange Rate Issues When Taxing Foreign Income section).

Around the world, there has been considerable attention paid to the unique tax and reporting issues of Americans who own foreign assets. As has been discussed elsewhere, this has led many foreign financial institutions to elect to cease to service accounts of individuals with U.S. residency. Furthermore, it has become much more difficult for U.S. citizens and residents to effect new purchases of foreign mutual funds. Of course, many people continue to own investment funds purchased many years ago, and foreign nationals can become U.S. residents after investing in such a fund. Additionally, anyone working abroad and contributing to a foreign retirement plan is likely to be accumulating PFIC investments, except in the unlikely situation where that foreign retirement plan is viewed as "qualified" in the United States per treaty.

So, it is quite likely that any U.S. taxpayer who holds a foreign investment account that contains stock or bond investment funds (including mutual funds and ETFs) has met the criteria for a PFIC investment.

Complex Reporting and Punitive Tax Treatment

A U.S. citizen or tax resident who holds shares in a PFIC investment fund is subject to difficult and lengthy reporting requirements and potentially punitive taxation treatment on his or her share of the income from within that fund. The tax implications of owning a PFIC are complex. The investor in a PFIC also loses the benefit of the lower tax rates on long-term capital gains and qualifying dividends, and will instead be taxed at higher ordinary tax rates (under the best of circumstances).

If you do choose to own PFICs, the best outcome will usually come from making the *mark to market* election, whereby you would be taxed annually based on the change in market value during that year, at ordinary tax rates. As an example, imagine you purchased shares in a mutual fund for $100,000, and the market went up during the year and those shares are now worth $120,000. If this were a U.S. investment, you would not pay taxes on that gain because you hadn't yet sold your investment. Under a mark to market approach, however, the $20,000 increase in value of the shares would be counted as ordinary income in that year.

A taxpayer can make a qualified electing fund (QEF) election to mitigate these tax rules. The QEF election allows a PFIC to be treated somewhat similar to a partnership, where the U.S. resident owner recognizes their share of the income earned in the fund annually even though it is not distributed, and gains from the appreciation in the value of the PFIC itself remain untaxed until they are realized. Income recognized annually as a result of a QEF election increases the investor's basis in the PFIC. Importantly, a QEF election is the only way to receive long-term capital gain tax treatment on any income from a PFIC investment. Unfortunately, this is an election that requires a significant amount of additional reporting by the fund itself, and most foreign institutions are unwilling or unable to provide the necessary information to facilitate the making of this election.

Given that the QEF election is likely not available, the mark-to-market election may be the best choice available. It may not sound like a good thing, but the alternative is potentially much worse! The only other alternative—known as the *excessive distribution method*—effectively forces the taxpayer to allocate the gain on an asset sale equally over the life of the investment. That annual gain is then taxed at the highest ordinary tax rates, and a healthy annual compounded interest charge is then added to the bill. It wouldn't take long for this calculation to reach 50 percent of the entire gain amount or more.

Advice on Foreign Accounts and PFIC

This is a tremendously complex area, but the bottom line is that if you are a U.S. citizen or tax resident, it becomes very inefficient to maintain investment accounts outside of the United States. If your goal is to build a worldwide portfolio—as we encourage you to do throughout this book—you should make those investments through pooled investment funds (like ETFs and mutual funds) located in the United States.

In this way, you will receive 1099 tax reporting, which will greatly reduce the complexity of your annual tax filing, and enable you to avoid the harsh tax treatment associated with PFICs. U.S. taxpayers need to know that the IRS taxes passive foreign assets differently than the foreign country where they are located might tax them. And, the IRS taxes the income the foreign assets produce differently than if it was earned from an investment located in the United States.

PFIC Rules Make Investing Within U.S. The Best Choice

When we talk with clients or prospective clients about liquidating their foreign investments and moving them to the United States, it can at times seem self-serving because, of course, at Worldview Wealth Advisors we have an interest in clients hiring us to oversee their portfolios. But the reality is that this advice generally leads to a much smarter approach. I know it can seem like an unfair burden for the United States to impose. Most foreign nations do not have rules that force immigrants to sell foreign assets and move those funds to within their borders, but regardless of the fairness of the PFIC rules, they are the law.

Foreign citizens who are likely to become U.S. tax residents face a more difficult dilemma, because they may not have any other good options for how to stay invested in a diversified way.

Note that the PFIC rules do not apply to most *individual* securities, so U.S. tax residents can still hold individual bonds or stocks located in foreign countries and not have these rules apply. Also, while there are certain foreign institutions that offer proper U.S. reporting on foreign investment funds, this is quite rare and generally is only available to very wealthy investors. Moreover, because of FATCA rules that require financial institutions to monitor the balances of U.S. persons and report on them back to the IRS, it's actually becoming increasingly difficult to even open an international account like this if you are a U.S.-connected person. That is, most banks are aware of the FATCA rules and would rather not have to deal with the complexity that comes along with serving someone connected to the United States, and in many cases such accounts have been or will be forcibly closed by foreign financial institution once they see a U.S. connection.

Finally, it should be pointed out that the larger international brokerage firms that provide access to foreign investment funds—the types that trigger the PFIC rules—also usually function as retail banks. So, while the PFIC-triggering investments discussed in this section should be avoided, the PFIC rules do not apply to the banking functions of these firms. That is, there is usually no reason not to use these firms for general banking purposes and for holding cash accounts (although be careful as foreign money market funds are typically considered to be PFIC as well).

In fact, you might find that while you can open a checking or savings account at a large foreign bank, that same bank might very well prohibit you from opening an investment account alongside of it. However, because of FATCA and other information-sharing regulations, some international firms are even refusing to offer U.S. tax residents even simple banking relationships.

Three PFIC Scenarios to Consider

This section presents three scenarios to give you a better idea of how someone can end up with PFIC holdings. Ultimately, this is one of those areas where seeking qualified professional help is absolutely essential.

Scenario #1

Let's consider a foreign individual who invested in foreign investment funds long before becoming a U.S. tax resident. When he or she first started investing in those funds, there may have been a notice that such funds were not open to U.S. residents. Of course that would not have mattered to this individual at the time. But after this person becomes a U.S. tax resident, he or she may now run into all of the difficulties mentioned previously. Making matters worse, any sale of those assets (assuming he or she takes the advice given in this book and moves the investment funds to the United States) would now be 100 percent taxable here in the United States, even if all of the gains had occurred long before the person moved here.

In this situation, the owner would be wise to sell all of these investments before becoming a U.S. tax resident. By doing so, the owner effectively avoids the punitive nature of the PFIC rules, while also avoiding U.S. state and federal income tax on any gains. This strategy may result in taxation in the foreign country of residence, but that is often is less costly than the tax treatment in the United States.

Scenario #2

It is a common practice in many foreign countries for wealthy families to place their investment holdings into a family holding company of some sort. Well, if any family member becomes a U.S. tax resident, or a U.S. tax resident inherits some or all of a family holding company, it is generally considered a PFIC no matter what type of investments are in it. So suppose someone who is from Malaysia creates a family holding company in Singapore—a known tax haven—and puts most of their assets (properties, stocks, bonds, etc.) into it. If that structure then touches the United States, because an owner has become a U.S. tax resident, it will be considered a PFIC and then potentially create substantial tax problems.

Scenario #3

Finally, consider someone who owns foreign investment funds inside of a foreign retirement plan (like a 401(k)). These investments may or may not be considered PFIC, depending on whether that retirement account is considered qualified in the United States based on treaty. In most cases, such foreign retirement accounts will not be respected and viewed as qualified in the United States, and in those cases, these investments are considered to be PFIC.

Foreign Asset Reporting and Tax Evasion

Over many centuries, people throughout the world have sought to avoid or minimize the payment of taxes to whatever local or foreign authority was seeking to tax them. In modern times, they've done this by hiding assets in offshore financial institutions, often through various anonymous accounts structures and foreign corporations.

However, as we continue to move toward a more globally connected world—driven by the globalization of business, technology, and travel—there has been an increasing focus by countries throughout the world on uncovering foreign assets and income so that they can be properly and fairly taxed. As discussed in Chapter 2, FATCA and other asset reporting laws are spreading fast, and it is increasingly difficult to avoid proper taxation. The 2016 Panama Papers leak, where the identities of thousands of prominent people associated with offshore shell corporations were leaked from a Panamanian law firm, only reinforces how difficult it is becoming to hide assets and evade proper taxation.

Foreign Bank Account Reporting (FBAR) Requirements

The United States, in particular, is taking the lead around the world in terms of enforcing the disclosure of foreign assets, and this has happened in a number of ways. One of the primary efforts is the Foreign Bank Account Reporting (FBAR) requirement of the United States Treasury, which was initially put into place around 1970 by the Bank Secrecy Act. It requires U.S. citizens and tax residents to report any interests in foreign bank accounts or other financial accounts to the U.S. Financial Crime Enforcement Network (FinCEN), through the submission of Form 114 (Report of Foreign Bank and Financial Accounts).

FinCEN requires that every U.S. tax resident who has a financial interest or signatory authority over any financial accounts in a foreign country—this includes bank accounts, brokerage accounts, retirement accounts, mutual funds, and many other types of financial accounts—must report that interest if the aggregate value of all of those accounts exceeds $10,000 at any point during the year. This requirement also applies to entities like corporations and partnerships organized in the United States, as well as to trusts or estates formed under U.S. laws. This form must be completed and received by the Treasury Department at a due date that conforms to the individual income tax return filing deadline, with extensions.

Numerous foreign assets are excluded from this reporting requirement, including hedge funds and private equity funds; real estate; and bonds, notes, or stocks issued directly to the owner by a foreign entity. For example, if you own shares of Nestlé directly with the company, you would not have to report on those shares. But if you owned shares of Nestlé inside of an investment account at a foreign institution, then you would have to report the account that holds the investment.

FBAR Penalties

FBAR is merely a reporting requirement, and there are no additional taxes owed as a result of filing the report. However, there are penalties for failure to file the FBAR report, penalties that in some cases can be severe. These penalties often have a subjective element, with a particular focus on whether the failure to report is deemed to be willful or nonwillful in the eyes of the examiner. The nonwillful failure to correctly report has an official maximum penalty of $10,000 per year, per account, unless a reasonable cause is found for the failure to report, such as if you told your tax preparer about the account and relied on the tax preparer to assist you with U.S. tax reporting. The IRS has been very clear that ignorance about the law does not represent a reasonable cause (such as when a taxpayer can show that he or she relied on a professional or made a good-faith attempt but missed something); however, the IRS may still waive penalties in certain situations, such as when an older person inherits an account and simply didn't know about the reporting requirement. In the nonwillful situation, even if taxpayers have multiple accounts that they have failed to report on, the authorities generally only impose one $10,000 penalty per year, unless the facts require them to impose separate penalties for each account. (This is the case at this time of this writing, but may not be true in the future.)

As for willful nonreporting—which is defined as knowingly and intentionally failing to report foreign assets—the official penalty is the *greater* of $100,000 or 50 percent of the balance of the unreported accounts at the time of the valuation. There is no defense for a "reasonable cause" in situations of a willful failure to report. In practice, where multiple years of willful nonreporting are at issue, the penalty is generally limited to 50 percent of the highest one-time balance. However, IRS examiners have discretion here, and the maximum penalty can in certain situations be more than 100 percent of the highest one-time balance. Willful violators can also be criminally prosecuted, so obviously, everyone should take this filing requirement quite seriously.

Other Foreign Asset Reporting: Form 8938

The Foreign Account Tax Compliance Act (FATCA) is a U.S. federal law enacted in March 2010 with a broad mandate to increase tax reporting and payment compliance, especially by those with foreign accounts or foreign assets. The bottom-line goal of FATCA is to enforce the requirements for all U.S. tax residents—including those living outside of the United States—to file yearly reports on their non-U.S. financial accounts. FATCA has numerous provisions, and importantly, it requires foreign financial institutions to survey all clients for U.S. connections and then report back to the United States on their financial affairs.

One part of the FATCA legislation is the Form 8938, Statement of Specified Foreign Financial Assets, a new reporting requirement that came into effect on April 20, 2011, and applies to all future tax years. Form 8938 requires individual U.S. taxpayers to report information about certain foreign financial accounts and assets in a filing, which is then attached to the annual federal tax return. Form 8938 applies to all U.S. citizens and tax residents, as well as to nonresidents who are filing a joint tax return with a U.S. resident.

In many ways, Form 8938 is like the FBAR on steroids. All of the accounts required to be reported on the FBAR must be reported on Form 8938, except that Form 8938 only deals with accounts in which the filer has a financial interest. (FBAR also includes accounts over which the filer has signature authority.) But many other foreign assets not part of FBAR must also be reported on Form 8938. Some of the additional assets that are reportable on Form 8938, but that are not reportable on the FBAR, include:

- Foreign hedge funds
- Foreign private equity funds
- Any interest in a foreign entity (businesses, trusts, and partnerships)
- Foreign securities (mainly stocks and bonds) held directly with a foreign issuer and not in a financial account
- Real estate that's held inside of a trust

Note that for now, real estate that is held directly—that is, real estate that is not in a trust or held by another entity—is still not required to be reported on Form 8938. But, given the significant amount of foreign property owned by U.S. citizens and residents, it would not be surprising if in the near future there is a requirement to report on all worldwide real property holdings.

Form 8938 Filing Requirements

The requirement to file Form 8938 is based on the aggregate value of interests in specified foreign financial assets owned by a U.S. taxpayer, and the reporting threshold amount is variable based on both (1) whether or not you are living in the United States, and (2) your marital and filing status.

If you are living in the United States, the thresholds are as follows:

- Single individuals must file if the total value of reportable foreign assets is more than $50,000 at the end of the year, or more than $75,000 at any time during the year.
- Married couples must file if the total value of reportable foreign assets is more than $100,000 if filing jointly ($50,000 if filing separately) at the end of the year, or more than $150,000 if filing jointly ($75,000 if filing separately) at any time during the year.

If you are living abroad, the thresholds are as follows:

- Single individuals must file if the total value of reportable foreign assets is more than $200,000 at the end of the year, or more than $300,000 at any time during the year.
- Married individuals must file if the total value of reportable foreign assets is more than $400,000 if filing jointly ($200,000 if filing separately) at the end of the year, or more than $600,000 if filing jointly ($300,000 if filing separately) at any time during the year.

Form 8938 Penalties

Even though Form 8938 has a much higher initial threshold for when it must be filed, it is also much more inclusive in scope, which makes it easier to reach its threshold. Failure to correctly file Form 8938 results in another set of potential penalties that are separate from, and in addition to, any penalties that result from failing to file the FBAR. If you are required to file Form 8938 but do not file it by the due date (including extensions), you may be subject to a penalty of $10,000, and after 90 days an additional $10,000 penalty applies for every 30-day period during which you fail to file (up to a $50,000 maximum).

Additional Foreign Asset Reporting

There are a variety of other forms that may be required to be filed along with your federal tax return which are likewise intended to further uncover offshore or unreported assets and income. Some of these forms are intended to uncover ownership interests in foreign entities, including foreign corporations and trusts. Still other forms are more focused on identifying gifts from any foreign persons or entities.

U.S. taxpayers who are beneficiaries of a foreign trust may not be aware that they also have U.S. tax reporting obligations on those assets. For example, suppose a brother and sister from a foreign country are beneficiaries of a large offshore trust with a variety of assets in it, including cash, property, business holdings, and investments. If either the brother or the sister moves to the United States and becomes a U.S. tax resident, there could be significant tax obligations. Overall, this is a highly specialized area, so consulting a professional tax advisor with foreign reporting experience is highly recommended, especially if a foreign-based family has significant wealth.

Voluntary Offshore Disclosure Programs (OVPD)

Since 2009, the IRS has offered several forms of voluntary offshore disclosure programs or initiatives, with the goal of making it easier for violators of foreign asset reporting laws to come clean and make things right. That is, the IRS has allowed qualifying taxpayers with previously undisclosed foreign assets and income to come forward and voluntarily make disclosures and pay back taxes owed. In exchange, the taxpayers receive reduced penalties and a promise that the IRS will not pursue criminal charges.

In June of 2014 the IRS announced several changes to the Offshore Voluntary Disclosure Program (or OVPD), which included increasing the offshore penalty from 27.5 percent to 50 percent for certain unreported accounts. At the same time, the IRS expanded its streamlined filing compliance procedures to offer an alternative—and generally less expensive—route to disclosure for those taxpayers willing and able to certify that their failure to report was not willful.

Other Forms of Taxation in the United States

There are a number of other taxes in the United States that can affect cross-border families, over and above regular taxes on earnings and investment income. Below is a summary of some of the more common taxes that you should be aware of.

Social Security Taxes

Many foreign nationals coming into the United States are rightly concerned about U.S. Social Security, since those who earn wages or self-employment income from their work in the United States are often subject to U.S. Social Security tax. Certain foreign workers in the United States may be exempted from U.S. Social Security tax, depending on their visa status and their country of origin.

American expatriates who are on a foreign assignment with a U.S. employer generally remain subject to U.S. Social Security tax, rather than the social taxes of their host country. If U.S. citizens or residents are local employees with a foreign corporation, they are generally not subject to U.S. Social Security tax, but are subject to the equivalent tax of the country where they are working.

Social Security Tax Calculation

The U.S. Social Security system comprises two different components, a Social Security tax and a Medicare tax, and these are imposed on both the employer and the employee equally, except in the case of self-employed people who pay 100 percent of these taxes. The employee portion of the Social Security tax is collected through a withholding tax equal to 6.2 percent of annual wages up to $118,500 for 2016, after which no additional tax is owed. The employee portion of Medicare tax is collected in the same way, and is charged at 1.45 percent of qualifying wages. However, unlike with the Social Security tax, there is no ceiling on wages subject to Medicare tax. The employer makes a matching contribution equal to the total amounts withheld from the employee.

Totalization Agreements

Sorting through cross-border social security taxes rules is complicated and must be determined on a country-by-country basis. Accordingly, the United States has entered into Social Security totalization agreements with a number of foreign countries to provide clarity in these situations and to avoid double social security tax obligations.

Totalization agreements have two primary elements:

1. *Relief from double taxation:* Totalization agreements state the rules that govern which country has priority to levy social security tax when someone is subject to such taxation in two countries. Consider, for example, a U.S. citizen who is on assignment abroad. How long can that individual avoid the local social security tax equivalent and only pay U.S. Social Security tax? And once they are subject to the foreign tax, how can they ensure they will not also be subject to U.S. Social Security? The rules found in the totalization agreements are generally pretty clear about how to proceed in these situations.

2. *Coordination of benefits:* These agreements define the continuity of benefits for individuals who have worked in multiple countries and therefore may only qualify for partial benefits in each of those countries. That is, even though they may not meet the traditional eligibility requirements of either of the countries, the totalization agreements ensure that they will have combined coverage.

Ultimately, then, the rules found in the totalization agreements provide for a period of time where a visiting worker can remain covered by their home country social security system before jumping into the system of the foreign country to which they have moved. And if they do jump from one system to another, and begin to accumulate social security–type benefits in two countries, those benefits will be coordinated.

Special Taxes on High-Earners

Starting with the year 2013, the IRS implemented two new taxes as added by the Affordable Care Act (ACA). These taxes are income based, and in general apply only to higher income taxpayers.

Additional Medicare Taxes on Ordinary Income

The Additional Medicare Tax applies to wages, compensation, and self-employment income above a threshold amount received in taxable years beginning after December 31, 2012. With it, a 0.9 percent incremental Medicare tax is assessed on earned income for single filers exceeding $200,000, and married filing jointly filers exceeding $250,000.

Importantly for many U.S. taxpayers living and working abroad, this additional tax is only due from taxpayers who currently have income subject to U.S. Social Security tax. Taxpayers living abroad who are not paying into Social Security are exempt from this tax.

Net Investment Income Tax (NIIT)

The net investment income tax (NIIT) is a tax on the net investment income (not earned income) of individuals, estates, and trusts that have total income (adjusted gross income or AGI) above the statutory threshold amounts. The NIIT is a 3.8 percent additional tax on net investment income exceeding a threshold amount based on your filing status ($200,000 for single filers, and $250,000 for married filing jointly filers).

Unlike the additional Medicare tax, the NIIT applies to all U.S. citizens and tax residents, even if they are living abroad and not currently subject to U.S. Social Security tax. Also, the Foreign Earned Income Exclusion (FEIE) must be added back to income for purposes of calculating the threshold—making a relatively large number of U.S. taxpayers abroad subject to the tax. The net investment income tax does not apply to nonresident aliens, unless they elect to be treated as a resident of the United States for tax purposes.

Unfortunately, the NIIT results in U.S. tax liabilities for many very-high-income U.S. taxpayers living abroad, including many people who may already live in a very-high-tax country. This is partly a result of the fact that foreign tax credits cannot be used to offset this tax in the United States (because it is technically not an income tax, but rather, a Medicare supplement). This means that in many cases, for U.S. taxpayers who are already paying very high tax rates in a foreign country (frequently greater than 50 percent), NIIT effectively raises their tax rates by 3.8 percent on a significant portion of their total income (the portion from net investment income).

Gift and Estate Taxes

In the United States, gift taxes and estate taxes are interlinked, and so it is important to discuss and consider them together. For families with significant wealth, the rules can be very complicated, and it is important to consult with a cross-border estate-planning attorney to ensure that these rules are correctly and optimally navigated.

The gift and estate taxes rules apply to all U.S. citizens and tax residents living in the United States. Note, however, that *not only do different rules apply to gift and estate taxation than to income taxation, but in general, the rules for determining income tax residency* (as described in Chapter 10) *are different from the rules that determine gift and estate tax residency.* The rules that determine gift and estate tax residency are based mainly on whether a foreign national is domiciled in the United States (i.e., whether they maintain a permanent home in the United States), and are therefore *broader* than those for determining income tax residency. Put differently, even if you are not a U.S. tax resident, you may still be *U.S. domiciled* when it comes to applying U.S. gift and estate tax rules.

Gift Taxes

Gift taxes are levied whenever a person who has a permanent U.S. domicile (anyone maintaining a permanent home in the United States) transfers property of any kind to another person without receiving adequate compensation (that is, without receiving adequate and fair consideration for the property that is transferred). This applies to any type of property that has value, including real property, personal property, cash, collectibles, and intangible property, and it does not matter what country the property is located in—that is, the property can be located in the United States or abroad. Put simply, the gift tax rules apply to any asset or indeed anything of value that is gifted without adequate and fair compensation.

There is an annual exclusion amount for gifts that can be made every year to an individual without incurring any gift tax. That amount is $14,000 for 2016. The donor can give a gift of this amount to as many people as he or she likes every year, and there is no requirement that recipients be related to the person giving the gift. For U.S. citizens who have a U.S. citizen spouse, that citizen and spouse can pool their gifting and effectively give $28,000 of their combined property to any individual without incurring gift taxes. Additionally, there is an unlimited exemption of the transfer of assets between spouses who are both U.S. citizens. That is, if you are

U.S. citizens, you can give your husband or wife as much as you want without incurring any gift tax. However, gifts to noncitizen spouses have their own annual limits ($148,000 for 2016).

Any gifts that are above these annual gifting limits are subject to gift tax. The amount of gift tax is determined by accumulating all the taxable gifts (above the annual $14,000 exclusion) made by an individual during his or her lifetime. That accumulated amount is then applied toward a lifetime gift and estate tax exemption, which for U.S. citizens and foreign nationals domiciled in the United States equals $5.45 million per individual for 2016. After the tax is calculated, a "unified credit" is then applied against the tax, which effectively shields the individual or estate from tax on an amount up to the gift and estate tax exemption.

This means that an individual can gift $5.45 million to his or heirs and pay no U.S. federal estate or gift taxes, keeping in mind that the total of all accumulated taxable gifts are also applied against this limit. Married couples who are U.S. citizens or foreign nationals domiciled in the United States can combine their individual exemptions into a unified $10.9 million exemption from federal estate and gift taxes as of 2016. This number rises with inflation annually.

Estate Taxes

Estate taxes are levied against an individual's total estate at the time of his or her death. But a determination as to which property is included in the total estate depends on whether the person is, upon his or her death, a U.S. domicile for estate tax purposes. U.S. citizens and tax residents are subject to U.S. estate tax. A nonresident for estate tax purposes is defined as a non-U.S. domiciled foreign national.

When an individual is a U.S. domicile for estate tax purposes, his or her total taxable estate includes all property owned around the world. On the other hand, nondomiciles for estate tax purposes are only taxed on any property they own that is located inside the United States.

After the value of all of the property included in an individual's estate is accumulated, that amount is then applied against his or her individual gift and estate tax exemption, as described in the preceding section on Gift Taxes, and amounts above that exemption are taxed at gift and estate tax rates. An unlimited marital deduction is applied to property passing to a spouse who is a U.S. citizen, but this marital deduction does not apply if the spouse is not a U.S. citizen.

Once the accumulated amount of the taxable estate is determined, a tentative tax is calculated using the gift and estate tax rates, which rises quickly to a 40 percent top tax rate.

Estate Taxes for Nonresidents

It is very important for nonresidents of the United States (nondomiciles) to know that they have a much higher exposure to U.S. estate tax (compared to U.S. domiciles, who are usually U.S. citizens and residents) on their U.S.-based assets. This is because the normal gift and estate tax exemption for U.S.-based assets ($5.45 million for an individual in 2016) is significantly reduced for nonresidents, down to a total of only $60,000. This means, then, that for nonresidents, estate tax will be due upon their death when their U.S.-based assets are valued above $60,000. Compared to the $5.45 million per person for U.S. citizens and tax residents, this is a huge difference. So, if you are a Green Card holder and you move back to, let's say, Spain, and you own a $5 million piece of real property in the United States, well, as long as you have kept your Green Card, your heirs will benefit from the $5.45 million exemption should you die.

The United States has executed a number of gift and estate tax treaties with other countries that may (a) expand the exemption afforded to nonresidents for estate tax purposes, (b) align the estate tax exemption with that of their home country, or (c) otherwise lessen their U.S. estate tax burden. As only a relatively small number of countries have such an estate tax treaty with the United States, it is once again very important to seek expert advice when your U.S. estate includes significant assets.

Expatriation Tax (Exit Tax)

All permanent tax residents (Green Card holders) considering leaving the United States need to be aware of the expatriation tax provisions, which apply to long-term holders of Green Cards who voluntarily surrender, or involuntarily lose, their U.S. residency (as well as to individuals giving up U.S. citizenship). These rules, which were originally meant to deter tax avoidance through the abandonment of citizenship or permanent tax residency, can potentially create a very high tax on people who are expatriating—in particular people who have accumulated significant wealth during their time as a permanent tax resident. This tax applies when someone has held a

Green Card in at least 8 of the last 15 years, ending with the year their tax residency ends; most typically, we see this when a foreign citizen has maintained a Green Card for more than 7 consecutive years.

Under U.S. law, any individual who has a net worth of greater than $2 million, or an average income tax of more than $160,000 for the five years immediately before expatriation (for 2015, indexed for inflation), and who renounces his or her U.S. citizenship or long-term permanent residency, is automatically assumed to have done so for tax avoidance reasons and is subject to the *expatriation tax* (these individuals are referred to as *covered expatriates*).

The calculation of expatriation tax is complex, and comprises two parts. The first is a tax on net unrealized gains of the individual's assets as if the property had been sold at fair market value on the day before expatriation (also called a *mark-to-market* tax). The gains on this deemed sale are offset by an exclusion amount of $680,000 (set in 2014 and indexed annually for inflation). Second, all deferred income (from stock options, 401(k)s, IRAs, deferred compensation, annuities, etc.) is deemed to be distributed (or realized) the day before expatriating. This is treated as ordinary income for tax purposes, and does not benefit from the $680,000 exclusion amount mentioned earlier.

If you are a long-term Green Card holder who has accumulated significant net worth, you should speak with a tax advisor prior to surrendering your Green Card or allowing it to expire.

Prearrival Planning

Before entering the United States and becoming a U.S. tax resident, a foreign person in effect has one chance to review his or her affairs to assess the impact of the worldwide tax exposure that will result upon arrival. Advance planning and preparation can help to mitigate potential pitfalls and help to save time, money, and hassle. Certain things can be done to either minimize tax exposure or otherwise improve his or her situation prior to coming to the United States. Unfortunately, many people are unaware of the worldwide nature and long reach of the U.S. tax net, or worse, they simply don't make the effort to consider all of this and take appropriate action before coming here.

If a cross-border professional is brought to the United States by a large multinational corporation, they will usually receive some personalized tax consultation from whatever tax firm works with their employer. Unfortunately, this consultation is generally not designed to review their entire financial picture in an effort to identify actions to optimize their wealth and tax situation—which is the goal of this book. Instead, they usually receive a brief, one-hour orientation as to how their income earned from their employer will be taxed once they've arrived in the United States, based on their individual situation and employment agreement. In fact, the tax advisors in these sessions generally avoid any discussion about the individual's goals and worldwide assets, because of the potential complexity and liability involved. Unfortunately, few people in this situation fully understand the importance of seeking expert cross-border financial advice at this moment.

The rest of this section will review a number of items that should be considered by foreign nationals who are entering the United States and becoming (or are likely to become) U.S. tax residents.

Accelerate Gift Planning

If you intend to make any gifts of assets from your estate, you may want to do so prior to your arrival in the United States. Otherwise, you will be subjected to U.S. gift tax rules, which can be complex and costly.

Accelerate Income When Possible

Income is generally taxable to individuals when it is received. It may be beneficial for a foreign citizen to receive foreign-sourced income while still a nonresident and before he or she becomes a U.S. tax resident, thus making the income exempt from U.S. tax. However, the timing of the income has implications for the foreign tax treatment, which should also be considered. For example, it would be better to receive income after coming to the United States if the applicable tax rate would be lower here than if received while a foreign resident.

Distribute Deferred Income When Possible

Before coming to the United States, international people should consider distributing any deferred income that will be taxable when they can elect to do so, assuming of course that doing so will result in a better outcome (i.e., their foreign tax liability will be lower than it would be once they are in the United States). For example, if someone lives in Singapore and would pay between 15 percent and 20 percent tax on incremental income, it would be better to realize that income before coming to the United States, rather than once the person is here and subject to higher tax rates.

Consider Realizing Gains Before Moving Here

Many places around the world do not levy taxes on the capital gains of various asset types, often including such things as real estate and investment securities. So, realizing the gains on these assets by selling them *before* entering the United States may result in no tax, or very little tax. But if an international person has for many years owned an investment asset that has seen significant appreciation, and if that person were to sell it the day after coming to the United States and establishing residency, the gain would be fully taxable in the United States (state and federal), even if all of it occurred long before the person arrived here.

As an example, a client of ours has owned a London flat for 20 years, originally purchasing it for £100,000. Today it is worth over £1,000,000, and the client was considering selling it, until it became clear that the IRS would tax them on the entire gain, even though he had only been living in the United States for less than one year. Similarly, another client who was moving to the United States from Singapore, where there is a very low tax rate on options gains, realized that if she arrived in the United States and then sold her options, she would be taxed heavily on the gains. Instead, she sold all her options several days before flying to the United States to start her new job, saving a substantial amount in taxes.

In addition to straight asset sales, there are also other methods available to raise the taxable basis of various assets before entering the United States so that only the appreciation that occurs after they become a U.S. tax resident will be taxable in the United States. Some of the ways of doing this are fairly complex, like asset transfer strategies that can be deemed a sale for tax purposes, or the use of foreign trusts or other structures for estate planning purposes. Families coming into the United States with significant preexisting wealth are wise to seek expert cross-border tax and estate planning advice prior to establishing U.S. residency.

Alternatively, if you own shares that have incurred a loss (after converting the purchase and sale into U.S. dollars) at the time of your move, you may want to hang on to them and sell them after the move, thus benefiting from the loss in the United States as an offset to other taxable gains (assuming that the losses are not more valuable when realized prior to the move).

Review Existing Asset Structures Before Arriving

Existing asset structures, like trusts and foreign corporations, should be reviewed to determine if there will be any adverse tax or compliance impacts once the foreign person moves to the United States. Examples of problematic structures may include offshore insurance-based investment programs, foreign retirement plans, foreign trusts, and foreign investment holding companies.

Review Immigration and Visa Alternatives

Before making final plans to come to the United States, immigration timetables and visa alternatives should be reviewed to optimize their tax situation. For example, by arriving in the second half of a calendar year, a foreign national might be able to avoid tax residency for that entire year, thus keeping his or her foreign assets out of the U.S. tax net for that calendar year.

PART

VI

Retirement Planning

13

Planning for a Global Retirement

Cross-border families generally face substantial challenges when it comes to planning for retirement and optimizing their future financial situation. Their assets are often scattered around the world, so correctly organizing them to maximize returns and manage risk takes diligence and perseverance. Importantly, cross-border families must understand that having assets and affairs in multiple jurisdictions, each with its own potentially complicated tax laws and regulations, means they are indeed likely to face many unique organizational and planning difficulties when it comes to preparing for retirement.

Fortunately, most successful international families tend to excel at saving, so the issue of whether they will have enough money to retire is, in our experience, not as prevalent for them as it is for most Americans (who often do *not* excel at saving). This isn't to say that the issue of whether there will be enough money for retirement doesn't come up for cross-border families, because nearly everyone wonders about this. But for the most part, the challenges that they face are less about having enough money and more about being optimally positioned to provide for their retirement when the time comes.

Where to Retire? A Common Dilemma

People who come from abroad to live in the United States are often uncertain about where their ultimate retirement destination(s) will be. Some will likely want to retire here in the United States, others will want to retire in their original home country, and still others will choose a third country to retire in, perhaps somewhere where they have also worked, or visited, or where they have family or close friends. Similarly, Americans who have spent substantial periods abroad are also often conflicted as to where they will want to live when they retire.

Overall, we've found that for successful people who have lived a global lifestyle, this is a difficult decision for a number of reasons. Those who have lived globally see the benefits, virtues, and problems in places where they've lived. Additionally, cross-border families tend to have assets in multiple venues and often have relationships with people who are important to them all across the world.

Being Near Family Is Most Important

We've found that by far the most important factor in the decision about where to retire is the location of family—parents and children in particular. For example, we've seen situations where clients decide to retire in three different locations: near their children, near their parents, and then also in a vacation destination of their choosing (think beaches or mountains). The bottom line is that *where* to retire is typically a much harder decision for cross-border families than it is for the typical American retiree.

Plan to Retire Anywhere, to Maximize Flexibility

Many cross-border families haven't ever really considered that they might retire and live in multiple places. Let's think about the many possible scenarios facing them. Perhaps they have a vacation home on the beach in their country of origin, yet they plan on continuing to live where they currently reside, or where one or more of their children reside. Ultimately, given the uncertainty and the many potential options before them, we think it's best for cross-border families to plan for a worldwide retirement, or put another way—to plan to retire anywhere.

Essentially, then, you should assume that you don't know where you're going to retire, because that will enable you to put together a plan that is truly global and that will work well for you regardless of where you end up. Planning for a worldwide retirement creates and preserves a wide variety of options, and makes it far easier to live in the place(s) where you want to be, when you want to be there, and in a manner that is economically sustainable.

Worldwide Planning Is Also Inherently More Complex

The good news about planning for a worldwide retirement is that it maximizes your flexibility and potential for living in and enjoying more than one venue over time. The bad news is that such worldwide planning is also inherently more complex. That complexity—and the additional issues, choices, and challenges that arise—will be addressed throughout this chapter.

A related issue concerns the pragmatics of periodically shifting from one location to another in retirement. A cross-border family with financial affairs in more than one country will ideally have maintained at least some of the bank accounts they had wherever they previously lived or worked. This will give them easier access to banking and cash management services when they need them. Also, in the very unlikely case that there is a national restriction on the ability to access one's wealth—for example, a law is passed in one country that limits or prohibits assets being taken to another jurisdiction—as an insurance measure, it might make sense to make sure that you have easily accessible assets in each jurisdiction of interest.[1]

Investing for Retirement

Part II discusses the importance of diversification for individuals likely to have a multicountry or global retirement. By spreading your assets across various countries and regions of the world, you are best insulated from economic shocks that may particularly affect one country or a specific currency.

Generally speaking, your portfolio investment allocation will need to be reconsidered from the perspective of someone entering their retirement years. Very often, this involves a shift from a focus on growth and appreciation to more of a focus on safety and reliable

---

[1] Similarly, many people assume that it makes sense to have one's assets split between more than one financial institution in case a major firm goes bankrupt or has its assets temporarily frozen. At least with regard to U.S. institutions, we don't see this as a major concern because U.S. accounts generally have several layers of insurance protection.

income, which usually comes from a shift to having more bonds, or a shift to stocks that are safer and more dividend oriented.

Having Enough Money to Retire

Almost everyone has some concern about whether they are "on track" for retirement, both as to whether they will be able to retire when they want to and whether they will have sufficient financial resources to sustain them throughout retirement. That is, whether there will "be enough." These questions are more common today than ever before, as the responsibility for funding one's retirement has fundamentally shifted in the last few decades on to each of us as individuals.

In the past, either employer pensions or government retirement programs could often be counted on to substantially fund one's retirement. Today, there is an increasing trend toward the responsibility for funding retirement to fall mainly on the shoulders of individual families. Like everyone else, then, cross-border families are very interested in questions of how much they will need for retirement, along with concerns arising from the additional complexity of worldwide retirement planning.

How Much Money Will You Need?

To understand with certainty whether or not you have enough money to retire, you need to answer three important questions.

First Question: What Will You Need to Live On?

The first question is how much money do you expect to spend in retirement? This can be a hard question, as it includes both nondiscretionary expenses like food, housing, utilities, and healthcare, as well as discretionary expenses like travel, entertainment, and many other personal expenses. And if you expect to have a more worldwide lifestyle in retirement, your travel expenses may be fairly high indeed. Put more simply, how much will you need to fund your desired lifestyle in retirement when considering the one or more places you will likely want to live?

Note that a conventional assumption found in many retirement guides (such as those for regular American citizens) is that since you are no longer working, many of your work-related costs (like dry cleaning, entertaining business associates, daily commuting, and so on) will go down significantly during retirement. From this assumption the "80 percent" replacement rule was born, that is, many financial planners suggest that you will need to "replace" only 80 percent of your preretirement income during retirement.

However, while some expenses may go down during retirement, others—including travel, healthcare costs, and any costs related to new pursuits or hobbies—may go up. So while the old 80 percent replacement rule can serve as a useful guide, there is no single formula that fits everyone.

In our opinion, the more important number is your expected living expenses in retirement. In a perfect world, retirees would have their primary residence completely paid off before entering retirement (and perhaps also a second home). From there, a simple budget can be prepared in today's dollars (before adjusting for future inflation), which would include everything from food, housing, and utilities, to travel and entertainment, to healthcare expenses. Of course, you can do a good job of estimating these numbers now, but no one knows how these expenses will grow over time. Likewise, there are bound to be unforeseen expenses throughout your retirement years, whether they are for health-related costs, home repairs, or financial support for a loved one, and for this reason it is always smart to build in a margin of safety.

Second Question: What Are Your Sources of Ongoing Retirement Income?

The second inquiry concerns making as accurate an assessment as possible about your various sources of ongoing income during retirement. That is, once you determine roughly what your desired retirement will cost you, your next step is to figure out whether you will have enough ongoing income to meet that level of expense.

You might, for example, have income from U.S. Social Security along with a governmental pension of some kind from another country, and perhaps a small pension from a former employer as well. You might also have a rental property that provides some income, or perhaps a small interest in an ongoing business of some kind. Even if you can only make educated guesses as to the amounts you expect from ongoing income sources, this is nonetheless a very important assessment to make.

Third Question: Will Your Retirement Savings Make Up the Difference?

Some international families will be able to cover their average monthly retirement expenses just from their sources of ongoing income. Many others, however, will need to supplement their retirement cash flow needs with assets they have saved throughout their working lives. This may come from income generated from their portfolio (such as interest paid on bonds and stock dividends), or from selling down parts of their portfolio that may (or may not) have appreciated over time. Most likely, it will come from a combination of the two.

This gap between your expected retirement living expenses and your ongoing retirement income is the amount that each of us is ultimately responsible for ourselves. We can't expect someone else's help! Furthermore, the size of this gap on average has been growing rapidly over the past few decades, with no end in sight.

For this reason, there is nothing more important to your retirement success than saving and accumulating retirement assets, and then making smart investment decisions with what you have saved.

Safe Withdrawal Rates: The 4 Percent Rule

Many people struggle to understand just how much money they can *draw* from their retirement portfolio, either through the spending of portfolio income or from the sale of certain assets (known collectively as the withdrawal rate). Many people would be surprised to learn that financial planners have long viewed the *4 percent rule* as a good guide for a sustainable withdrawal rate. This means that a retiree can draw out about 4 percent of a diversified portfolio every year, and be reasonably certain that their money will last. Of course, many people who have not saved enough do not have the luxury of maintaining the value of their portfolio into the future. Someone drawing 6 to 8 percent or more from a portfolio can expect that portfolio to eventually be drawn down completely.

This 4 percent number may seem low to you, but you should understand that it is designed to *maintain the purchasing power of the assets after inflation in perpetuity*. This is certainly an ideal goal for many, but unfortunately, very few people can realistically afford this luxury. To explain, imagine if you had a $1,000,000 portfolio at the start of retirement; this would mean you could comfortably draw $40,000 per year from that account to supplement your retirement cash flow needs. If we assume that the account earns a return above 4 percent, then by leaving the remaining growth in the account, over time you should see the portfolio continue to grow in value. This continued growth would ensure that in 20 years, the portfolio would have as much or more purchasing power as it does today.

For example, returning to our $1,000,000 portfolio, let's assume that after drawing out the 4 percent, we reinvested the remaining average growth, which totaled 2.5 percent per year (a rate that is close to the expected rate of inflation). Twenty years from now, that portfolio would be worth $1.65 million, although the actual purchasing power would be roughly the same as $1 million today.

How Much Can You Really Draw Every Year?

Our clients at Worldview Wealth Advisors often ask us what is the maximum they can safely draw from their portfolio annually. This is a difficult question to answer, as there has been significant debate about how much can be safely drawn from a portfolio in retirement. In the past, stock and bond returns were higher, and a 4 to 5 percent withdrawal rate seemed realistic and possible. In today's world, with very low bond yields and lower expected returns for the stock market, we are recommending that those who want to maintain their wealth (their purchasing power) throughout retirement should withdraw less than 4 percent from their portfolio annually.

What Is a Successful Retirement?

It should be said that many people do not aspire to maintain the value of their net worth throughout their retirement, often only to leave their legacy to their children after they are deceased. Many people would rather enjoy their lives to the fullest during their retirement years, and they are willing to accept that the purchasing power of their wealth will decline over time. It is, in fact, quite possible to have a successful retirement even while slowly spending down one's portfolio assets. However, because investment returns are unpredictable, and one never knows how long they will live, spending more heavily through retirement does raise the risk of one day potentially running out of money.

The Important Role of Financial Planning

Planning and budgeting for retirement is important, and you should be prepared to take the time and effort to carefully think through how much you will need in retirement, whether you do this on your own or with the help of a wealth management or financial planning professional. Going through a detailed planning process with an experienced financial planning professional—such as someone who has earned the CFP™ (certified financial planner) credential or perhaps an accounting or legal accreditation—can provide you with tremendous benefits and insight.

Whereas in the past many *financial planners* were really insurance salesmen in disguise, today, financial planning has evolved into a sophisticated profession unto itself. The digital tools now available make it much easier to perform sophisticated analysis in areas such as budgeting and cash flows, saving strategies, risk profiling, investment return projections and simulations, tax planning strategies, estate planning, and so on.

Longevity Risk Is Alive and Well

Another important factor to consider is called *longevity risk*—that is, the risk of living longer than you originally expected or planned for. People today are living considerably longer than they did in past generations. This is especially true of members of better-educated and more successful families, which includes many cross-border families (probably including your own), who generally have sufficient financial resources and access to high-quality medical care. Even if no extraordinary medical breakthroughs happen in the next few decades, the general trend for well-off people has been and continues to be toward longer lifespans.

The downside (if it can be called that) of such longer lifespans is the increased risk of fully depleting your financial resources during retirement. In most cases, the amount of money you need to have when you begin retirement must be substantially greater if you are going to live substantially longer. Simply put, you generally will need a good deal more assets if you are going to have not just a 5- to 15-year retirement, but instead, a 20- to 25-year retirement or longer.

Unfortunately, the most likely outcome of increasing longevity is that most people will need to work significantly longer before they can afford to retire.

Inheritance: Plan for It, But Don't Count on It

As you plan for retirement, you should also consider—but not overly rely on—the potential for inheriting assets. Some people are quite sure that they will be receiving a substantial sum from their parents or other relatives, while others of us are fairly confident that there will be no such inheritances forthcoming. If you think you are likely to receive an inheritance, it might be useful to make estimates of the likely amounts and timetables so that your planning can be as comprehensive as possible. But always keep in mind that inheritances are never guaranteed.

Organizing and Optimizing Worldwide Income and Assets

When planning for retirement, it's important for cross-border families to keep the "big picture"[2]—with all of its worldwide ramifications and details—in mind. In this section, we will review the wide variety of items that you need to organize ahead of time to ensure that you are ready and prepared for retirement.

Assessing Sources of Income in Retirement

One of the first things we suggest that international families understand in as much detail as possible is their various sources of guaranteed income in retirement. *Income in retirement* generally refers to the following:

- *Social Security* in the United States;
- *Other governmental pensions* (similar to Social Security) that have been earned in countries outside of the United States;
- *Private employer pensions* from employers that offer a pension benefit (also known as a *defined-benefit plan*);
- *Private pensions and annuities;* these are not very common, but it is possible to purchase a guaranteed income stream for your lifetime or for a specific number of years; and
- *Other stable income sources;* ignoring portfolio investments for now, these include other reliable income streams such as real estate rental income.

---

[2]Another aspect of the "big picture" of retirement planning involves going beyond questions of money to also consider questions of *meaning,* that is, what will you do and how will you live your life in retirement so that it is meaningful for you? All too often, individuals arrive at retirement without having given much thought to what's really important to them and how they want to spend their remaining years.

Caution! Avoiding Bad Employer Pension Pay-Outs

As previously mentioned, private employer pensions are becoming less common as we move forward into the twenty-first century. According to the *Washington Post*, roughly one-quarter of Fortune 500 companies still offer pensions to new hires, but this is down from 60 percent in 1998.[3] Furthermore, the typical payout terms for the remaining pensions available are much less generous compared with pensions of the past. The strong trend away from such pensions continues, and employees who are owed pensions frequently find themselves receiving offers to convert their pensions—which essentially are lifetime annuities—into a one-time distribution payment (usually a tax-qualified distribution which is then rolled into a 401(k) or IRA).

We recommend that those who are offered these one-time payouts be very cautious about accepting them. Although the offer may *sound* like a lot of money—$200,000, $500,000, even $1,000,000—very often it turns out that the one-time payment substantially undercuts the true value of the lifetime pension. And, of course, if you live longer than the average lifespan, it will have turned out to be a very bad deal for you. Conversely, if you expect that your life expectancy will be below average, then perhaps you should seriously consider the offer, as it would likely increase the size of your estate for your heirs.

Organizing Your Assets

Organizing your net worth—the overall wealth and net worth that you have been able to accumulate over your lifetime—is extremely important. In addition to understanding your various sources of retirement income discussed previously, you will want to consider all of the assets that you own.

Depending on the type of asset, you want to have a firm sense of:

- What the asset is—that is, exactly what it is that you own;
- What the asset is worth;
- How the asset is invested (if a financial asset), what the level of inherent risk is, and whether the investment fits in well with your overall financial plan;
- Where the asset is located (what country or jurisdiction, and in what currency);

---

[3]See Jonnelle Marte, "Nearly a Quarter of Fortune 500 Companies Still Offer Pensions to New Hires," *Washington Post* (September 5, 2014), https://www .washingtonpost.com/news/get-there/wp/2014/09/05/nearly-a-quarter-of-fortune -500-companies-still-offer-pensions-to-new-hires/.

- How to gain access to the asset and whether it can it be liquidated easily; and
- Any special rules, limitations, timing, or tax issues with regard
  to cashing in some or all of the assets before its full maturity
  date.

The most common types of assets include:

- *Cash and cash equivalents*—safe liquid funds, perhaps in various
  currencies;
- *Qualified investment accounts*—tax-deferred or tax-advantaged
  in some way, also known as a "defined-contribution" accounts;
- *Nonqualified investment accounts*—not tax advantaged, also
  called taxable or brokerage accounts;
- *Concentrated stock and stock options*—generally a highly concentrated and more risky asset;
- *Real estate*—including residences and income property; and
- *Alternative investments*—including private investment funds,
  collectibles, and other often-illiquid assets.

Cash and Cash Equivalents

Here we are talking about cash and cash equivalents such as
short-term government bonds, certificates of deposit, and money
market funds. It is important to know what currencies your cash is
held in, and the interest rate or yield that they earn. Depending on
the type of cash equivalent you own, there may also be penalties for
early withdrawal, something you definitely want to be aware of and
avoid if possible.

Qualified Accounts: 401(k)s, IRAs, and Other U.S. and Foreign Retirement Accounts

Qualified accounts are generally U.S. and foreign retirement savings
accounts, which have some form of tax-advantaged element to them.
The most common type of account, both in the United States and
abroad, are pretax salary deferral programs where you are able
to defer a portion of your earnings before taxes are applied into
a capital account that is then invested into a diversified portfolio.
These programs, which are also known as "defined-contribution"
accounts, are extremely valuable because they allow for funds to
be invested before taxes are assessed, and then to benefit from
tax-deferred growth, ideally over a very long period of time.

In many places around the world, these programs are obligatory, that is, you are required to contribute a healthy percentage of your income into a savings account for your future, often with an additional contribution from either the government or your employer. Given the previously discussed worldwide trend away from pensions—which pushes primary responsibility for retirement directly onto individuals—in most cases it makes sense to make substantial use of these types of accounts when they are offered.

Individual Retirement Accounts: A Good Start, But Not a Solution

As we have said before, there is a powerful trend around the world to push the responsibility for funding retirement down to the individual (usually through the various forms of tax-advantaged salary deferral programs, or *defined-contribution plans*), rather than having employers or the government do it for them. Unfortunately, from our perspective, these kinds of plans are *not* a panacea and cannot be an effective replacement for the defined-benefit pension systems that have historically filled this role around the world.

Substantial research shows that the *majority* of people will not be successful under this system. First, we know that the average person will not save enough income every year to adequately fund retirement. Perhaps this can be partially solved by *requiring* that individuals and their employers make regular contributions to their plans, as is done in many other countries around the world.

Second, research further shows that most people will poorly manage the funds that they've been able to save. On average, most individuals earn returns that are well below market averages, mainly as a result of poorly diversified portfolio construction and emotionally driven investment decisions (such as buying in when prices are high, and selling out when markets are in correction).

Instead, we would like to see another solution that is obligatory yet takes some of the investment decision making and control out of the hands of individuals. Unfortunately, this may be too big of a challenge to solve easily. Perhaps the best we can hope for is to make incremental improvements to the current system to ensure at least a basic minimum retirement income for everyone.

Nonqualified Investment Accounts—Generally Holding Stocks and Bonds

Many families are able to build up savings with after-tax funds over time. At some point, some of these savings are often invested into financial assets like stocks and bonds (usually through a pooled fund structure like a mutual fund). For many families this after-tax retirement savings becomes a large and important element of their retirement plan. However, this is also an area where many people make the biggest investment mistakes, by either failing to properly diversify in order to minimize investment risk, or trying to trade stocks or otherwise time the market (often based on their own emotional reactions to the current market environment). Most people would greatly benefit from working with a good fiduciary financial advisor, who really puts their best interests first.

Concentrated Stock and Stock Options

Many people own concentrated stock and stock options, where over time they have accumulated shares of stock or options in the company or companies where they have worked. One thing to avoid is *overconcentration* of your wealth in any one particular company, industry, or currency. That is, if a significant percentage of your portfolio is made up of shares of stock in one company, or multiple companies that are very similar to each other in terms of industry or region, then you want to diversify out of that concentration, as discussed in Chapter 4.

Real Estate

Real estate holdings, including both personal residences and investment property, are a critical element of a strong retirement plan. Not only does a residence provide a roof over your head, but it also represents a store of wealth that can usually be easily liquidated and used elsewhere (to buy another home, for example, or to fund the cost of an assisted living care facility later in life). With regard to income properties, how much income do these properties generate, and how much management time do they require?

Also, while real estate ownership has generally proven to be a good investment over many decades, it is dangerous to have too much of your net worth in this asset class. Most people from outside the United States have a strong desire to own real estate, which we fully support. However, even though real estate prices have increased substantially over the past few decades, there have also been long periods of time throughout history where real estate has performed poorly. Diversification is key!

Alternative Investments

This class of assets includes many different type of things, from private partnership investments, to commodities and precious metals, to art and other collectible items of value. These assets are generally less liquid than the other types of assets mentioned above, and they usually do not provide an ongoing income. Certain alternative assets have delivered exceptional rates of return over time. But for most people, these assets are less reliable and are more of a hobby investment or something that they receive enjoyment from beyond the actual investment value.

Currency Exposure: A Real Retirement Risk

When planning for your retirement, it's very important to consider *currency exposure.* Essentially, you need to make sure the currency you actually use to pay for your lifestyle expenses is aligned with your ongoing retirement income and investment assets. It's important to avoid a mismatch where, for example, your pension is paying you in euros but you are living in the United States in a dollar-based economy.

Suppose, for example, that you have an ongoing income stream of 5,000 euros a month for life, but you live in a place where dollars are the official currency. In this situation, if the euro were to decline by 25 percent, the pension that you were relying on to fund your retirement expenses would have suffered a 25 percent loss of purchasing power in dollars. One strategy to employ in this example might be to shift a large majority of your other portfolio assets into dollar investments, thus providing a measure of protection against changes in the dollar/euro exchange rate.

This is a real risk that is especially dangerous for those who do not understand the potential magnitude of the risk, and who have not built into their wealth a certain level of currency diversification. Even if you cannot avoid this kind of currency exposure risk entirely, you should hedge against that risk by having income, investments, and cash in all the currencies in which you are likely to be spending in retirement.

CHAPTER 14

Considerations for Cross-Border Retirees

Tax Planning for Retirement

Tax planning for retirement is, of course, vitally important. Understanding how you will be taxed on each element of what you own, or what is due to you, can make a tremendous difference in providing for the kind of retirement you hope to have. Moreover, as explained in Chapter 2, if you plan to remain a U.S. tax resident in retirement, it's important to understand the wide-reaching nature of U.S. tax law and its potential effects on your retirement future.

Taxes on Pension and Social Security Income

To begin with, you need to gain an understanding of how any pension and social security income will be taxed. In part, the answer to this question will depend on where the pension originates and what tax treaties are in place, assuming you live in a different country. In many tax treaties, pension payments are taxed first in the country in which you reside, as opposed to in the country in which those payments originate from. This subject is discussed further in Chapter 7.

Taxes on Investment Income and Gains

Similarly, with regard to investment income and gains, you will need to understand how interest income, dividends, and appreciation (realized capital gains) will be taxed. If you have investment accounts in different countries, then those different countries may impose different tax rules on your assets and the income they generate, depending on the local laws and the tax treaty between your country of residence and the jurisdiction in which the investments are located. Depending on the details, you might decide to relocate some of your investments to another jurisdiction to gain more favorable tax treatment.

For example, you might have a diversified portfolio that, shortly before retirement, you decide to reallocate into a much more income-oriented investment approach, that is, a more safe and stable portfolio that is focused on generating reliable income. However, it may be that tax laws in the jurisdiction where those assets are located are particularly well suited for an investment strategy focused on appreciation, but are not so well-suited for an income-focused portfolio. If indeed the jurisdiction the assets are in has a punishingly high tax rate on investment income, it might make sense to move that account to another jurisdiction that has a much lower tax rate.

Of course, if you are planning to remain a U.S. citizen or tax resident throughout retirement, then you can never escape the baseline floor of the U.S. tax system (adjusted for foreign income exclusions). However, it is very possible, depending on where you are living, that you will incur a higher tax burden in retirement than what would be owed to the IRS (remember there are no state taxes if you reside abroad). In these situations, even though being a U.S. resident will cause complications and an annual tax-filing burden, it will likely not lead to additional tax liabilities.

Taxes on Distributions from Qualified Accounts

Qualified accounts, such as U.S. 401(k)s and IRAs, are generally funded with pretax money, and the proceeds are then taxable when money is withdrawn. The key to being successful here and limiting unwanted surprises is making sure that the various tax-deferred or tax-free structures that you have in place will still work if you move from one jurisdiction to another. Furthermore, distributions from pretax savings accounts are generally taxable to you in the country in which you reside; however, this tax treatment is governed by the tax treaty between the two countries involved, and therefore requires careful consideration and study. This subject is discussed further in Chapter 6.

Taking Retirement Accounts with You

A related question is whether qualified accounts can be fully liquidated or taken with you if you move away without substantial consequences. Suppose you lived and worked in three or four different countries throughout your lifetime, and you have tax-advantaged savings accounts in multiple jurisdictions. It may be a hassle to manage these accounts in different countries, so you might be tempted to take them with you when you move to another country. Unfortunately, most of these accounts cannot be withdrawn or taken away outside of the country in which they originate without significant taxes and penalties applying.

Tax-qualified accounts in some jurisdictions, however, provide for more lenient portability. Consider a Swiss Pillar 3 pension, which is similar to a 401(k). These accounts can be fully withdrawn early and moved outside of the country while paying a special lower tax rate, provided that you are leaving the country for good (emigrating). But U.S. accounts, like 401(k)s and IRAs, cannot be taken outside of the United States unless you fully withdraw all funds and in so doing, face all of the tax liability from that income in addition to a 10 percent penalty for early withdrawal (if before the age of 59 and a half).

Cash Management and Account Administration

It is clearly very important to be able to easily access your funds no matter where in the world they are and no matter where in the world you are. Begin by asking yourself where your accounts are located, and then determine how easy they will be to access from different places around the world. It's important to realize that if you have funds located in certain countries, they will be more difficult to manage and access.

Note that it is becoming increasingly more difficult to easily interact with international financial institutions. This is especially true if someone has a direct connection to the United States, such as being a citizen or a Green Card holder. The new FATCA regulations, which were previously discussed in Chapter 2, require foreign financial institutions to carefully look at their clients for U.S. financial connections. If they find a client with U.S. connections, they're obligated to report the details of their accounts back to the U.S. Treasury, which as we'll now explain, has had some negative consequences.

FATCA Fallout: Harder to Deal with Big International Banks

Given the overall intention and momentum of FATCA, cross-border information sharing between governments and international financial institutions will only increase over time. Not only will it generally become more difficult to deal with these financial institutions—at least in the short-term—but in some cases, these institutions will simply refuse to take on what they view as higher risk clients and accounts. In fact, many international financial institutions are now already refusing to take on certain types of cross-border families as clients (especially U.S. citizens and permanent residents).

Over a longer period of time, however, it's likely that the laws, rules, and regulations relating to FATCA and similar measures will become clearer and more refined, and the mechanisms for cross-border information sharing will become smoother, ubiquitous, and easier to follow. But for the time being, cross-border families, whether they're Americans abroad or foreign nationals in the United States, will have to deal with special challenges as far as access to and the administration of international accounts. As they say in the travel business, "Expect delays."

Accessing Your Money

Once you are retired, what will the technical mechanics of accessing your accounts look like? From a purely functional perspective, how will you arrange to supplement whatever ongoing income you may be receiving so that you can meet your ongoing cash flow needs and maintain your desired lifestyle in retirement? Clearly, this is something you want to consider and have a firm understanding of.

The goal here is to be able to not just access your various accounts, but to bring together funds in a simple, low-cost way in the functional currency of the place or places where you will most likely be spending. If you simply retired to the same country where most of your funds are located, then creating automated linkages and withdrawals on a monthly basis is relatively easy. But if you are drawing from three, four, or even more sources in different countries in order to bring together your 10,000 euros every month into your primary spending account, well, things can become quite complicated and expensive, and are often quite difficult to arrange.

Foreign Exchange Costs—Minimize Translations

Keep in mind that it can be very expensive to convert money to different currencies and to move money around through international wire transfers. Retail banks handle most foreign exchange for individuals around the world, but they are often one of the most expensive places to convert money. Very often, the cost can be as much as 3 percent or more above the current interbank exchange rate, which amounts to a significant cost indeed.

While certain multicurrency accounts may offer somewhat better conversion rates, it is often hard to tell exactly what their costs are and how much you are being charged without simultaneously comparing an offer from your financial institution with the most recent interbank exchange rate. This is because the cost of exchange is generally embedded in the bid-ask spread, which is essentially invisible to the customer.

Certain large private banks that regularly work with international families may have access to currency exchange services that are ordinarily only available to very wealthy families. These platforms may end up costing as little as 1 to 1.5 percent over the interbank exchange rate, and for larger transfers the costs come down even more, which is a much more reasonable charge for currency exchange transactions.

Efficient Cross-Border Money Transfers

Additionally, because of the cost of currency conversations and foreign transfers, it can be inefficient to set up money transfers on a *monthly* basis (often, the typical setup for most retirees). In many cases, it is far better to arrange for the necessary movement of funds once or twice a year to replenish a cash reserve account that can be easily accessed—typically a local bank in local currency. These funds can then be slowly used up over a 6- or 12-month period. Then, as they are exhausted, more funds will be moved to once again replenish that pool. Doing things this way will limit transactions fees and mitigate inefficiencies in the process of transferring funds.

Another option is to utilize one of the many online currency exchange firms that specialize in offering a better rate on currency transfers. The services of these firms are well worth exploring, especially if you will be making larger transactions—that is, you will get a much better exchange rate if you are moving $100,000 than if you are moving $5,000, and an even better rate if you are moving even larger amounts. Again, this is in alignment with the idea of not undertaking monthly transfers, but instead, bundling your transfers periodically.

Additionally, you should consider a plan that keeps assets divided into currencies that might not be the functional currency of where you are living, but that can be used to pay expenses and bills that come due that are in that other currency. For example, you might have an ongoing pension coming to you in British pounds, in addition to keeping a home in the United Kingdom. You could then allow these funds to accumulate in a U.K. bank, then use those funds for expenses related to your U.K. residence as well as any additional expenses that you incur while you are visiting there.

Social Security and Foreign Government Pensions

It can often be difficult to understand the exact amount of U.S. Social Security or other foreign government pensions that you are entitled to receive. The United States and most other countries use a variety of complex formulas to calculate social security benefits. These formulas can often be difficult to decipher and apply to your own situation. Not only are the rules and regulations complicated and nuanced, they are subject to fairly frequent legislative and administrative change, making them even more difficult to understand and quantify.

On top of all that, it's not uncommon for a cross-border professional to have accumulated public pensions from more than one country, each written in a different language and following a different formula. Additionally, oftentimes cross-border professionals will have earned only limited benefits from the public pension plans that they paid into. Very often, the most significant part of public pension benefits only come to someone who has worked a full career in a particular country. So if you only worked 8 years in one place, 12 in another, and then 15 in the final country, you may receive only limited benefits from each of them. That is, this is a case where the sum of your public pension parts will be less than the whole that would have been due to you had you worked (and paid into) the pension system in only one country.

The United States does have bilateral social security agreements with 25 countries. As discussed in Chapter 12, these agreements improve benefit protection for workers who have divided their careers between the United States and another country.

Social Security Benefits Earned Are Usually Yours for Life

The U.S. Social Security system provides a wide array of benefits to eligible individuals. The system provides old age and disability benefits to workers, benefits to dependents and survivors of retired and disabled workers, and medical benefits to the elderly.

There are no stated citizenship or residency requirements imposed for an individual to receive social security retirement, survivor, or dependency benefits. For U.S. citizens, benefits earned in the past are generally yours no matter where you move (except that the Social Security Administration will not send payments to certain restricted countries like Cuba and North Korea). Foreign citizens who worked in the United States for some length of time will usually continue to receive the benefits they earned in retirement, even if they've left the United States and are no longer a U.S. tax resident. However, there are number of situations where this is not the case.

For foreign residents, if you are a citizen of one of the 25 countries with which the United States has a social security agreement, then you will continue to receive your benefit payments. There are another approximately 60 countries in which you will continue to receive U.S. Social Security payments, unless you are receiving your payments as a dependent or survivor. If you are a citizen of most other foreign countries, your U.S. Social Security payments will stop after you have been outside the United States for six consecutive calendar months, unless you meet an exception to the Alien Nonpayment Provisions of the Social Security Act. There are quite a few additional exceptions to the Alien Nonpayment Provisions based on how long a foreign citizen worked in the United States, the nature of that work, and other relevant provisions of the international treaty.[1]

So then, we can say that for those living in *most* major foreign countries, whatever social security benefit you've earned generally belongs to you. More simply, if you've paid into the system and earned a benefit, then it is your property whether or not you stay in the United States or remain a U.S. taxpayer in any capacity. Even

---

[1]See https://secure.ssa.gov/poms.nsf/lnx/0302610010.

if you move abroad and give up your U.S. residency and become a nonresident alien, you are still entitled to the benefits you earned while working in the United States, in most cases.[2] Of course, these rules and the various international agreements that are involved are complex and always evolving, so it is best to check with the Social Security Administration regarding the rules relevant to the country where you are likely to retire.

Possible "Windfall Elimination" Reduction to Benefits

You should also be aware that there are certain possible reductions to your social security benefits if you have worked for an employer who did not withhold social security taxes from your salary. The *Windfall Elimination Provision* often comes into play if you have worked for a private employer or government agency in a foreign country, and contributed to another pension system other than Social Security during that time. This provision affects how your retirement or disability benefit is calculated. It implements a modified formula to calculate your benefit amount, generally resulting in a lower Social Security benefit than you would have otherwise received.

The Windfall Elimination Provision primarily affects people who earned a public pension benefit through a job where they did not pay Social Security taxes, and also worked in the United States long enough to qualify for a Social Security retirement or disability benefit. If you think you might be affected by this provision, you can start with one of the U.S. government's online calculators.[3] However, this entire area can be pretty daunting, so if you have any doubts about it, we recommend you consult with the Social Security Administration.

Long-Term Viability and Ongoing Changes

Of course, as anyone who watches the news knows, U.S. Social Security is in flux, and there are significant doubts about the future long-term viability of the program because of the increasing longevity of recipients and a likely inability of the program to fund itself. To keep the program viable, there are likely to be numerous adjustments to it in the future.

---

[2]See https://www.ssa.gov/pubs/EN-05-10137.pdf, entitled "What Happens While You Are Outside The United States," for more details.

[3]See, e.g., https://www.ssa.gov/planners/retire/anyPiaWepjs04.html.

One fix that has already been implemented is to raise the full retirement age of participants, thus lowering the payments made over the total benefit period. Traditionally, the full benefit age was 65, and early retirement was first available at age 62 (at a 20 percent reduction to the full benefit). Currently, the full benefit age is 66 for people born in 1943 to 1954, and it will gradually rise to 67 for those born in 1960 or later. The reduction in benefit for those taking early retirement at age 62 has increased gradually to 30 percent for those born in 1960 or later. Another possible remedy may be a means test, where benefit payments are somehow limited for people with higher income or net worth (their "means"). In our opinion, it is inevitable that further reductions in benefits will occur in the future, either through a means test, a further rise in the full retirement age, or by some other method.

Filing for Benefits Early, on Time, or Late?

A question that frequently arises concerning U.S. Social Security is whether to: (a) file to start receiving benefits before full retirement age, (b) wait for full retirement age, or (c) wait beyond full retirement age so that you can accumulate additional benefits. Our general recommendation is that if you don't have an urgent need for the benefits you are owed, it's best to wait until full retirement age. There is substantial discounting that occurs if you file for benefits early (usually a full 30 percent discount at age 62), so waiting until full retirement age is in effect a good investment.

An Opportunity Cost to Waiting Beyond Full Retirement Age

Many people advocate for continuing to build up additional Social Security benefits by waiting beyond your full retirement age—that is, perhaps waiting all the way up until you are age 70 (after which no additional benefits accrue). At Worldview Wealth Advisors, we generally do not recommend delaying benefits far beyond full retirement age. We've found that many of the analyses into the benefits of waiting are overly simplistic. These calculations usually do not take into consideration that, in effect, you have a benefit termination date—that is, the date you will die. Therefore, while it is true that for every year (actually, for every month) you wait beyond your full retirement age you will receive a certain percentage increase in your monthly payment, you will also have given up an entire 12 months of payments on the front end while you wait, which amounts to a considerable opportunity cost—what you could have earned on that money over the years had you received it. Thus, waiting to draw your benefits for one more year *does not* actually yield an X percent increase in your monthly benefit (which, from a simplistic perspective, might seem reasonable), because you in fact had to give up receiving the lower monthly benefit for a full year in order to get it.

The bottom line here is that if in fact you should end up living not as long as you originally planned on or hoped for, then waiting until age 70 to start receiving benefits will, in retrospect, turn out to have been a poor choice. If you knew for sure ahead of time that you were going to live well beyond your actuarial date of death, then waiting a few years beyond your full retirement age to collect benefits would generally make sense. But since we can't know when we will die, waiting until age 70 to start receiving benefits can be a bit of a gamble.

Foreign Government Pensions

The same types of considerations as described above with respect to U.S. Social Security are also relevant for most foreign public pension programs. Each will have unique features and decision points that can be difficult to understand, especially if the rules and regulations are only accessible to you in a language that is not your primary language. Without question, you will want to consult with someone who has specific expertise in the foreign public pension in question.

Drawing on Tax-Deferred Accounts

Most international professionals who end up living and working in multiple countries over the course of their lifetime tend to accumulate a variety of tax-advantaged accounts (known as *qualified accounts*) in multiple countries. Most of these programs allow for the accumulation of assets in a pretax manner, so the funds are invested over a long period of time, with the effect of income taxes deferred until such time that funds are withdrawn. These tax-deferred accounts often end up being a large percentage of the nest egg that people plan on using to support their retirement. At some point, most people will eventually need to draw from these accounts during retirement.

There are some unique issues around strategizing a plan to draw on one's various tax-deferred accounts around the world. You need to know where all of the accounts are, of course, and you need to understand all of the various rules around withdrawals. For example, at what age can you begin to make withdrawals without any penalty?

The Ordering of Withdrawals

One issue concerns the ordering of withdrawals. For example, you may have three different tax-deferred savings accounts in three different countries. Suppose, for example, that you have determined that in addition to all of your sources of ongoing income in retirement, you will need to take about $2,000 a month from the combination of these three accounts. Should you take that amount evenly from all three, or should you start drawing down from only one until it is completely empty, and then start drawing down from the next one? Based on taxes, penalties, and other factors, the order and percentage amount that you draw down from your tax-deferred accounts can make a big difference.

One of the factors we look at is the efficiency and growth potential of the account—essentially, the quality of the investments offered and the expenses within each plan. For example, many retirement plans, particularly international ones, are built inside an insurance structure, which can have much higher internal expenses. These types of plans can also provide you with more limited investment choices. For that reason, you might decide to draw from these accounts first in terms of the order of withdrawals.

Tax ramifications are also important. As discussed in Chapter 6, most tax treaties state that tax-deferred account distributions are taxed first in the country in which a person resides. However, in some cases the country where the account is located may assert the primary right to tax that distribution. That means it is possible that drawing from differing retirement accounts will result in differing taxation rates. So you might decide to first draw down from the accounts that have the lowest taxes associated with them, depending on where you are residing. Similarly, you might decide to draw down a particular account only up to a certain level, because drawing down at a higher level would kick you into a higher tax bracket, and then take everything else you need from other accounts where withdrawals have a lesser tax impact.

Conclusion

As promised, *The Cross-Border Family Wealth Guide* provides a comprehensive review of issues and opportunities relating to taxes, investing, real estate, and retirement. To our knowledge, the information presented in this book has never before been collected in one place, which means that as an internationally oriented person, you now have a substantial opportunity before you.

Specifically, if you have read through the book, you have likely gained a reasonable understanding of—or at least caught a glimpse of—the particular wealth management problems and challenges facing you and your family in both the short and long run. To reduce the likelihood that you have overlooked anything of great significance, this short concluding chapter will very briefly review some of the most important highlights from the guide's core content parts. What follows, then, will be a short recap of some of the major points that we want to make sure you understand, take to heart, and then take action on if desirable or necessary.

An Overview of Key Points

Part I, Financial Challenges of a Cross-Border Life, defines cross-border individuals and lays out the challenges placed before them. It discusses the unique reach of the U.S. tax system, including the Foreign Account Tax Compliance Act (FATCA).

Part II, Saving and Investing, begins with the fundamental principle that we all need to learn to take care of ourselves financially for the long run. Gone are the days when you could rely on an employer or the government (of nearly any country) to take care of you through a pension or some other means in your old age. Going forward, everyone who wants to arrive at and have a financially stress-free retirement must learn to first accumulate wealth for themselves and their family, and to then properly diversify and grow that wealth.

To this end, Part II spends a good deal of time explaining the primary role of the three most important classes of assets: stocks, bonds, and real estate. These three asset classes will constitute the vast majority of most people's wealth, and so the more you know about them, the better. Further, given that stock market holdings are an important component of most families' net worth, the chapter further presents a set of core guidelines for how to invest in the stock market. These guidelines are based on having a diversified and *truly* global investment outlook that is put into place through a low-cost and tax-efficient investment process.

Part III, 401(k)s, IRAs, and Other Pensions and Savings Plans, directly follows up on Part II's focus on the importance of each of us needing to take care of ourselves financially. These sorts of retirement plans—whether a 401(k) or IRA based in the United States or an equivalent foreign plan—are among the only places where you can save meaningful amounts of money for retirement in a pretax (and therefore highly advantageous) structure. For this reason, these plans should be fully taken advantage of by *everyone* who has access to them and the ability to make contributions. Of course this also means that everyone should fully understand the unique rules and regulations that govern them. Complications can arise if you move from one country to another, or have retirement plans in more than one country, and as always, it's best to be aware of potential problems ahead of time.

Once you have accumulated a significant balance in your 401(k) or equivalent plan, it then becomes extremely important for you to properly invest those funds. Not only should you build a portfolio that is low-cost, diversified, and has a true globally oriented exposure, but you also want to *make sure that you aren't invested too conservatively*— a common problem, especially for foreign families who are less familiar and comfortable with stock market investing. Since the very nature of these tax-favored retirement accounts tends to favor a very long time horizon (most structures restrict or penalize early withdrawals), it's important that these retirement accounts include a significant enough allocation to stocks to ensure long-term growth.

Finally, once you are about to enter retirement, it's very important to understand the unique rules and tax consequences of drawing on various retirement accounts. Given the complexities of cross-border tax regimes, the exact timing and way in which you access your funds throughout retirement can make a big difference.

Part IV turns to Real Estate, and there are three important points for you to understand here. First, owning your primary residence should be a goal for most people. If your circumstances allow for it, owning your primary residence will often provide you with certain tax advantages, the potential for substantial long-term capital appreciation (i.e., the value of your home will likely rise), and the pride of ownership and sense of community that comes from being a homeowner.

Second, real estate investment can be an excellent choice for many cross-border families, given the inherent stability of the asset and the predictability of cash flow from rental income. However, people need to understand the management responsibilities and commit to spending the time needed to select, manage, and oversee this kind of investment. Alternatively, in some cases a good choice will be to invest in passive fractional interests in real estate through professional real estate investment managers.

Third, because real estate ownership is familiar and culturally desirable, many cross-border families tend to hold a large—and sometimes the largest—portion of their wealth this way. It's important to make sure, then, that you are not so heavily invested in real estate that you are taking too much risk by being overexposed to it. Instead, make sure the totality of your wealth is diversified, with real estate being only one (even if a very significant) portion. As a general rule of thumb, we suggest that clients seek to limit real estate equity to no more than 50 percent of their net worth, with the remainder primarily divided among stock market investments and other stable assets like bonds and cash.

Part V focuses on Cross-Border Taxation, which in some ways underlies and ties together all of the material in this book. The first thing to make sure you understand is that exposure to the U.S. tax system—which can happen more easily than you might imagine—can and likely will greatly increase the complexity of your financial affairs. Importantly, in many situations you will be affected quite differently, depending on whether you are an American abroad, a foreign person in the United States, or a foreign person abroad with assets in the United States.

A second point (and corollary to the first) is that before moving to the United States and becoming a tax resident—before you expose yourself to the wide-reaching U.S. tax net—it is vital for you to undertake systematic preplanning, especially if you are older or more accomplished and already have significant preexisting assets. For example, the exact timing of when you sell a highly appreciated foreign residence can make a huge difference and either cost or save you large amounts in taxes.

Additionally, anyone who is indeed required to pay U.S. taxes—the tests for whether you fall within the very wide U.S. tax net are described in detail—must be very careful about investing in financial assets of *any* kind outside of the United States. Doing so can immediately lead to increased reporting requirements and significant complexity, as well as potentially higher tax burdens. As emphasized in Chapter 2, we are entering into a new world of cross-border information sharing, led and enforced primarily by the United States, so it's very important that all investors with U.S. tax reporting remain in strict compliance with any foreign bank account reporting and foreign asset disclosure laws.

Part VI, Retirement Planning, is the last core content section. Consider the premise that there is an emerging class of successful families who are truly cross-border. For these internationally oriented individuals or couples, it's quite common to plan on retiring in more than one country, with the United States being one of those countries. Figuring out how to plan for and optimize one's retirement in this situation can be quite difficult, and often leads to a variety of special challenges as discussed throughout the chapter.

One particular problem faced by cross-border families who are retiring internationally is the problem of account administration and cash management. That is, it can be very difficult to access and manage your wealth in a convenient and low-cost way, so Chapter 14 offers a variety of practical suggestions for approaching this. Another problem arises for those who have earned some type of government pension, or the equivalent of U.S. Social Security, in more than one country. The rules concerning how to best take advantage of benefits in multiple countries are complex and varied, so determining what those rules are and strategically applying them can make a big difference to your retirement picture.

Final Thoughts and Words of Encouragement

The community of cross-border people in the United States—like cross-border people throughout the world—is growing very rapidly. By and large, cross-border professionals are smart, competent, and driven to succeed. However, when it comes to taking optimal advantage of the wealth that they are generating and have accumulated, they are stymied by the lack of readily available information concerning the complex rules, systems, and investing options facing them.

Our hope is that for those readers who have an international orientation, investing a relatively small amount of time here, within the pages of this book, will yield large dividends. Ultimately, if you are able—with or without the assistance of a competent and caring financial advisor—to benefit from even *one* of the hundreds of topics or pieces of advice given in this book, you will have done yourself and your family a great service. Taking even just one meaningful action as a result of what we've discussed here can easily recoup the price of this book many times over. Doing so can also potentially lead you to significantly better long-term financial outcomes, and improve the quality of life that you and your family hope for and deserve. Good luck, and cheers to your personal and financial success!

Index